REDISCOVERING GANDHI

VOLUME 8 : Gandhian Economics and Its Contemporary Relevance

Series Editor: ***Prof. R.P. Misra***

Vol. 1. Hind Swaraj: *Gandhi's Challenge to Modern Civilization*—***R.P. Misra***
2. Ahimsa: *The Way to Peace*—***Jonathan K. Crane & Jordi Agusti-Panareda***
3. Satyagraha: *Gandhian Approach to Conflict Resolution*—***Jainarain Sharma***
4. Consensual Democracy: *Gandhi on State, Power, and Politics*—***Ashu Pasricha***
5. Humanizing Science and Technology: *Some Case Studies* —***Vinnie Jauhari and Parul Goyal***
6. Gandhi and Jesus : The End of Fundamentalism—***Wolfgang Sternstein***
7. How Relevant is Gandhi Today? A Japanese View—***Yamaguchi Hiroichi***
8. Gandhian Economics and Its Contemporary Relevance —***R.P. Misra and D. Gopal***
9. Conflict Resolution and Peace Building: The Gandhian Way —***R.P. Misra and D. Gopal***
10. Mahatma Gandhi: The Man, His Vision and Mission—***R.P. Misra***

About the Editors

Prof. R.P. Misra, born in 1930, Prof. Misra did his BA (1952) and MA (1954) at the University of Allahabad, and Ph.D. at the University of Maryland, College Park, Md., USA in 1964. Author of 15 books and editor of over 30 volumes on Gandhian thought, local and regional planning, environment, and human development, Prof. Misra specializes in economic geography, urban and regional planning, sustainable development, Gandhian studies and peace research. After joining the University of Mysore, Department of Geography in 1965 as its head, he launched an interdisciplinary Institute of Development Studies (IDS) in 1968 and took over as its founder Director (1968-79).

He made a name in the field of Geography and local and regional planning both in India and abroad and was invited as Vice-Director of the United Nations Center for Regional Development (UNCRD), Nagoya, Japan (1979-83). Earlier, he was consultant/advisor at the United Nations Research Institute for Social Development, (UNRISD), Geneva, and UNDP, Teheran, Iran. Prof. Misra was Vice-Chancellor of Allahabad University (1984-87) and Professor of Regional Planning at Delhi School of Economics, Delhi University (1987-95). He was honoured with prestigious Bhoogol Ratna award by the Bhoovigyan Vikas Foundation, India.

Prof. D. Gopal, Prof. Darvesh Gopal hails from Gulburga, Karnataka. At present, he is Professor of Political Science, Director of School of Social Sciences, and Coordinator of Gandhi and Peace Studies Programme in Indira Gandhi National Open University (IGNOU), New Delhi. He has been serving IGNOU for the last 25 years and has more than 30 years experience in teaching and research. Prof. Gopal earned his M.Phil. and Ph.D. degrees in International Relations from JNU, New Delhi and M.A. (Political Science) from Karnataka University, Dharwar. He developed MA degree course in Peace Studies and Conflict Resolution and brought out course material to suit learners of the subject on ODL (Open and Distance Learning) Mode.

Prof. Gopal is involved in the development of curriculum on "Gandhian Approach to Conflict Resolution and Peace building" in selected Colombian universities. He is a Visiting Professor or Fellow at several reputed Universities in India and abroad, including Hawke Research Institute, University of South Australia, Adelaide; and Malviya Centre for Peace Research, BHU, Varanasi, India. He has authored and edited 10 books and published more than thirty research papers in various journals and books.

REDISCOVERING GANDHI

Series Editor
Prof. R.P. Misra

Volume 8

Gandhian Economics and Its Contemporary Relevance

Edited by
R.P. Misra
D. Gopal

CONCEPT PUBLISHING COMPANY PVT. LTD.
NEW DELHI-110059

ISBN-13: 978-81-8069-374-8 (Series)
ISBN-13: 978-93-5125-236-8 (Vol. 8)

First Published 2018

Published and Printed by

Concept Since 1974

Concept Publishing Company Pvt. Ltd.
A/15-16, Commercial Block, Mohan Garden,
New Delhi-110059 (INDIA)
T : 25351460, 25351794
E : publishing@conceptpub.com *W* : ww.conceptpub.com

Cataloging in Publication Data--Courtesy: D.K. Agencies (P) Ltd. <docinfo@dkagencies.com>

Conference on Gandhi and Peace Studies (2014 : New Delhi, India)

Gandhian economics and its contemporary relevance / edited by R.P. Misra, D. Gopal.

pages cm. — (Rediscovering Gandhi ; volume 8)

"Most of the papers included in this volume were presented and discussed in a Conference on Gandhi and Peace Studies organized by the Gandhi Centre, Indira Gandhi National Open University, New Delhi during 2014"--About the book.

Includes bibliographical references and index.

ISBN 9788180693748 (series)

ISBN 9789351252368 (vol. 8)

1. Gandhi, Mahatma, 1869-1948—Congresses. 2. Economic development—India Congresses. 3. Economic development—Congresses. I. Misra, R. P., 1930- editor. II. Gopal, D. (Darvesh), editor. III. Indira Gandhi National Open University. Gandhi Centre, organizer. IV. Title. V. Series: Rediscovering Gandhi ; volume 8.

LCC HC435.C66 2014 DDC 338.954 23

Preface

In the present era of globalization, liberalization and privatization, how relevant is Gandhian economics is a question that haunts all those students, teachers, research scholars and others interested in economic development and social change. This book tries to answer this question. It covers various aspects of Gandhian economics and points to its contemporary relevance in India and the world.

The economic philosophy of Gandhi was inspired by the philosophy of simple living and high thinking in general and *Bhagavat Geeta* that preaches *Aparigraha* in particular. Two western thinkers: John Ruskin (1819-1900) and Leo Tolstoy (1828-1910) influenced Gandhi immensely. Ruskin's book *Unto This Last* inspired Gandhi so deeply that he established Phoenix Settlement near Durban in South Africa in 1904 to demonstrate how a good society can exist and function peacefully. Gandhi was also inspired by Leo Tolstoy and his book *The Kingdom of God Is within You*. Tolstoy believed that the aristocracy was a burden on the poor, and that the only solution to live together in peace was through anarchism. He opposed private property and advocated an egalitarian social order.

Gandhi did not subscribe to the nineteenth century doctrine of *laissez faire* which constitutes the political basis of capitalism; to him labour was superior to capital. Nor did he subscribe to Marxism which was opposed to capitalism but made the government so supreme that people had no rights. No wonder then that Gandhi was against industrialism and mass producing machines although not against machines as such. He considered decentralized economic system down to the village communities. A progressive society would ensure that the means of production such as land must be in the hands of the tillers. Gandhi was pained to see the misery of the Indian farmers and hence he formulated his well known Constructive Programme for improving the life and living conditions of the common man. He wanted cottage industries to go along with farming to ensure that villages were as self-reliant as possible in matters of their day-to-day needs. Redistribution of land or cooperative farming together with the production of *khadi,* i.e., handmade cloth was his major thrust in the revival and rejuvenation of the Indian village communities. He considered *khadi* as the symbol of *swadeshi,* i.e., self-reliance.

Bread labour was one of the central themes of Gandhian economic philosophy. He felt that every individual should do enough labour to produce goods and services to meet his basic needs. This would not only ensure food, clothing and shelter for all, it will also promote equality and lead to social structure without poverty for the most and affluence for a few. Although this idea was also mooted by St. Paul, St. Augustine, T.M. Bonareft, Leo Tolstoy and Peter Kropatkin in the west earlier, Gandhi made it a part of his life's philosophy and he not only preached but also practiced it in his South African days and later in his *ashrams* in India.

Another basic element of Gandhian economics is the concept of Trusteeship. This concept has its roots in *Geeta*'s concept of *Aparigraha* (non-possession). To begin with, it was a moralist view but as time passed Gandhi made it an essential element of his economic and socio-political philosophy. He went to the extent of resorting to *satyagraha* against the holders of wealth. In 1938, he said, 'A trustee has no heir but the public.' The underlying concept of trusteeship was to make rich people realize that their wealth was nothing but what they could grab from the people lawfully or unlawfully and, therefore, it was their responsibility to return to the people whatever was in excess over and above their needs. It would not only make the society at large extended family but also engender love and affection among the people. At the same time it would restrain the government from amassing too much power to overpower the people.

Relevance of Gandhian economics can be gauged from the fact that modern economics has neither been able to solve problems of production nor of distribution. Even in developed countries like the

USA, there are ups and downs in economic growth and there are rich and poor people. And if the current reigning capitalist approach to economics continues, the problem of distribution would never be resolved. Gandhi resolved this problem by prescribing that wages should be the same irrespective of the work people do. All should get the necessities of life and thus he introduced a revolutionary doctrine of equality of wages for lawyers, doctors, teachers and scavengers as a panacea for socio-economic evils of the society. It was also the view of Ruskin.

These ideas may appear to us impractical, unrealistic and irrelevant but a deep contemplation thereon brings us to the conclusion that unless we have an ideal we cannot move forward in right direction. Unfortunately, we have no ideals before us today. The ideal, if any, is faster economic growth in the hope that increasing productivity and production would trickle down to the poor too in the long run, if not in the immediate run. We ignore the fact that no country has so far been able to remove poverty and income disparities by following this course.

Gandhi lived and advanced these ideas at a time when technology was in its primitive stage of development. The situation has altogether changed in twentyfirst century. Farmers no longer want to till the soil with the help of bullock-drawn ploughs. In fact the youth no longer wants to live in the village where social and economic conditions continue to be age old. There is mass scale distress migration from rural areas. People prefer to live in the slums of cities and earn livelihood by working as daily wagers leaving their aged parents at home in the village. There is labour shortage in villages and mushroom growth of slums in cities. Today nearly 42 million people of India live in slums. Half the population of Mumbai lives in slums. Dharvi is perhaps the biggest slum of the world. Its population is about a 1,00,000. The only city that competes with Mumbai in this respect is Karachi in Pakistan.

This being the current situation, is Gandhi still relevant? Is it still possible to ensure economic security for all and to build self-reliant rural communities? Cities are already over-crowded; there is still some scope to build vertically and spread horizontally in adjoining rural areas. But the time when vertical and lateral spread of ever growing cities will create massive transport and service delivery problems, is not far off. The problem gets more complicated in countries like India and China which have more than a billion people each and most of them are village based and dependent on agriculture.

According to the Human Development Report 2007, the poorest 40 per cent of the people of the world get only 5 per cent of global income. The richest 20 per cent account for 75 per cent of world income. Much of the population (80%) lives in countries where income differentials are widening. In matters of consumption, the situation is equally alarming. According to World Bank Development Indicators 2008, the share of private consumption of the richest 20 per cent of the world was 76.6 per cent in 2005 while the share of the poorest of the world was just 1.5 per cent. The Remaining 21.9 per cent was shared by 60 per cent of the middle income people. The poorest 10 per cent accounted for 0.5 per cent of consumption and the wealthiest 10 per cent accounted for 59 per cent of all consumption.

According to the UNICEF (2008), 22,000 children in the world die each day of the year because of poverty. More than a quarter of the children of the developing world are underweight or stunted. 72 million children of primary school age in the developing world did not go to school; 57 per cent were girls. Almost a billion people were illiterate in 2000 AD. Interestingly, less than 1 per cent of world expenditure on weapons would be enough to put every child in school.

Share of world's private consumption, 2005

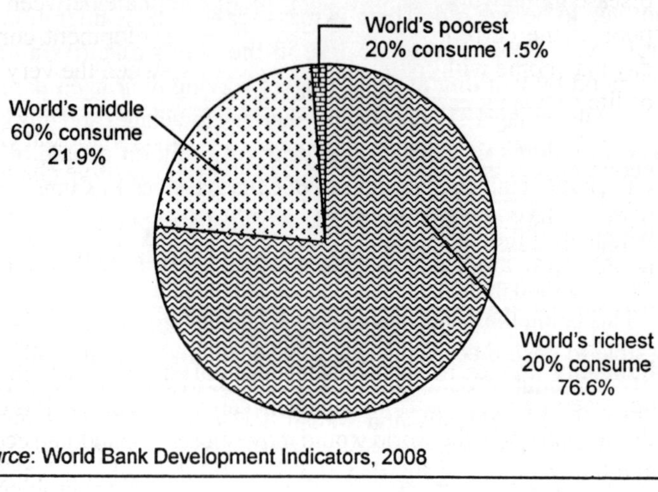

Source: World Bank Development Indicators, 2008

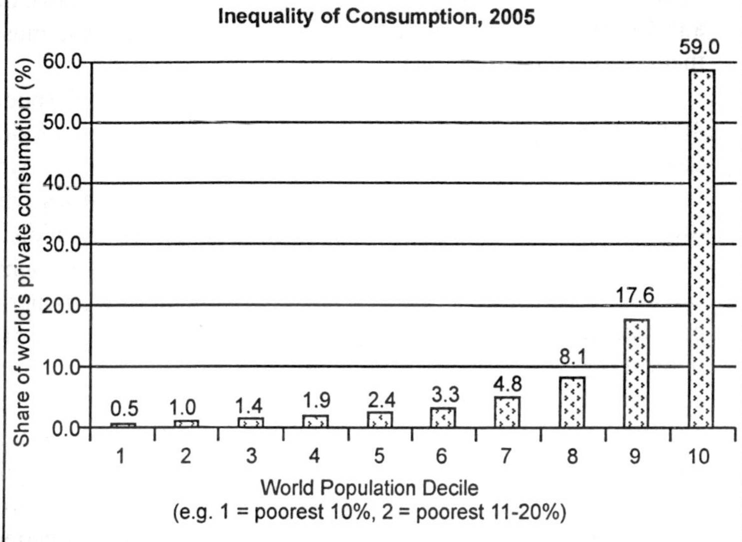

Source: World Bank Development Indicators, 2008.

Modern economics cannot handle the problem of environmental degradation, a problem that is already knocking at the doors of humanity. Environmental degradation caused by the economic policies of production and distribution kills more people than any single disease in the world today. It does not discriminate between rich and poor. If the current policies of economic development continue, a day may come within the next 50 years or so when the very survival of life on planet earth would be jeopardized.

It is in this context that we need to have a fresh look at Gandhian economics. It is the only way to bring about a positive change in the minds of the people and in the society at large. Think of a situation in which all billionaires and millionaires of the world create charitable trusts and use the proceeds of these trusts in helping the poor and investing in projects that benefit all equitably. In our view without the adherence to the basic principles of Gandhian economics, humanity is sure to face hurdles and catastrophes which modern approaches to economic management can never resolve. It is our hope that as years pass the world would move closer to Gandhian economics and thus be more egalitarian and peaceful than what it is today.

The papers included in this volume look at Gandhian economics from various perspectives and together present a picture that makes Gandhian approach to economic development easy to understand. The volume consists of 20 chapters including an Introduction by the editors. We appreciate the authors for participating in the discussion and contributing the papers included in this volume. We would also like to thank Concept Publishing Company (P) Ltd., New Delhi for publishing the volume in Rediscovering Gandhi series.

New Delhi
June 1, 2015

R.P. Misra & D. Gopal

Contents

Preface v
Contributors xiii

1. Introduction 1

PART I
UNDERSTANDING GANDHIAN ECONOMICS

2. Wholistic Vision of Gandhian Economics 29
Gita Srivastava
3. Relevance of Gandhian Economics in a Globalized World Economy 40
Anup K. Mishra
4. Gandhian Perspectives on Economy and Society 49
Hetal Mehra and *Kirti M. Vyas*
5. Gandhian Idea of Economic Independence 58
A.N. Panda
6. Five Myths about Gandhian Economics 74
Koilpillai J. Charles
7. Contemporary Relevance of Gandhian Economics 85
S.D. Subba Reddy
8. Gandhian Economics in the Context of Globalization 93
Poonam Bawa and *Ram Chandra*
9. Gandhian Economics in the Context of Emerging Rural Scenario 107
G.K. Singh
10. *Hind Swaraj*: A Source Book for Corporate and Business Ethics 115
Anurag Gangal

PART II
GANDHIAN MODEL OF ECONOMIC DEVELOPMENT

11. Gandhian Model of Economic Development: A Vision for an Inclusive Society 127
Rudra Prasad Sahoo

12. Economic Development: The Gandhian Way 145
Ashutosh Pandey

13. Bridging the Development Gap: The Gandhian Way 162
Ramdas Bhatkal

14. Relevance of the Concept of *Swadeshi* in the Era of Globalization 169
P.L. Devaraj

15. Minimizing Ill-effects of Market Economy on Social Fabric: Gandhian Ethics as a Counter Force 178
Sheoraj Singh

16. Can *Swadeshi* Help Solve Contemporary Economic Problems? 192
D.M. Diwakar

17. Journey of *Khadi* and Village Industries: From 'Livery of Freedom' to 'Fabric of Livelihood' 218
Raunak Ahmed

18. Relevance of the Concept of Village Republic in a Globalised Economy 237
Vandana Sinha

19. Concept of Village Republic: Gandhi, Nehru and Ambedkar 251
Pradeep Kumar Jha

20. Kibubutzim and Moshavim: Israel's Village Republics 261
R.P. Misra

Index 285

Contributors

Ahmed, Raunak: Ms. Raunak Ahmed is a Senior Research Teaching Assistant (SRTA) in Gandhian Studies Programme, Faculty of Political Science, School of Social Sciences, Indira Gandhi National Open University, New Delhi. She can be contacted through e-mail: raunakahmed@gmail.com

Bawa, Poonam: Dr. Poonam Bawa is Professor and Head, Department of Political Science, J.N.V. University, Jodhpur. A double Gold Medalist, she is author of two books: "Hindu Revivalism, Its ideological Roots of Nationalism" and "Power Politics and Women in India". She is Editor of *Indian Journal of Political Studies* published by the Department of Political Science, J.N.V. University, Jodhpur. e-mail: poonambawa@gmail.com

Bhatkal, Ganesh Ramdas Educated at the University of Mumbai, Dr. Ramdas Ganesh Bhatkal (b. 1935) is publisher of books (Popular Prakasan Ltd.) in English and Marathi since 1952. He has edited Political Alternatives in India, Snakes and Ladders and Alternate Strategies of India's Development. His research work includes doctoral dissertation 'Gandhi and His Adversaries with special reference to Savarkar and Ambedkar'. His translation of Gandhi's English *Hind Swaraj*: Indian Home Rule tries to grapple with small but significant differences between original Gujarati and English.

Charles, Koilpillai: Dr. Charles (b. 1926 at Madras) was Professor of Economics in American College, Madurai (1952-1956); received his Ph.D. degree from McGill University, Montreal, Canada in 1958; and served as a lecturer in McGill University (1958-1959) and Associate Professor at University Manitoba, Winnipeg, Canada (1959-1966). He then served the Lakehead University, Thunderbay, Canada as Professor of Economics, Chairman Department of Economics (1966-1991). Since, 1994, he associated with the Centre for Research in Economic and Social Development, Chennai as Professor of Economics.

Devaraj, P.L.: Dr. Devaraj is Academic Coordinator, M.A. GPS Programme (IGNOU). Chair for Gandhian Studies & Research, University of Calicut, Kerala, 673635. (Mobile) 09447418573, e-mail: pidevaraj@ rediffmail.com.

Diwakar, D.M.: Dr. Diwakar is a Professor of Political Science and Director, A.N. Sinha Institute of Social Sciences, Patna-800 001. He can be contacted at tel No. 0612-2219856 & 22286226; e-mail: dmdiwakar@yahoo.co.in

Gangal, Anurag: Dr. Anurag Gangal is Professor of Political Science and Director, Gandhian Centre for Peace and Conflict Studies, University of Jammu, Jammu-180006, J&K. He can be contacted at Mobile: 9419116171, e-mails: anuraggangal18@gmail.com, anuraggangal@live.in

Mehta, Hetal J.: Ms. Mehta is Principal of Swami Sahajanand College of Commerce, Management & Social Work, P.G. Centre of MSW & MHRD, Bhavnagar University, Gujarat. Phone: (R) 0278-2471046, (O) 0278-2512252, (Mobile) 09825553149, E-mail: hjmehta@rediffmail.com

Misra, R.P.: Prof. Misra is a Gandhian scholar and former Vice Chancellor of Allahabad University. He is closely associated with Gandhi and Peace Studies programme of the IGNOU. He can be contacted at
e-mail: sdf.misra@gmail.com and (Mobile): 9450869688.

Mishra, Anup K.: Dr. Anup K. Mishra is Assistant Professor of Economics at DAV College, Banaras Hindu University, Varanasi.

Panda, A.N.: Dr. Panda is Reader in the Department of Political Science in Panchayat (Government) College, Bargarh, Odisha-768028

Pandey, Ashutosh: A Ph.D. in Political Science, from the University of Allahabad, Dr. Pandey is Assistant Professor of Political Science at the Amar Singh (P.G) College, Lakhaoti, Bulandshahr (CCS University, Meerut). His areas of specialization include Indian Government and Politics, Women Empowerment, Ecology and Human Rights.
He can be contacted at e-mail: ashuparsiya@rediffmail.com

Reddy, S.D. Subba: Dr. Reddy, MA, Ph.D. was a lecturer and then the Principal of the Govt. P.G. College, Khairtabad, Hyderabad. e-mail: drsdsr@yahoo.com, Fax: 040-27074000, Mobile: 9177787456.

Sahu, Rudra Prasad: Dr. Sahu is Assistant Professor and Assistant Director of Centre for the Study of Social Exclusion and Inclusive Policy (CSSEIP), Babasaheb Bhimrao Ambedkar University, Lucknow.

Singh, Girish Kumar: Dr. Singh (b.1974) is associated with the Department of History, Amar Singh P.G. College, Lakhaoti, Bulandshahr, UP. The College is affiliated to CCCS University, Meerut. His areas of specialization include environment protection, indigenous people and peace. He has just completed a study on *Concerns for Environment Protection and Rights of Indigenous People.*

Singh, Sheoraj: Dr. Singh is Assistant Professor of Physics at Govt. College of Education, Chandigarh. He holds Master Degree in Physics Education from Patna University and MA Distance Education from IGNOU and has Ph.D. in Education from Punjab University. Gandhian Philosophy and value-education are his special areas of interest besides Theoretical Physics and Physics Education.

Sinha, Vandana: Dr. Sinha is Professor in the Department of Social Work, M.G. Kashi Vidyapeeth, Varanasi, UP. She specializes in Medical and Psychiatric Social Work. She has one book and over 15 research papers to her credit. She can be contacted at: e-mail: drvandana888@gmail.com and mobile no. 9450223145.

Srivastava, Gita: Educated at Allahabad, Dr. Gita Srivastava did her doctoral research on Indo-Italian History from University of Rome. She was granted Ph.D. degree by Meerut University. She joined Meerut University in 1978 as a lecturer and retired as Prof. & Head, Department of History in 2008. She was Director of the UGC sponsored Gandhian Centre. She has written several books and has published about 50 research papers in Indian and foreign journals.

Vyas, Kirit M.: Dr. Kirit M. Vyas is Administrative Officer, Nataraj Research Centre & Training College, PNR Society for Relief & Rehabilitation of the Disabled Kaliyabid, Bhavnagar-364002, Gujarat. Phone: (R) 0278-2211194, (o) 0278-3202470, (Mobile) 09824027898,
e-mail: drkiritvyas@rediffmail.com

1
Introduction

In this era of globalization, liberalization and privatization, Gandhi and his economic thoughts do not appear to be relevant. Gandhi sounds like a moral philosopher whose place rests in the realm of religion and philosophy, not in academic and policy discourses in mundane fields like economics. Economics, as practically all the text books say concerns the allocation of scarce resources for optimum material or monetary returns. Adam Smith, the Father of Classical School of Economics, said in 1776 that people acting in their own self-interest produced goods and wealth that benefited the whole society. He did not want governments to interfere in markets because the latter are self-regulatory and, thereby, produce wealth at maximum efficiency. Classical theory forms the basis of capitalism, the ruling economic system in the world with modification brought in by Keynes who suggested the governments to act within capitalistic economies to promote economic stability. It called for reduced taxes and increased government spending when the economy became stagnant and increased taxes and reduced spending when the economy became overly active. This theory strongly influences global economic policy today.

Marxism, on the other hand concludes that capitalism will eventually fail because factory owners and CEOs exploit labour to amass wealth that belongs to workers. Karl Marx, the propounder of this theory believed that the exploitation of labour in the production of goods and services leads to class conflict and social unrest. To ensure social and economic stability, he theorized that the labour class or proletariat as he branded them should own and control the means of production. Although this model has been widely rejected all over the world as an alternative to the capitalistic system, the flaws it points out in capitalism remain relevant to this day.

Gandhian economics is an alternative economic model. It rejects both Capitalism and Marxism, for they both concern only with economic aspects of human life. To treat man as a bundle of wants and his life as a means to satisfy those wants amounts to reducing him to an animal. While allocating resources to produce goods to satisfy human needs, man is not bereft of moral aspects of his life and living. While satisfying his own needs and wants, he has to opt for only morally acceptable means and products. Resources robbed from fellow beings should be morally unacceptable although they may help render material benefits. To make profit and amass wealth by cheating others would amount to being immoral. But if economics has no place for morality and ethics and it aims only at using natural and human resources to multiply goods and services, the economic system would be similar to an engine that guzzles diesel to produce electricity to light homes and streets while polluting the environment with CO_2 and thus destroying the forests, killing the animals and making human survival and development impossible.

"The ultimate purpose of economics is to increase the possibilities of civilization for our grand children" said Keynes. If economics must enhance the possibilities of human civilization, it cannot be outside the realm of culture that constitutes the foundation of civilization. If civilization is the material expression of culture, culture is the moral foundation of civilization. No civilization has ever lasted long without morality and hence by corollary, economics without ethics is a dangerous proposition.

Capitalism and socialism, the two opposing economic systems are by and large devoid of ethics; they appear scientific and beneficial but only in the short run; in the long run they prove disastrous. No wonder then that Marxism has almost disappeared from the earth and capitalism is in the grip of perpetual crises. We appear to have forgotten the heaven that Marx offered for the proletariat. Today, there is no country in the world that follows Marx for the heaven it offered is now buried in the history of the USSR. The only countries that still appear to adhere to Marxian economics are North Korea and China. The former is a drop in the ocean and the latter has distorted Marxism to such an extent that even the dictatorship of the proletariat has turned into the dictatorship of the party of elites. It follows Marxian politics intertwined with capitalist economics.

Who knows what fate is awaiting capitalism. With increasing suffering and deprivation of people in both developing and developed countries on the one hand and growing number of millionaires and billionaires and black money account holders, it would not take much time for the same fate to befall the 'actually-existing capitalism.' It is not the capitalism of Keynes and Mills or even of Adam Smith. The present Marxist politico-economic system constitutes capitalist economic core fitted in a Marxist political frame.

This being the present scenario, people tend to lose hope, and ask themselves 'where can we turn for alternatives?' Alternatives do exist, in Gandhian economics and decentralized development from below. There was a time, when local initiatives and even local currencies were prevalent all over the world. Even in days of British in India, there was a cooperative movement and every village had a cooperative society. What happened to those societies? Modernization has wiped them out. Grameen Banks could grow in Bangladesh as model local initiative; the Amul could grow in India as cooperative endeavour to help the poor produce milk jointly. One can cite many such examples in India but none could take the form of a national movement. The globalization, privatization and liberalization would not allow such endeavours to survive and grow.

Let us go deeper into the theory and practice of capitalist, socialist and Gandhian economic paths and find the strengths and weaknesses of each.

THE CAPITALIST PATH

The Wealth of Nations[1] by Adam Smith formed the launching pad for modern academic discipline of economics. Smith based much of his theory on self-interest and competition to satisfy those interests. Although he remained controversial economists as his approach was too materialistic, it helped the British in eighteenth century retain their superiority among the industrial countries of Europe. As the British Empire grew, it used its power to spread its model around the world, characterized by open markets, and relatively barrier free domestic and international trade.

George Stigler[2] attributed to Smith proposition that the owners of the three basic resources, e.g., labour, land, and capital would use them most profitably when there is perfect competition resulting in an equal rate of return in equilibrium for all uses minus of course of the cost of such factors as training, trust, hardship, and unemployment. Paul Samuelson, another noted classical economist found Smith's use of supply and demand to determine wages, rents, and profit as the basis for the general equilibrium modelling of Walras a century later.

But there were others like Joseph Schumpeter who dismissed Smith's propositions as illogical "His very limitation made for success. Had he been more brilliant, he would not have been taken so seriously. Had he dug more deeply, had he unearthed more recondite truth, had he used more difficult and ingenious methods, he would not have been understood. But he had no such ambitions; in fact he disliked whatever went beyond plain common sense. He never moved above the heads of even the dullest readers. He led them on gently, encouraging them by trivialities and homely observations, making them feel comfortable all along."[3]

And thus emerged the "labour theory of value" which in due course time brought Maxian theory elaborated in his famous book *Das Capital*[4] published in German in 1867. According to the labour theory of value, the value of a thing was determined by the labour that went into its production. It was unlike Smith's view that value of a thing was determined by what one is willing to pay for it.

Adam's theory was reinvented as New-classical economics or "marginalized" during 1870 to 1910. Marshall was the leading proponent of this thesis. It used mathematical methods to systematize supply and demand as co-determinants of price and quantity in market equilibrium, affecting both the allocation of output and the distribution of income. It dispensed with the labour theory of value of which Smith was most famously identified within classical economics, in favour of a marginal utility theory of value on the demand side and a more general theory of costs on the supply side.

The bicentennial anniversary of the publication of *The Wealth of Nations* was celebrated in 1976. During this celebration the precursor of Smith's *Wealth of Nations* was brought to prominence. It was *The Theory of Moral Sentiments*[5] published before his *The Wealth of Nations* was published. Thus, Adam Smith came to be known as the founder of not only the science of economics but also of a moral philosophy. Thus, his homo economicus (economic man) was simultaneously a moral person. David Levy and Sandra Pearl in their *The Secret History of the Dismal Science* make this point clear when they point to Smith's opposition to beliefs in economic, social and racial inequality and hierarchy. He was also against slavery, colonialism, and imperialism. They also cite Smith's opposition to the often expressed view that science is superior to common sense.

Explaining the relationship between growth of private property and that of civil government, Smith had said:

> "Men may live together in society with some tolerable degree of security, though there is no civil magistrate to protect them from the injustice of those passions. But avarice and ambition in the rich, in the poor the hatred of labour and the love of present ease and enjoyment are the passions which prompt to invade property, passions much steadier in their operation, and much more universal in their influence. Wherever there is great property there is great inequality. For one very rich man there must be at least five hundred poor, and the affluence of the few supposes the indigence of the many. The affluence of the rich excites the indignation of the poor, who are often both driven by want, and prompted by envy, to invade his possessions. It is only under the shelter of the civil magistrate that the owner of that valuable property, which is acquired by the labour of many years, or perhaps of many successive generations, can sleep a single night in security. He is at all times surrounded by unknown enemies, whom, though he never provoked, he can never appease, and from whose injustice he can be protected only by the powerful arm of the civil magistrate continually held up to chastise it. The acquisition of valuable and extensive property, therefore, necessarily requires the establishment of civil government. Where there is no property, or at least none that exceeds the value of two or three days' labour, civil government is not so necessary. Civil government supposes certain subordination. But as the necessity of civil government gradually grows up with the acquisition of valuable property, so the principal causes which naturally introduce subordination gradually grow up with the growth of that valuable property. (..) Men of inferior wealth combine to defend those of superior wealth in the possession of their property, in order that men of superior wealth may combine to defend them in the possession of theirs. All the inferior shepherds and herdsmen feel that the security of their own herds and flocks depends upon the security of those of the

> great shepherd or herdsman; that the maintenance of their lesser authority depends upon that of his greater authority, and that upon their subordination to him depends his power of keeping their inferiors in subordination to them. They constitute a sort of little nobility, who feel themselves interested to defend the property and to support the authority of their own little sovereign in order that he may be able to defend their property and to support their authority. Civil government, so far as it is instituted for the security of property, is in reality instituted for the defence of the rich against the poor, or of those who have some property against those who have none at all." [6]

If each individual pursued his own economic goals, there will ultimately be equality among peoples and regions provided of course there is free and competitive environment. In the long run economy will be at equilibrium wherein:

1. Growth rate of GDP will go up;
2. Income of the people and nations will increase;
3. The natural resources will be exploited to the fullest extent;
4. There will be no poverty as perfect competition would equalize every thing;
5. All will have equal access to goods and services as there will be no shortage of goods;
6. There will be no ecological and environmental fallout as technology will take care of it.
7. People will be happy as they will possess whatever goods and services they aspire to have.

Adam smith pointed to the possibilities of moral derailment but this aspect of his theses was ignored in the mad rush for economic growth. And thus what the capitalist can be characterized today is:

1. Universal inequity-interpersonal to global;
2. Increasing unemployment;
3. Shortage of resources;
4. Environmental degradation;
5. Arms race; and
6. Globalization of violence, diseases, hatred and poverty.

SOCIALIST PATH

A school of economic thought based on Karl Marx's semina! book *Das Kapital* published in 1857 evolved in Europe which can be said to be antithetical to Capitalist path. Marxian economics focuses on the role of labour in the development of an economy and is critical of the classical economic approaches to wages and productivity as developed by Adam Smith. Marxian economics argues that the specialization of the labour force, coupled with a growing population, pushes wages down and that the value placed on goods and services does not accurately account for the true cost of labour.

Marxian economics is based on three principles:

1. Stage theory of economic development,
2. Dialectical materialism, and
3. Labour theory of value.

According to the Stage Theory, human society is to evolve in five stages. These are:

1. Graeco-Roman Slavery (ancient times),
2. Feudalism (medieval times),
3. Capitalism (nineteenth century),
4. Socialism, and
5. Communism.

The second principle that forms the core of Marxist economics is Dialectical Materialism. It was based on the Hegelian view that historical progress is achieved through the clash of opposites and their ultimate resolution in the form: thesis *vs.* antithesis > synthesis. This has led to the theory of class struggle as the central historical dynamics that leads any society to pass through the above five stages. Each stage has a different ruling class and the antithetical or opposing class which, through violent conflict bring about the destruction of that ruling class.

The third principle is derived from Labour Theory of Value: that labour is the sole source of value in production. According to *Das Capital* "....the exchange value of a commodity is determined by the quantity of socially necessary labour contained in it. .... The Quantity of Socially Necessary Labour, as the common denominator determining the equality of exchange, is the average amount of time required for the production of a commodity under normal conditions, with an average degree of skill and intensity of labour, utilizing the contemporary, most advanced technology available. Thus: 'no more time than is socially necessary'. Marx did recognize that technological changes enhanced the productivity of labour. Thus: "the greater the productivity of labour, the less labour time is involved in the production of the commodity, and the lesser will be its value, or the lower will be the price of the commodity.' Or: 'The value of a commodity.. varies directly as the quantity (of labour) and inversely as the productiveness of the labour incorporated in it."[7]

The labour-value of a commodity considered not just the final manufacture of a commodity but also all the previous expenditures of 'labour power' involved in the production of the final goods. For example, the labour cost of the manufacture of a chair includes the labour involved in the production of all the raw materials and finished goods including the cost of transportation and marketing and finally the amount of socially necessary labour time required for the creation of that labour power, in terms of the subsistence (food, clothing, shelter, etc.) of the worker and his family and of his education.

In Marxian economic theory, the funds that a capitalist uses in the production of the commodities he sells constitute 'capital'. It is of two types: Constant and Variable. Constant capital is non-reproductive while the Variable capital is reproductive. For example the cost of raw materials and machinery are constant; they become intrinsic to the product manufactured. The variable Capital is "that part of capital represented by labour power, which both reproduces the equivalent of its own value and also produces an excess, or a surplus value, which itself varies…This part of capital is continually being transformed from a constant into a variable magnitude."[8] That is to say that the variable capital is labour power

On the Concept of Surplus Value, Marx said: "The consumption of labour power is at one and the same time the production of commodities and of surplus value."[9]. "The surplus of the total value of the product, over the sum of values of its constituent factors, is surplus of the expanded capital over the capital originally advanced."[10] Surplus Value represents the Capitalist's profit. It is created solely by labour-power but is expropriated solely by the Capitalist because he has purchased from the worker all of his labour-power and, therefore, has purchased the rights to the fruits of that labour-power, namely the surplus value he creates.

In Marxian sense, profit is actually composed of three elements:

1. Interest on capital;
2. Rent on land and physical capital; and
3. Entrepreneur's 'normal profit' or what is often called the 'wages of entrepreneurship.'

We can now sum up Marx's view of the role of constant capital, machinery and technological change, in his own words: 'In order to enable one portion of a capital to expand its value by being converted into labour power, it is necessary that another portion be converted into means of production' [machinery]. Thus constant capital must be advanced in proper proportions 'given by the special technical conditions of each labour process.'

Both classical school of economists (Adam Smith, Malthus, Sismondi, David Recordo, and J.S. Mills) and Marx concluded that the historical tendency of profit (interest, rent, profit) was to fall, but not because of the same reasons. Thus as capital grew, the capitalist would invest more in constant capital rather than in labour. Thus the constant capital would grow but the variable capital would proportionately decline. To quote Marx "In the course of accumulation, a point is reached at which the development of the productivity of social labour becomes the most power level of accumulation;"[11] and so the contribution of labour in production, as a proportion of the total means of production, must fall.

Pointing to the internal contradiction of the capitalist process, Marx said: "The nature of the capitalist process of accumulation... implies as a matter of course that the increased mass of the means of production, which is to be converted into capital, must always find on hand a corresponding increase of labouring people for exploitation."[12] But that becomes increasingly difficult if the capitalist process necessarily means technological advancement and increased scales of production so that constant capital must inevitably increase at a faster rate than variable capital, and thus bring about an inevitable fall in the rate of profit.

The creation of surplus value leads naturally to capital accumulation, which leads to amalgamation in the form of very large capitals, which through competition will gobble up smaller capitals, and so lead to the concentration of capital in few hands as monopolies. Monopoly capitalism must result, since the larger capitals with their superior economies of scale and superior technologies will cheapen commodities at a faster rate than will smaller capitals, and so drive the latter out of production, or simply absorb them through purchase.

All of the attempts of large capital to counteract the falling rate of profit can be only temporary palliatives. And in this process the chief source of escape for the capitalist will be intensifying the exploitation of labour: that is to continue driving down wages to augment surplus value. Both the unemployment caused by technological change, by machines displaying labour, and the population growth stimulated by the economic development will create a 'reserve army of the unemployed' which will permit the capitalists to depress wages further and further to the point of immiserising the working classes.

Growth of monopoly capitalism by hastening the expansion of constant capital at the expense of variable capital, will hasten this process of 'immiseration' and oppression of the working classes to the point of revolution, of sparking a revolutionary explosion by which 'the expropriators are expropriated.' hence the ultimate internal contradiction of capitalism[13].

GANDHI'S CRITIQUE OF CAPITALIST AND SOCIALIST PATHS

Gandhi was not an economist in a formal sense to put his thoughts in formats economic theoreticians do, nor did he apply rigorous economic theory to give structure to his thought. He did, however, formulate clearly and logically his basic principles. An attempt is made here to express these principles in mathematical equations to justify calling these principles a complete alternative system.

Here are the six basic principles of Gandhian economics:

1. Humans are no longer animals; they have body, mind and soul; they need nourishing food and enough exercise to keep their body fit; intellectual input to keep their mind alert, sharp and inventive; and spiritual nourishment to move away from their animal past an inch closer to their superconscious future.
2. Nature is not a resource for exploitation; it is a life supporting

system evolved through time and essential for human survival and development; it has to be used and conserved at the same time;

3. Meeting the basic needs (food, clothing, shelter, education, health, and peace, both inner and outer) of each and every individual must be the first charge of the social, political and economic institutions created by man;
4. Technological progress is a must for human development but it should not lead to power for some and poverty for others;
5. In order to equitably serve the interest of all, the governance system should neither be centralized nor in the hands of a select few; and
6. Planning and development activities should be top down and bottom up at the same time. The bottom up process should take care of the micro-economics and ensure the satisfaction of the basic needs of all while the top down process should take care of macro-economics and concentrate on managing the macro policies and programmes including of course the international relations.

These principles cancel out completely the assumption that primary aim of economics is to maximize the efficiency of production of goods, whether these goods meet the basic needs of the people or the comforts and luxuries of a few. It also cancels out the Marxist view that production of capitalist goods should get priority over the consumption goods so that more goods get into the hands of the people in future. Both capitalist and socialist economies are based on technology-intensive rather than labour-intensive production. Gandhian economics reverses this preference and lays emphasis on full employment of the people. Technology should be such that it is accessible to all. All resources, natural, human or technological should be so used that they are conserved for the future uses.

The first goal of Gandhian economics is to so organize the production and distribution system that all are fully employed and their basic needs are satisfactorily met. This could be achieved only if technology instead of displacing labour conserves it. Thus, Gandhi was not against technology; he advocated a proper mix of technology-intensive and labour-intensive production. This proper mix will be determined by the economists using various tools and techniques of analysis and people themselves. Thus, population increase or decrease will have bearings on type of technology to be used. Foreign trade of a country would not deprive the nationals of their basic needs including the opportunity for work.

Marxism is on the verge of disappearing as a politico-economic system but its replacement by capitalism does not auger well for the world. Capitalism cares least for the poor and deprived; they become tools in the hands of the capitalist for exploitation. Luxury goods get least priority, if at all in the Gandhian economic regime because the goal of life is not to amass wealth but to become a better human being. This means that the motto of simple living, high thinking and peaceful living and devotion to the arts and sciences, and spiritual pursuits would be a part of the life style. The gap between needs and wants would narrow down and thus there would be no poor or super rich and there would be no environmental problem either. People would adhere to the principle of voluntary simplicity.

The meaning of Gandhin Economics was made clear by Gandhi himself when he addressed the professional economists gathered at the Muir Central College Economic Society at Allahabad a century back in 1916. This lecture clearly reflects Gandhi's approach to economics. While going through the speech we have to keep in mind that he was addressing a most distinguished gathering of Academicians, British Officials and Rajas and Zamindars.

> "You are an economic society. You have chosen distinguished specialists for the subjects included in your syllabus for this year and the next. It seems to be the only speaker ill-fitted for the task set before him. Frankly and truly, I know very little of economics, as you naturally understand them. Only the other day, sitting at an evening meal, a civilian friend deluged me with a series of questions on my crankisms. As he proceeded in this cross-examination, I being a willing victim, he found no difficulty in discovering my gross ignorance.... To his horror and even indignation, he found that I had not even read books on economics by such well-known authorities as Mill, Marshal, Adam Smith.... In despair, he ended by advising me to read these works.... He little knew that I was a sinner past redemption."
>
> "Every human being has a right to live and, therefore, to find the wherewithal to feed himself and where necessary to

> clothe and house himself. But, for this very simple performance, we need no assistance from economists and their laws".[14]
>
> "There come to us moments in life when about some things we need no proof from without. A little voice within us (leads us to the Truth)".

As the audience was predominantly from a Christian background, he quoted extensively from the *Bible* in support of his thesis, and ended by stating what he regarded as the most fundamental law of economics:

> "Let us seek first the Kingdom of God and His righteousness and the irrevocable promise is that everything will be added with us. These are real economics. May you and I treasure them and enforce them in our daily life."

What did he mean by saying 'everything will be added' unto us? Was he referring to 'goods and services' in the usual economic sense of the term? He explained this in another context thus:

> "Modern science is replete with illustrations of the seemingly impossible having become possible within living memory. But the victories of physical science would be nothing against the victory of the Science of Life, which is summed up in Love which is the Law of our Being."[15]

Gandhi saw man having three dimensions in his life and living; physical—represented by his body; mental—represented by his capacity to think, remember and recall and spiritual—represented by his urge to love. Man in his primitive stage of evolution considered himself only as physical being. As he evolved further, he considered an intellectual to be more powerful than a wrestler. And finally, he realized that his spiritual realm was superior to even his mental realm. Gandhi came to the conclusion that if we human beings made spiritual pursuit our primary pursuit, we would not only have peace within but also outside. Then, there would be no hatred, jealousy, conflicts and wars.

Let us take the example of the greatest scientist the world has ever produced, i.e., Albert Einstein. Behind his quantum theory was his spiritual urge. "I want to know how God created this world. I am not interested in this or that phenomenon, in the spectrum of this or that element. I want to know His thoughts, the rest are details."[16] And Schrödinger laid far more emphasis on the spiritual nature of his work:

> "Within a cultural milieu ('Kultukreis') where certain conceptions (which once had or still have a wider meaning amongst other peoples) have been limited and specialized, it is daring to give to [my] conclusion the simple wording that it requires. In Christian terminology to say 'Hence I am God Almighty' sounds both blasphemous and lunatic. But please disregard these connotations for the moment and consider whether the above inference is not the closest a biologist can get to proving God and immortality at one stroke.
>
> "In itself, the insight is not new. The earliest records, to my knowledge, date back some 2500 years or more. From the early great Upanishads the recognition ATMAN=BRAHMAN (the personal self equals the omnipresent, all-comprehending eternal self) was in Indian thought considered, far from being blasphemous, to represent the quintessence of deepest insight into the happenings of the world. The striving of all the scholars of *Vedanta* was, after having learnt to pronounce with their lips, really to assimilate in their minds this grandest of all thoughts.
>
> "Again, the mystics of many centuries, independently, yet in perfect harmony with each other (somewhat like the particles in an ideal gas) have described, each of them, the unique experience of his or her life in terms that can be condensed in the phrase: DEUS FACTUS SUM (I have become God)."[17]

The well known equations of Einstein and Schrödinger were first philosophical breakthroughs and then only as technological breakthroughs expressed in the language of mathematics. In the words of Schrödinger, this breakthrough came when he felt that the electrons were asking him "so, Mr. Schrödinger, you are trying to figure out if I am a particle or a wave or what. But, who, Mr. Schrödinger, are you?"[18] and if no further development has taken place in the field of Quantum Mechanics during the last 80 years, it is because the worldview of science has gone back to Newtonian physics and become materialistic; instead of producing something that nuclear bombs.

Gandhi was asking human beings through his countrymen to change their world-view and give spiritual progress a priority and self-realization the goal of life. The violent technologies should be replaced by non-violent ones. The physical needs of the body and mind would be automatically taken care of if spiritual progress became the goal of life. In that situation, there would be no rat race for material gains; nor there social inequities and environmental degradation. In Gandhi's own words, "the victories of physical science would be nothing against the victory of the Science of Life, which is summed up in Love which is the Law of our Being."[19]

Gandhi aimed at creating a Kingdom of God in world so that our creative energies are unleashed to make this earth a heavenly abode. His mission began in 1916 in South Africa and continued all through his life; it ceased only on 30th January, 1948 when his *atma* became a part of *Parmatma* and his body merged in the five elements (*Tatwas*) i.e., *Chhit*, *Jal*, *Pavak*, *Gagan*, and *Samir* (land, water, fire, outer space and atmosphere). So, what Gandhi was suggesting to his audience in 1916 was: if we make the Kingdom of God our goal in life, then the creative energies that will be unleashed will help us positively to achieve all that we need on this earth.... It would create technologies that would be sensitive to ecology and environment and bring about a society where poverty would be a thing of the past. And small would become beautiful once again. Implementation of the concept of Trusteeship wherein those who earn more than the national per capita income would constitute Charitable Trusts to contribute in social causes and to serve those who lag behind economically, socially or otherwise.

Is it possible to recapture Gandhi's vision of Sarvodaya where spirituality is the goal and physical labour and intellectual power as the means to create a world of happiness? Even at the time when Gandhi's leadership was unchallenged in India, there were many leading figures in the country who did not subscribe to Gandhian approach to development. Leave aside Jinnah, even Jawaharlal Nehru and Jayaprakash Narayan did not subscribe to his views in full. Nehru was his follower but not wholeheartedly. He believed in the socialist mode of production wherein large scale industries played a key role in the economic resurgence of India. Nehru stood for mechanization but Gandhi thought "It is machinery that has impoverished India". And he added:

> "That economics is untrue which ignores or disregards moral values. The extension of the law of nonviolence in the domain of economics means nothing less than the introduction of moral values as a factor to be considered in regulating international commerce."
>
> "My ideal is equal distribution, but so far as I can see, it is not to be realised. I, therefore, work for equitable distribution."
>
> "I suggest that we are thieves in a way. If I take anything that I do not need for my own immediate use, and keep it, I thieve it from somebody else. I venture to suggest that it is the fundamental law of Nature, without exception, that Nature produces enough for our wants from day-to-day, and if only everybody took enough for himself and nothing more, there would be no pauperism in this world, there would be no man dying of starvation in this world."
>
> "It is open to the world ... to laugh at my dispossessing myself of all property. For me the dispossessing has been a positive gain. I would like people to compete with me in my contentment. It is the richest treasure that I own. Hence, it is perhaps right to say that though I preach poverty, I am a rich man!"
>
> "No one has ever suggested that grinding pauperism can lead to anything else than moral degradation. Every human being has a right to live and, therefore, to find the wherewithal to feed himself and where necessary to clothe and house himself. But for this very simple performance we need no assistance from economists or their laws."
>
> "The rich cannot accumulate wealth without the co-operation of the poor in society. If this knowledge were to penetrate to and spread amongst the poor, they would become strong and would learn how to free themselves by means of nonviolence."[20]

SOCIALISM AND CAPITALISM HAVE FAILED ON THE HUMAN FRONT

Neither socialism nor capitalism has achieved what Marx and

Smith/Keynes had envisaged. The socio-economic system of the world is in the mess. No country is in peace. Violence in varied forms prevails all over. There are rich (developed) and poor (under-developed) nations; there are poor and rich regions, cities and villages. In the midst of multi-storeyed concrete jungles called cities there are hells called slums. What made this disparate life and living in a world that has more money than the world needs to meet the basic needs of all? It is lack of moral and ethical foundations of the economic and social system of the world.

According to some estimates, the 'black money' that rich people of India have stashed in foreign banks and in their pillows, mattresses and real estate would be enough to raise the per capita income of the people of India by at least five times. It may be an estimate but no one can deny that corruption reigns supreme in India and other countries of the world and if the people are poor, it is not because there is shortage of resources to root out poverty but because the resources are maldistributed and foul means are used to corner the available resources by a few.

The situation is none better in a so-called Marxist country like People's Republic of China which has now become Rich People's Republic of China. And Putin, the present President of Russia is perhaps the richest head of the state of the world today. He allegedly owns assets worth $ 10 billion. The tiny North Korea, a Marxist and one of the poorest countries of the world is known for dictatorship of the unproletariat.

The internal contradictions of both capitalist and socialist systems are rooted in Newtonian, Cartesian, and Darwinian scientism. It sees the universe as a mechanical system; the human body as a machine; and life as an unending competitive struggle for survival. Its goal is economic growth with the most effective use of resources, both natural and human. In the pursuit of economic growth many problems emerge that negate much of what economic growth promises to offer. The individual is lost in the industrialism it promotes; he becomes a cog in the weaving machine and shunted from right to left and left to right. He loses his individuality, a sense of place and community for the material pleasures of a few. Violence threatens human existence; wars, terrorism, crimes and vandalism have grown beyond control. We consume 3,500 million tonnes of fossil fuels annually and the environmental problems it creates threaten the very existence of life on planet earth. And the amount of biomass, water, and land we use or consume is beyond the capacity of the earth to replenish. Earth is on receiving end of the cruelty that man inflicts on the earth is already beyond its carrying capacity to absorb.

Much (86%) of the private goods consumed in the world is gobbled up by 20 per cent of the population. The bottom 20 per cent of the people use just 1.3 per cent of these goods. Americans use more on advertisement and the British on ice cream in a single year that is needed to provide basic education and sanitation to one-third of global humanity living below the poverty line (1998 Human Development Report). Is then globalization, liberalization and privatization the real answer to poverty and hunger? Can these problems of poverty and inequity be solved by technological changes? Technology, as we know is not neutral to social structure. As such it always favours the rich.

The problems are really cultural, not technological or developmental. Development is a process of getting more goods and services to consume and technology is a means to produce these goods and services. How these goods and services would be produced and used would depend on the values people cherish and the human relations they maintain. Man changes as he acquires new knowledge and tools to manage his affairs. At every stage of his life he calls himself more civilized and his perceptions, values and visions of his own and the society at large change and mould the developmental and technological processes in particular directions. He is caught in a trap of conflict between what he wishes, aspires, feels and does. This conflict is not a marginal problem to be brushed aside. It has stressed his life and living so deeply that he is at perpetual unease. That is the reason, why some of them renounce everything and becomes saints. But most of them live under a constant fear of losing what they have amassed. They keep themselves busy in hiding and protecting their material possessions.

Socialists want to dispossess the elites of the wealth they have accumulated by exploiting the working classes. But once the proletariats grab power, they are not immune from all those crimes they abuse the capitalists to commit. Corruption was rampant in the USSR of the past, as in Russia of the present. And it has taken deeper roots in Communist China today and Democratic India.

So, both capitalism and communism have failed to create a society which can take man to a state of contentment and happiness. The world in which we live today is full of conflicts; conflicts among nations, conflicts among societies, conflicts among religions, and of course, conflicts among individuals and inside the individual. There are world wars, regional wars, local wars and wars within each individual. Man is torn apart from top to bottom. Once a given problem is solved, new problems crop up. Even a temporary peace has become a chimera.

GANDHIAN CRITIQUE OF SOCIALISM AND CAPITALISM

Gandhi on Socialism

"Nearly fifty years ago, when I was practicing law in South Africa, many people used to call themselves socialists. But they were less of socialists than I was. I used to work among the labourers. I made this part of my life's work. This is true socialism. I have always considered myself a true servant of the peasants and of the workers. .... I am of the opinion that even a king can be a socialist by becoming a servant of the people."[21]

Addressing the Delhi Provincial Political Conference on July 9, 1947, Gandhi said "Socialism is a beautiful word and so far as I am aware, in socialism all the members of society are equal—none low, none high. In the individual body, the head is not high because it is the top of the body, nor are the soles of the feet low because they touch the earth. Even as members of the individual body are equal, so are the members of the society. This is socialism."

"In it, the prince and the peasant, the wealthy and the poor, the employer and the employee are all on the same level. In terms of religion, there is no duality in socialism. It is all unity. Looking at society, all the world over, there is nothing but duality and plurality. Unity is conspicuous by its absence. This man is high and that one is low, that is a Hindu, that a Muslim, third a Christian, fourth a Parsi, fifth a Sikh, sixth a Jew. Even among these there are subdivisions. In the unity of my perception, there is a perfect unity in the plurality of designs".

"But, in order to reach this state, we may not think philosophically and say that we need not make a move until all are converted to socialism. Without changing our life, we may go on giving addresses and forming parties and hawk-like seize the game when it comes our way. This is no socialism. The more we treat it as a game to be seized, the farther it must recede from us."[22]

Gandhi on Capitalism

Gandhi's *Hind Swaraj* (*HS*) is the fundamental text for understanding of the man, his philosophy and his mission. Gandhi considered civilisation a moral enterprise, a route to make man a better human being: "Civilisation is that Mode of conduct, which points out to man the path of duty"[23]. Thus he challenged the western view of civilization as a mode of life and living that empowers man to secure his rights by subduing nature and his fellow human beings. Gandhi considered 'might is right' and the 'survival of the fittest' the two basic principles at the core of modern concept of civilization. The first is inherent to the politics of power expounded by Machiaveli and the second to the economics of self-interest proposed by Adam Smith. Deviations from these two principles in the west are rare and those who charted a different path like Tolstoy and Ruskin were treated as unrealistic and off the track.

The four themes that Gandhi repeatedly refers in *Hind Swaraj* which he thought were the by-products of capitalism are:

1. Rationalism,
2. Materialism,
3. Industrialism, and
4. Colonialism.

While Gandhi was neither against science nor against technology, he certainly was against uncompromising rationalism. Reason too has its limitations as "Just as dirt is matter misplaced, reason misplaced is lunacy! I plead not for the suppression of reason, but for a due recognition of that in us, which sanctifies reason itself'[24]. The supremacy of reason over faith, Gandhi thought was the bane of western civilization, although he pleaded for cross checking of one by the other.

The age of reason has led the western civilization to destructive paths. Gandhi never allowed his faith to go untested on the anvil of reason or his reason to override his faith in all circumstances.

Science and technology are the products of rationalism and spiritualism and religion are the products of faith. Science and technology lead to materialism that negates the spiritual and religious worldview. Gandhi put Truth at the centre of all that exists; it is something that cannot be perceived by the human senses and since reason is the product of human senses, it cannot give a final answer to the reality. Truth, to Gandhi is a transcendent reality that gives meaning to our life and living.

Although all religions are united on this perspective of the reality Gandhi envisioned, it was Hinduism that impressed him most. No wonder then that he proclaimed himself a *Sanatani* Hindu. In a so-called secular world today, people may not subscribe to this worldview. Yet, if we look at the moral degradation that prevails in the so-called rational world today, we cannot fail sympathize with Gandhian view in this respect.

Colonialism, in Gandhi's view was the byproduct of rationality and materialism both in the west and India. The English were pursuing their rational urge to have more land, more wealth and more prosperity. Indians discarded their own world view and failed to face the challenges posed by the west. "The English have not taken India; we have given it to them. They are not in India because of their strength: but because we keep them"[25]. Gandhi knew that colonialism was a by-product of materialism that ruled supreme in the west and it could be combated only by the spiritual power of India. Gandhi felt that Indians were also infected by the values of western civilization and unless this 'Intimate Enemy' was exorcised and exiled, unless we recovered the Self, we would remain enslaved by foreigners or Indians. Gandhi was thus against colonialism whether external or internal.[26]. Colonialism was branded as a civilising mission. Gandhi rejected the western civilization branded as modern civilization and thus subverted the legitimacy of the colonial enterprise at its base.

Capitalism in Gandhi's view lay at the core of western civilization and hence the dynamic force behind colonial imperialism. Unlike Marx, Gandhi rejected capitalism because he disliked or even abhorred a system which impoverishes labour for profit and which values machines more than humans. He was so pained by this state of affairs that he said: "Machinery is the chief symbol of modern civilisation; it represents a great sin"[27]. He uttered the word sin because it concentrated wealth in few hands and displacing workers. He did change his views a bit in subsequent years, but he remained steadfast on his basic thesis in this regard and even extended his critique to the professions like medicine and law[28] because the poor hardly benefited from these services; more often than not they become their victims. He suggested their nationalisation[29]. If we look at the medical and legal services today, Gandhi not only expressed what was emerging then but also foresaw the situation as it prevails today. To ensure that he was not misunderstood as a man against machine, he said, how can I be against machine when my own body is like a machine?

CONCLUSIONS

To some, Gandhi's critique of modern civilisation sounds like questioning of the role of science and technology in shaping the future of the humanity and the world. Even Parekh thinks so and feels that but for these two instruments of inquiry and the human control over nature together with modern organisational capacity, world would have not made the progress it has made so far. The dedication with which they were pursued was not without certain 'spiritual dimension' that Gandhi seems to have missed (Parekh, 1997:35). While the focus of his criticism is modern civilisation of a specific period, the fundamentals of this civilization have not changed nor would they ever change. And hence his criticism was time specific. His condemnation of colonialism too is not time-specific. While earlier, it was inspired by imperialistic design, today it is inspired by politico-economic design to control. His rejection of industrialism had two bases: capitalist mode of production wherein the small man did not have a place. Gandhi stood for decentralized mode of production so that each individual and community worked for itself and its neighbours more than for export to foreign lands in so far as the basic necessities of life were concerned.

But to say that all that Gandhi said and did was final and there can be no change in it will amount to denigrating Gandhi's personality. Time and again he emphasized that he was a living being always evolving and, therefore, what he said last should be taken as his final word. As such to quote Gandhi from *Hind Swaraj* or any other book he wrote prior to his eternal rest in January 1948 would not do full justice to him. Yet, deep analysis of Gandhi's views and thoughts expressed from time to time have one common thread that never changed largely because it was based on a judicious mixture of spirituality and science; faith and rationality; and eternal truth and physical reality.

Thus if we take the principles which Gandhi followed in his life, we can better assess his relevance for us today. Gandhi's rejection of the civilising mission of colonialism questions the legitimacy of any country overpowering other countries politically, economically or militarily at a fundamental ethical level. Gandhi wanted India to unlearn much it had learnt from the British. But it did not happen. The British left India but the British mentality remained engrained in Indian mind.

It is so clearly apparent in the post-colonial era not only in India but all over the world. Globalization is leading to a unipolar world; FDI is defended tooth and nail by the government ignoring at the same time the issues of empowerment and disempowerment, dependency and interdependency, and rural and urban have gained more urgency both at home and abroad. The fear of external colonialism has receded because no country is powerful enough to colonize any other country, but internal colonialism has set its foot down dividing the country into Bharat and India, Upper Caste and Lower Caste, the rich and the poor, urbanites and ruralites, the toiling masses and the privileged classes, the common man and the VVIPs, the minority and the majority. Thus our post-colonial world can best be described as a neo-colonial world, internationally divided into developed and developing nations, and intra-nationally divided between privileged and underprivileged. Gradually, these divisions have received cultural sanctions; they are considered natural for they are based on the principle of might is right.

To most Indians west is still the centre of the world; young minds consider it a privilege to study and work in the west. Our colonial mentality has remained intact. Gandhi worked hard to reverse this damage to our collective psyche by redefining courage as inner power and demonstrated by throwing the mightiest empire of the world out of India non-violently and thus giving us a new identity as a nation, as a culture and as a people. But we receded back. We have once again lost our identity that binds every Indian together and imbues him with a sense of nationalism that cuts across religions, castes, creeds or linguistic identities.

The ethics of industrial capitalism has not undergone any change. As such the hope that the post-industrial mode of production would usher in freedom from the monotony and dehumanizing work has been completely belied. Profit motive and market mechanism have ushered in compulsive consumerism. We may laugh at Gandhi's idea of trusteeship for it sounds impractical, but we have no alternative model to present to the world to bring freedom and dignity to the toiling masses. We have caged ourselves in the 'iron cage' of our own making.

We have stopped thinking in long terms and the systems way. What would happen in the long-run, and how the step we take will affect the freedom of others, we are not concerned. If someone makes me blind by one eye, I go for his both eyes. Gandhi warned against such thoughtless actions and reactions as they would turn the whole world blind. A bright example of this is the environmental crises the world faces today. We used certain technologies thoughtlessly and polluted the environment. And now we are looking for new technologies to repair the damage done by the older ones. Gandhi had warned us of the consequences of the so-called modern technology and modern thinking and modern science and technology. But his ideas were branded as anti-modernist.

Post modernism on the surface seems to reverse the gear. But it has rather added incongruities and irrationalities. Gandhi was not against rationality; he was against modernist rationalism that had no concern for human values. Gandhi was, therefore, equally opposed to a post-modern rejection of rationality. Gandhi was thus looking and pleading for a concept of rationality within reasonable bounds without an irrational revolt against reason itself.

REFERENCES

1. Smith, Adam (1776), *An Inquiry into the Nature and Causes of the Wealth of Nations*, 1st ed., London: W. Strahan.
2. George Stigler (1975), *Citizens and the State: Economic Theory of Regulations*. See also his, *The Economist as Preacher, and Other Essays*, Chicago: University of Chicago Press, 1982.
3. Joseph A. Schumpeter (1942 & 2010), *Capitalism, Socialism & Democracy*; See also his *Can Capitalism Survive? Creative Destruction of the Future of the Global Economy* (1942 & 2010), New York: Harper & Collins; and Bonar, J. (1926), The Theory of Moral Sentiments by Adam Smith, *Journal of Philosophical Studies*, Vol. 1, pp. 333-353.
4. *Das Capital* (first published in German, 1867), Marx/Engels Internet Archive (marxists.org) 1995, 1999.
5. Adam Smith, *Moral Sentiments,* first published 1959.
6. Adam Smith, *The Wealth of Nations,* Book 5, Part II, Chapter 1.
7. Karl Marx, *Das Kapital*, I, pp. 41-55.
8. *Ibid.*, 225-33.
9. *Ibid.*, 187-90.
10. *Ibid.*, 225-33.

11. Karl Marx, *Das Kapital*, I, 681-3. Also see, D.K. Fieldhouse, (ed.), (1967), *The Theory of Capitalist Imperialism,* London, pp. 1-44.
12. Karl Marx, *Das Kapital*, III, pp. 247-60.
13. *Ibid.*, I, 685-703; III, pp. 308-10.
14. D.G. Tendulkar, *Mahatma*, Vol. 7, Gandhi's Speech at Muir Central College, Allahabad in 1916.
15. *Ibid.*
16. Einstein, Albert *http://www.einsteinandreligion.com/godcomments.html*
17. Schrödinger, *op. cit.*
18. *Ibid.*
19. M.K. Gandhi, *All Men are Brothers,* Ahmedabad: Navjivan Publishing House.
20. *Ibid.*
21. D.G. Tendulkar, *Mahatma,* Vol. 1, p. 37, Address at the Delhi Provincial Political Conference on July 9, 1947, p. 38.
22. M.K. Gandhi, *Hind Swaraj*, Ch. 13.
23. *Collected Works of Mahatma Gandhi*, *op. cit.*, 6, p. 106.
24. M.K. Gandhi, *Hind Swaraj*, Ch. 7.
25. *Ibid.*, Ch. 4.
26. *Ibid.*, Ch. 19.
27. *Ibid.*, Ch. 11, 12.
28. *Collected Works of Mahatma Gandhi*, New Delhi: Government of India, 68, p. 97.
29. *Ibid.*

PART I
Understanding Gandhian Economics

2
Wholistic Vision of Gandhian Economics

Gita Srivastava

The first and the foremost cause of human suffering is the economic system of the world. It concentrates economic power in the hands of a few nations and few people. It does not matter which political system they follow: democratic or communist. It is the rich who dictate the processes of development and turn the wheel of globalization. Human values are set aside and misuse and waste of natural resources have increased and so have the crimes, corruption, alienation in the society. Cut-throat competition has created fear and insecurity. In this unending and ever escalating war, the weaker party, whether a nation-state or an individual suffers most. Poverty, unemployment, illiteracy and ill-health rule supreme in developing countries of Asia and Africa.

Since, the nineties of the last century and disappearance of the communist world led by the USSR, globalization as the means to develop an economy has become a new buzz-word. Greater access to the markets and technologies of developed countries holds out promise of improved productivity and higher living standard. It has also thrown new challenges like growing inequality across, and within nations, volatility in financial market and environmental deterioration. It has not only affected the economic aspect of human life but also took in its whirlpool all other aspects of human life. Ecomomic crash in U.S.A. led to world-wide market crash and closure of many industries and factories, leading to unemployment, inflation, starvation and suicides all over the world. Large-scale violence, totalitarian behaviour of the super powers and corruption in high places, racial discrimination, ethnic clashes, economic deprivation and criminalization of politics are some of its non-economic side effects. It is in this context that Gandhi's views on economic development within the overall framework of human development and modified to meet the present contexts and challenges can help resolve problems humanity faces today, economic problems intensified by globalization included. In the absence of morality and ethics, economics can prove to be a dangerous proposition as it has done so far.

In this context, Gandhi's economic views point to a solution. He proposes a non-violent and non-exploitative socio-economic system. In his scheme of things, there is place for poverty and unemployment. South Africa and India were Gandhi's experimental grounds from where he transmitted his message of truth and nonviolence to the entire world. In his design of the future, 'all men are equal'. "Even as members (organs) of the individual body are equal, so are the members of the society"[1]. He prepared this design of 'Equality' not only for India but for the entire humanity. This chapter delineates the economic views of Gandhi and how these views can be used for the welfare of humanity even in this era of globalization.

GANDHI'S STRESS ON MORAL PROGRESS

Gandhi regarded economic aspects of human life important but not over-riding. To him, evolution of man from animal made him a moral and spiritual being and rendered him superior to animals, which have physical might alone. As man evolved, he added material possession to his innate desire to be physically strong. And thus a new norm evolved under which richer a person is, more advanced he is. This has come to be known as modern civilization. So the evils associated with modern civilization touch practically every aspect of human life. Progress of science and technology in the two centuries has given man far more mechanical power to control nature than in the rest of human history. But this achievement, far from making man wiser or happier, has proved to be a great misfortune. Material progress has spelt moral ruin of man. In 1909 in *Hind Swaraj* Gandhi characterized "modern civilization as a 'disease' and a 'nine day wonder', for it takes note neither of morality nor of religion"[2]. This moral lag expresses itself in man's inordinate love of wealth and power. This blind worship of wealth and violence cannot go on indefinitely, without the human race relapsing into savagery. But Gandhi was not a pessimist. He held that "Modern civilization is not an incurable disease. It requires a drastic revolutionary remedy". This remedy, according to him, was the "cultivation of nonviolence in all spheres of life"[3].

To understand Gandhi's economic views let us go back to his writings. Gandhi more or less foresaw the problem that humanity faces today. In his view, increasing stress on material production and consumption unmindful of its implications for human development would eventually lead to immorality and loss of ethical values, which in turn would lead to socio-economic inequity, and violence. The emerging economic scenario is marked with rising standard of living and declining standard of life; widening gulf between poor and rich nations; between villages and cities; and between groups of people and individuals. Gandhi was opposed this lopsided progress and said, "I hold that economic progress in the sense I have put it, is antagonistic to real progress"[4]. Later, on 22nd December, 1916, while speaking in 'Economics Society' of Muir Central College, Allahabad University on "Does economic progress clash with real progress?" Admitting that he was not an economist and had not read well known economists like Mill, Marshall, and Adams Smith but he cannot equate economic progress, i.e., rise in the standard of living of the people with real (moral) progress that raises the standard of life of the people. "By economic progress we mean material advancement without limit, and by real progress we mean moral progress, which again, is the, same thing as progress of the permanent element in us"[5]. Defending the real (moral) progress Gandhi added, "They say that before we think or talk of their moral progress, we must satisfy their daily wants. With them they say material progress spells more progress. And then is taken a sudden jump. What is true of thirty millions is true of the universe…."[6] In *Hind Swaraj*, Gandhi said as early as 1909, "With its emphasis on material comforts, physical pleasures, mechanized system of production, sophisticated and more destructive arms, speedy communications and means of transport, this civilization, is more a disease than anything else…."[7]

To Gandhi increasing consumption of material goods alone was not a source of human satisfaction. A human being is not only a body and mind, but also a spirit. Unity of life follows through and from human spirit or soul. The development of human spirit, and an appeal to it, is through caring, love and sharing. Love involves service to others. Real progress relates to the progress of soul force; for real progress, moral laws are essential. "Man's duty is to do unselfish service to others…. because it is the very nature of the being"[8]. The moral law also requires that strong men of a community or a nation should consider it as their permanent duty to protect the weak and the oppressed. If all men realized the obligation of service, they would regard it as sin to amass wealth, and then, there would be no inequalities of wealth and, consequently, no famine or starvation.[9]

For Gandhi love is the binding force. "The world is held together by bonds of love. History does not record day to day incidence of love and service. It only records incidence of conflicts and wars. However, acts of love and service are more common in this world than conflicts and quarrels. We find innumerable villages and towns flourishing in the world. Had the world been always full of quarrel and discord, they could not possibly exist".[10] Love is expressed most acutely in the institution of a family and from family to a neighbourhood, to a community, to a village and on to a nation. This economic idea is applicable to global community also. Tolstoy wrote to Gandhi during his stay in South Africa "That love, which is the strong force for the union of human souls and actively derived from it, is the highest end only law of human life….This law was proclaimed by all…by the Indians and by the Chinese, Hebrew, Greek and Roman sages of the world".[11]

Gandhian economic order is based on the principles of truth, purity of means, *ahimsa* or non-violence and truth force. Gandhi sees two basic contradictions in the market economy: firstly, there is an elite-mass contradiction and secondly, the national elites exploit national masses and international elites exploit masses all over the world[12]. So long as these contradictions exist in any society, "the desired state of society" cannot be achieved. Gandhian economic thoughts and practices aim at minimizing and eventually eliminating these contradictions.[13]

Gandhi considered modern society being divided into two: elites and masses. The elites of both the rich and poor countries join hands and follow the policies and strategies that promote their welfare often at the cost of the masses. Economic growth and development in low income countries benefit the rich countries and elites among the low income countries. This growth takes place at the cost of the masses all over the world and thus promotes income inequality among the countries[14]. This inequality is set to increase as the globalization process moves forward. Number of millionaires and billionaires is growing, while a very large part of the world population lives under conditions of poverty. Poverty is not absent even in rich countries like the USA.

GANDHIAN ECONOMICS

Gandhian economics is based on certain moral and ethical principles that ensure the development and welfare of all: individuals, communities, societies and humanity as a whole irrespective of where they live, what religion they follow and what activity they are engaged in so long as they tread on the path of truth and nonviolence. We can outline the Gandhian economic model in following terms.[15]

1. Natural and financial resources should be used to promote the welfare of all human beings (individuals, families, communities, nations and societies).
2. The state should so manage the economy that each and every adult of the country—man as well as woman—is assured employment.
3. Small-scale agriculture and industries especially the handicrafts are protected from the onslaughts of individual and corporate entrepreneurs.
4. The state should ensure corruption-free administration; it should observe austerity and not indulge in wasteful public expenditures.
5. The administrative and implementing agencies should be accountable for the quantity and quality of development works carried out by them
6. People should be encouraged and helped to initiate grass root planning and development from below.
7. The energies of the people should find scope for regeneration and recognition.
8. Efforts should be made to promote local talent, expertise and initiatives and to rectify any deficiency that crops in the system and avoid induction of foreign ideas and ideals without proper examination.

The following six concepts incorporate the above eight requirements and thus constitute the foundation of Gandhian Economic model:

(a) *Swadeshi*,
(b) Bread labour,
(c) *Aparigraha*,

(d) Trusteeship,
(e) Equality, and
(f) Non-exploitation.

All the above concepts are based on certain moral and ethical principles; they are not mutually exclusive. *Swadeshi* is defined as self-reliance in matters basic needs with the proviso that it leads to optimum use of natural and human resources; it encourages cooperation among producers and consumers; and it promotes efficiency as well as moral progress. *Swadeshi* is to be practiced at all levels: individual, village, city, and nation. *Bread labour* is a socio-economic doctrine. Gandhi once observed that bread was a scarce commodity in India; poor had to go almost without it; sometimes having one meal a day and sometimes, none at all.[16] "If all laboured for their bread and no more, then there would be enough food and enough leisure for all. Then, there would be no cry of over population, no disease, no such misery as we see around. Such labour will be highest form of sacrifice....This may be an unattainable ideal. But we need not cease to strive for it. Even if without fulfilling the whole law of sacrifice, that is, the law of our being, we performed physical labour enough for our daily bread, we would go a long way towards the ideal"[17].

Aparigraha is non-possession of things which are trivial and irrelevant; it also means that all have access to and/or possess things in question. If people lead a life of *aparigraha*, there would be no shortage of goods that meet the baic needs of the people. The concept of *Trusteeship* was emerged from Gandhi's experience in South Africa as well as in India. Knowing that the poor and oppressed would never be able to counter the mighty forces of rulers and exploiters with violence, he wrote in 1927, "Each and everyone of you should consider himself to be a trustee for the welfare of the rest of the fellow labourers and not be self seeking. You must be and remain nonviolent under circumstances however grave and provoking...."[18] He further wrote, "If Indian society is to make real progress along specified lines, there must be a definite recognition on the part of the moneyed class that ryat also possesses the same soul that they do and that their wealth gives them no superiority over the poor. They must regard themselves ....as trustees holding their wealth for the good of their wards, the ryats. Then they would take no more than a reasonable amount as commission for their labours."[19]

Criticizing the Western civilization, he wrote in *Hind Swaraj* in 1909, "The aim of the Indian civilization is to elevate the moral being and that of the Western civilization is to propagate immorality. The latter is Godless, the former is based on belief in God.[20] Theory of trusteeship circumscribes privilege and power by sacrifices in favour of the under-privileged. It implies equality and decentralization. Gandhi's concept of equality did not mean that everyone should literally possess same amount of wealth. It simply meant that everybody should have enough for his or her own needs: "To each according to his needs."[21] He further said, "...The contrast between the rich and the poor, as it exists today, is a painful sight. The poor villagers are exploited by the foreign government and also by their own countrymen, the city dwellers. They produce the food and they go hungry. They produce the milk and their children go without it; it is disgraceful. Everyone must have balanced diet, a decent home to live in, facilities for the education of one's children and adequate medical relief."[22]

Gandhi's concept of a world without exploitation was based on his idea that the national elites exploited the masses all over the world. So long as this contradiction existed in any society, it would be impossible to bring about an equitable socio-economic order. And so long as inequities reign supreme in society, there would be no peace and harmony.

ECONOMIC SECURITY AS CONCEIVED BY GANDHI

Gandhi has written voluminously on various aspects of social, economic and political problems humanity faces today. He arrived at several concepts almost intuitively. Human existence, human survival and human development are the three cardinal elements of economic security and economically secured human life.[23] The economic crisis humanity faces today has given rise to economic disorder and imbalance, in that section of the population of the world which is marginalized and lives below the poverty line. For Gandhi, economic progress bereft of economic security had no meaning. Economic security implied freedom from economic violence and consisted of human rights of individuals:[24]

(a) to lead an economically secured life,
(b) to be employed to earn enough to sustain himself and his family,

(c) to maintain good health of his own and his family,
(d) to educate his children, and
(e) to ensure that the needs of the old age parents are met and they lead an honourable life.

If Gandhi's concept of economic security is extended to the nation-states, then the problems of human survival and development the world faces today would be gone once for all. Much would depend on how the nation-states use their economic resources and mechanism to ensure the welfare of all. If a nation follows Gandhi's concept of economic security, it will be able to ensure political, economic, social, cultural and ecological security for its citizens.

The looming threats of nuclear proliferation and ecological devastation are having a chastening effect on political leaders and development specialists. The grave socio-cultural and ecological stresses, the byproducts of runaway technology and unbridled economic growth, have cast a shadow on the long term viability and even wisdom of Western model of development. In many developing countries like China, a great majority of the people live below the poverty-line, building up of scientific, industrial, and technological infrastructure notwithstanding. Gandhi in his own time had warned that "machine must not make atrophied the limbs of man ....the mad rush for the wealth must cease and the labourer must be assured not only of a living wage but a daily task that is not mere drudgery.[25] In 1935, he said, "I would prize every invention of science made for the benefit of all. There is a difference between invention and invention. I should not care for the asphyxiating gases capable of killing masses of men at a time. The heavy machinery for the work of public utility, which cannot be undertaken by human labour has its inevitable place, but all that be owned by the state and used entirely for the benefit of the people. I can have no consideration for the machinery which is meant either to enrich a few at the expense of the many, or without cause to displace the useful labour of many."[26]

Gandhi at times seemed indulging in hyperboles. But he was right in the same way as Jacques Ellul was with respect to his *Technological Society*; Herbert Marcuse to his *One Dimensional Man*; and Jurgen Hebermas to his *Towards a Rational Society*. They have shown how 'technique' instead being the slave has become the 'master' of man. Similarly, Ivan Illich in *Tools for Conviviality* has shown how "machine has enslaved men."[27] The intractability of the socio-economic problems in developing countries and emergence of new tensions and dangers in the affluent West, are inducing a mood of introspection and sending thoughtful men back to Gandhi. Aldous Huxley wrote in the 'Gandhi Memorial Peace Number' of *Vishva Bharti Quarterly* of October 1949 "Gandhi's social and economic ideas are based upon a realistic appraisal of man's nature and the nature of his position in the universe."[28]

On thc occasion of the opening ceremony of Magan Museum of Khadi at Udyog Bhawan, Wardha, in 1938 someone asked Gandhi "whether cottage industries and the big industries can be harmonized?" Gandhi said, "Yes, if they are planned to help the villages. The key industries, the industries which the nations need, may be harmonized."[29] Referring to paper industry, he said "I believe that every village can produce its own paper ... I would expect to protect all the papers that villages can make."[30] To the question "What is meant by protecting the villages?" Gandhi said that "Protecting them against the inroads of the cities. In any case, under my scheme nothing will be allowed to be produced by the cities which can be equally well produced by the villages. The proper function of cities is to serve as clearing houses for the village products."[31]

During a discussion with M. Frydman, a Polish Engineer, Gandhi asserted that all the clothes we need can easily be produced in villages. Frydman replied, "The ultimate ideal of having self-sufficient villages is, of course, there, but that can come only when everyone is cultured in the Indian sense of the word. Does industrialization not serve to level the ground? Is not a sheer waste of energy merely to oppose it?" Reacting to Frydman, Gandhi said "As I look at Russia where the apotheosis of industrialization has been reached, the life there does not appeal to me. To use the language of the *Bible*, What shall it avail a man if he gains the whole world and lose his soul"? In modern terms, it is beneath human dignity to lose one's individuality and become a mere clog in the machine. I want every individual to become full blooded and fully developed member of society. The village must become self-sufficient. I see no other solution if one has to work in terms of *ahimsa*."[32]

Although Gandhi was conscious of the compromises he was making. "Railways are there, I do not avoid them. I hate motor cars, but I make use of them willy-nilly all the same. Again I dislike fountain pens, but just now I am making use of one...compromise comes in at every step, but one must realize that it is a compromise, and keep the final goal constantly in front of the mind's eye."[33]

Expressing his economic views to an American journalist in Sevagram in 1940, Gandhi had said "India has seven lakhs villages which take in ninety per cent of her population. America has to think of these.... My views on the national planning differ from the prevailing ones. I do not want it along the industrial lines. I want to prevent our villages from catching the infection of industrialization. American exploitation has added neither to the moral height of the exploited countries, nor of the exploiting country. On the contrary, it has impeded their march towards spiritual progress and had deadened America's real spirit of philanthrophy."[34] "Phenomenon like the one that America witnessed, cannot happen in India. I mean the destruction of tons of sugar and other agricultural products. You might have supplied to the other countries the sugar and the wheat or fed America's own unemployed." What a tragedy! Recently in India millions of tonnes of wheat kept in the open became unfit for human consumption. But the Government would not distribute it to the poor free of charge. Gandhi would never have dreamt that this would also happen in India—his dream of a free India

REFERENCES

1. D.G. Tendulkar, 1990, *Mahatma, Life of Mohandas Karamchand Gandhi*, Vol. VIII, New Delhi: Publications Division, p. 38.
2. *Hind Swaraj*, Ahmedabad, 1909, pp. 20-22, 92.
3. *Ibid.*, p. 22.
4. Ramjee Singh, Sundaram, S. (ed.), 1996, *Gandhi and the World Order*, New Delhi, 1996, p. 131.
5. D.G. Tendulkar, *op. cit.*, Vol. I, 1988, p. 192.
6. *Ibid.*, p. 194
7. J.N. Uppal, 1965, *Gandhi Ordained in South Africa*, New Delhi, p. 296.
8. Ramjee Singh, S. Sundaram, *op. cit.*, p. 131.
9. *Ibid.*
10. *Ibid.*
11. C.F. Andrews, 1995, *Mahatma Gandhi—His Life and Ideas*, New Delhi, p.195.
12. Ramjee Singh, S. Sundaram, *op. cit.*, p. 132.
13. *Ibid.*
14. *Ibid.*
15. Ratan Das, 2005, *The Global Vision of Mahatma Gandhi*, New Delhi, 2005, p. 133.
16. Ramjee Singh and S. Sundaram, *op. cit.*, p. 114.
17. D.G. Tendulkar, 1991, *op. cit.*, Vol. IV, p. 36.

18. D.G. Tendulkar, *op. cit., Ibid.*, Vol. II, p. 297.
19. *Ibid.*, p. 380.
20. M.K. Gandhi, 1909, *Hind Swaraj*, Ahmedabad, p. 2.
21. D.G. Tendulkar, 1990, *op. cit.*, Vol. VII, p. 47.
22. *Ibid.*, p. 47.
23. Amlendu Guha, *Economic Security and Peace*, in Gandhi *Prasang*, Vol. VIII, No. 1, October 2, 2005, p. 76.
24. *Ibid.*
25. B.R. Nanda, 2002, In *Search of Gandhi, Essays and Reflections*, New Delhi, p. 260.
26. D.G. Tendulkar, 1962, *op. cit.*, Vol. IV, p. 28.
27. B.R. Nanda, *op. cit.*, p. 260.
28. *Ibid.*, p. 261.
29. D.G. Tendulkar, *op. cit.*, Vol. V, p. 8.
30. *Ibid.*
31. *Ibid.*
32. *Ibid.*, p. 9.
33. *Ibid.*
34. D.G. Tendulkar, 1996, *Mahatma, Life of Mohandas Karamchand Gandhi*, Vol. VIII, New Delhi: Publications Division, p. 335.

3

Relevance of Gandhian Economics in a Globalized World Economy

Anup K. Mishra

Modern economic system is marked by globalization which was supposed to bridge the widening gaps between rich nations and poor nations at the international level and between rich people and poor people at the national, regional and local levels. The experience of the last two decades, however, tells a different story. The economic and human development gaps between rich and poor nations and peoples have widened. These unexpected consequences of globalization force us to look for alternatives.

One of these alternatives is Gandhian economics. Amidst the great thinkers of the twentieth century, Gandhi, the Father of Our Nation, shines with a peculiar lustre. His vision was broad and he considered economics as a means of human development, rather human beings as means of economic development. He recognized economics as one of the decisive forces in human life but refused to treat it as its determinant[1]; he tried to make economics serve the people rather than the other way round. And if human life must be founded on certain moral principles and values, economics cannot be allowed to over-ride these principles and values[2]. "Economics, for Gandhi, to be worth anything, must be capable of being reduced to terms of religion or spirituality.... that economics is untrue which ignores or decreases moral values"[3]. Unlike many earlier Indian economic thinkers, Gandhi repudiated many of the concepts and tenets of western economics and developed his own and that too not in the isolation of the real problems of life in India and their effective solutions.

THE PARADOX OF GLOBALIZATION

Nearly two decades have passed since the term globalization came in currency. This period is long enough to trace how far it has achieved the aims and objectives it was expected to achieve. It aimed at converting the world into a global village: a village marked by interdependence, love and affection, peace and harmony, and economic and social equality. But after two decades, it has created a world which is conflict-ridden, divided into rich and poor nations and peoples. Instead of prosperity spread across nations, societies, communities and individuals, it has given rise to more billionaires and more deprived; instead of bridging the gap between rich and poor it has widened the social, economic and technological gaps among them; instead of creating work opportunities to people, it has led to more unemployment; instead of eliminating chronic diseases, it has let loose many new contagious diseases (AIDS, Hepatitis, etc.); instead of maintaining peace, has led to more conflicts and wars; instead of sustainable development, it has disturbed the environmental balance; instead of respecting cultural values and traditions, it has crushed these values; and instead of sharing economic and political power, it has concentrated these powers in the hands of a few nations, regions and individuals.

These trends are well indicated by the Human Development Reports (HDRs) of the UNDP. The HDRs highlight that the top three billionaires in the world have now assets greater than the combined gross national products of 48 least developed countries of the world and inhabited by 600 million people. The richest of the world increased their net worth from US $400 billion in 1998 to two and half times in just four years[4]. Unfortunately in the same period over 80 countries have fallen below what they had as per capita incomes only a decade ago. A glance at the widening income gaps between the rich and the poor countries reveals the shocking facts that income ratio between the richest and poorest countries which was about 3:1 in 1820, 11:1 in 1913, 35:1 in 1950, 44:1 in 1973, 72:1 in 1992, 74:1 in 1997 widened to 80:1 in 2005.[5] These facts force us to remember and revive the concept of economics as a means of human development Mahatma Gandhi propounded.

Poverty and Hunger

Poverty, unemployment and low productivity are the highest concerns of most developing countries including India. In South Asia, 30 per cent of the babies are born underweight. Child mortality rates continue to be high (200 per 1000 live births); female child mortality is particularly high. The world has abject poverty in the midst of plenty. Of the world's six billion people, 2.8 billion live on less than $2 a day and 1.2 billion, on less than $1 a day. And 44 per cent are those who live on less than $1 a day, live in South Asia. As against this, the rich countries of European Union and Japan spend $2.5 and $7.0 a day for a cow, respectively.

In rich countries less than 1 per cent of children die before they reach their fifth birthday. As against this, in the poorest countries as many as a fifth of the children do not cross their fifth birth day. And while in rich countries fewer than 5 per cent of all children under five are malnourished, in poor countries as many as 50 per cent are malnourished.[6]

Disparities in Consumption

It is instructive to have a look at the consumption disparities in the beginning of the twentyfirst century. In the globalised world 20 per cent of the world's richest people account for 86 per cent of the total private consumption expenditure, the poorest 20 per cent consume only 1.3 per cent. The richest fifth consume 45 per cent of all meat and fish, the poorest fifth consume only 5 per cent of same. In energy consumption the richest fifth have the lion's share of 58 per cent, the poorest fifth are left with less than 4 per cent[7]. Viewing the above fact we admire the Gandhian perception of consumption. We find an entirely different approach which stresses on minimizing of wants and relates this principle to some of the major issues and concerns in development economics and policies.

Gandhi put forth the golden principle of "minimization of wants and/or consumption" and found that resources are "abundant enough" to satisfy the needs of all in a comfortable way. Instead of maximizing utility, consumers have to set their goal to satisfy their needs.

Global Economic Scene

While globalization has created unprecedented opportunity for some, a great majority of people have been left behind. There are still around 1 billion people living at the margins of survival on less than US $ 1 a day, with 2.6 billion—40 per cent of the world's population—living on less than US $ 2 a day. Around 28 per cent of all children in developing countries are estimated to be underweight or stunted. If India's high economic growth is unequivocal good news, the bad news is that this has not been translated into accelerated progress in cutting under-nutrition. One-half of all rural children are underweight for their age. About 10 million children die each year before the age of 5, the vast majority from poverty and malnutrition.

Infectious diseases continue to blight the lines of the poor across the World. An estimated 40 million people are living with HIV/AIDS claiming 3 million deaths in 2004. Every year there are 350-500 million cases of malaria with 1 million fatalities. Africa accounts for 90 per cent of malarial deaths and African children account for over 80 per cent of malaria victims worldwide. These deficits in human development draw attention to deep inequalities across the world. The 40 per cent of the world's population living on less than US$ 2 a day accounts for 5 per cent of global income. The richest 20 per cent account for three quarters of world income.

Income inequality is also rising within countries. Income distribution influences the rate at which economic growth translates into poverty reduction. More than 80 per cent of the world's population lives in countries where income differentials are widening. Skewed income distribution intersects with wider inequalities. Child death rates among the poorest one-fifth of people in the developing world are falling at half the average rate for the richest, with deep disparities between rural and urban population. Rural areas account for three in every four people living on less than US$1 a day and a similar share of the world population suffering from malnutrition. However, urbanization is not synonymous with human progress. Growth of urban slum is outpacing urban growth by a wide margin.

Realizing the above facts, now we can say that Gandhian ideas successfully expose the inherent weaknesses of the conventional approach and its irrelevance to the basic problems of mass poverty, hunger and unemployment in the developing parts of the world. These intolerable international disparities are rationalized by economic theory as unavoidable in a growing economy. The fault lies with the iniquitous socio-economic system maintained by the brute force of the class-dominated states.

India too is a Victim of Modern Economics

In India too, the growth has not benefited all sections of population. High rate of per capita income growth with very little reduction in poverty is itself a sufficient proof of the iniquitous character of growth. Some recent estimates[9] show that Gini coefficient of consumption expenditure has increased substantially both in rural and urban areas during 1993-94/2004-2005. According to estimates made by Asian Development Bank, Gini coefficient which was 0.326 in 1993 and rose to 0.368 in 2004. The ratio of income of the top 20 per cent to that of the bottom 20 per cent increased from 4.9 to 5.5.[10] Does it mean that growth has not 'trickled down' to the sizeable group of population? In fact, the notion of 'trickle down' does not seem to be a relevant now-a-days and hence the term 'inclusive growth' has been used in India in the latest government economic policy statements.

During the Tenth Plan of India (2002-2007), Indian economy grew by 7.8 per cent, but the growth rate of agricultural sector has been only around 2.0 per cent. Agriculture still employs 55 per cent workers and is the major source of livelihood for almost 60 per cent of population of the country. The industry and service sectors, which experienced much faster growth, i.e., 9 and 10 per cent, have not been able to pull people away from agriculture. With slower growth of agriculture and higher share of population dependent on it, the rural population has remained insulated from the benefits of the high aggregate growth of GDP. Their exclusion has been further reinforced by the fact that urban-centered and high technology-based subsectors in industry and services have been the main engines of economic growth in recent years.[11]

And the Gandhi's fear comes true when we visualize the above facts. In *Hind Swaraj* (1909) he opposed the use of machines which renders millions of people unemployed.

MODERN WORLD NEEDS GANDHI

Any discussions on globalization would remain incomplete unless we recall Gandhi. It is quite easy to come to an instant conclusion that Gandhi, despite the historic role he played in our freedom struggle, was old-fashioned, someone who could not fit well into the ethos of the new age. Indeed, his insistence on ascetic principles, his inclination to the centrality of the village in our socio-economic life, and his discomfort with modern machine, Railways and the legal system might give the impression that Gandhi is irrelevant. Even Nehru—a disciple and admirer of Gandhi—could not resist expressing his disagreement with him. He was not comfortable with Gandhi's blueprint of development, his 'glorification of poverty and suffering'. It is the spirit underlying what Gandhi said and did not the external forms and symbols he used to express his views. It is this spirit, to be used creatively to alter the trajectory of the prevalent form of modernity.[12]

Swaraj: The Ultimate Goal

Gandhi's notion of *swaraj* is highly relevant today. He wanted us to regain the power of 'soul-force', and become independent of the huge techno-economic enterprise that rule the economic landscape today. Gandhi's politico-economics leads to an ideal state which is not yet achieved anywhere in the world. People also doubt if it is ever achievable. But Gandhian thought persists in the possibility of achieving this state, if the means we adopt are right and in consonance with the goal. For the individual, it may be *Moksha* or *Nirvana*; and for the society, it would be *Swaraj* or the *Ramrajya*. In *Swaraj* or *Ramrajya*, everyone is ruled by one's own self and not by anyone else. In such a state, people enjoy freedom in all sectors of their life. This society is based on principles of Truth and Non-violence. The conditions laid by Gandhi to attain this goal are rather stringent. One has to pass through the path of *satyagraha,* the law of love. It is without anger and urge to retaliate even if the opponent is violent. This law of love is a law of truth as without truth, there is no love.[13]

We have seen how modernity elevates the power of the techno-scientific structure and the nation-state. It is not our contention to deny that these modern structures including globalization have made human life comfortable. But then, these very structures have also created an 'iron cage' or an 'administered totality' that tends to paralyze our power of self-rule. In other words, we become increasingly dependent on the 'expertise' solutions emanating from the techno-bureaucratic elites. This, as Gandhi warned, has belittled man. "If people were to settle their own quarrels, a third party would not exercise any authority over them. Truly, men were less unmanly when they settled their disputes either by fighting or by asking their relatives to decide for them. They become more unmanly and cowardly when they resorted to the courts of law. It was certainly a sign of savagery when they settle their disputes by fighting. Is it any the less so, if I ask a third party to decide between you and me? Surely, the decision of a third party is not always right. The parties alone know who is right. We in our simplicity and ignorance, imagine that a stronger, by taking our money gives us justice"[14]

"Likewise, if I fall sick, I am incapable of looking after myself, and altering my life-project. Instead, I begin to rely more and more on the medical expert. Indeed, the doctors induce us to indulge, and the result is that we have become deprived of self-control, and have become effeminate."[15] Gandhi sought to alter it. He thought that we must cultivate our 'soul force'—our moral/spiritual power—to revitalize ourselves, our villages, and our communities. In a way, Gandhi's notion of *Swaraj* was far deeper, not just the replacement of one kind of authority by another.

Human Values Must Accommodate Globalization

In a non-violent socio-economic order of Gandhi, modern economics and its by-products like accumulation of wealth by some and poverty for many would not be the rules. Gandhi was a vehement and consistent critic of economics in the form it is practiced today. He denounced the endless pursuit of materialism, which gave only sufferings and hardships to human beings. He aimed at improving the quality of life; wealth and income were to function as the means of human welfare and not as ends in themselves. Stressing that ethical and spiritual values were superior to materialistic goals, Gandhi disfavoured modern industrialization, mechanization, centralization and urbanization processes which entailed evils like slums, child labour, endless pursuit of profit, destruction of the spirit of cooperation, unemployment, decay of small, agro-and handicraft industries, exploitation of labour, disruption of self-reliant and self-contained village life, moral degradation, class-conflict, etc.

Gandhi rejected as a positive means to develop the economy. The USA is the most industrialized country in the world, but has failed to banish poverty and violence within and in other parts of the world. He favoured cooperation and best utilization of manpower.[16]

Gandhi has exposed the inherent weaknesses of conventional approaches, and their irrelevance in resolving the problems of mass poverty, hunger and unemployment in the world. The rich are becoming richer and the poor are left alone to fend for themselves and live on the leftover. This iniquitous socio-economic system is maintained by the brute force of the class-dominated state.

TO CONCLUDE

Gandhi was indeed a visionary. But dubbing Gandhian economic theory as utopian and rejecting his approach to development as mystic, value-loaded, primitive and, therefore, irrelevant is simply to overlook many aspects of the existing economic situation in the world. Depletion of natural resources—destructions of forests, pollution of air and water—emergence of new diseases, colossal waste of resources, widespread corruption in public life, monopolization of gains by a few and conspicuous consumption by them, and decaying moral values, are the direct results of modern economics. Gandhi has warned that the time is running out and unless man changes his economic route, the world would face more serious problems in years to come.

In the next 25 years, the world would have far more millionaires and billionaires than it ever had and would witness far more violence and iniquitous social, economic and technological development it ever had. The only way to get over the impending problems is to adopt the Gandhi's route of '*Swaraj*' that in essence means economic and technological changes circumscribed by eternal human values—truth and non-violence.

Globalization has indeed done a lot of good to humanity but it has also caused severe damage to our life and environment. We, the moderns would lose nothing except our arrogance if we learn a couple of lessons from Gandhi's visionary insight.

REFERENCES

1. Sethi, J.D. (1992), *Gandhi Today*, New Delhi: Vikas, p. 63.
2. Singh, Ramashankar (1991), "Elements in Gandhian Economics", *Gandhi Marg*, Jan-March, p. 454.
3. Hare A.E.C. "First Principles of Industrial Relations", Quoted in J.S. Mathu, (ed.) *Economic Thought of Mahatma Gandhi* (1962), Allahabad: Chaitanya, 1962), pp. 30-34.
4. *Human Development Report (1999)*, UNDP, Oxford University Press.
5. *World Development Report* (2007-08), UN Publication.
6. *Ibid.*, 2000-01.

7. Stieglitz, J. (2002); *Globalization and its Discontents*, New Delhi: Penguin Books.
8. Himanshu (2007), "Recent Trends in Poverty and Inequality: Some Preliminary Results", *Economic and Political Weekly*, February, 10.
9. ADB (2008), *Key Indicators*, Manila: Asian Development Bank.
10. Dev and Ravi (2007), "Poverty and Inequality: All India and States," *Economic and Political Weekly*, February, 10.
11. Gandhi, M.K. (1909), *Hind Swaraj or Indian Home Rule*, Ahmedabad: Navajivan Publishing House, p. 51.
12. Papola, T.S. (2008), "Disparities in Development", Trends in Regional variations in High Growth Period, Presidential Address at Fourth Annual Conference of UPUEA, DBS College, Kanpur, November 2008.
13. Pathak, Avijit, 2006, *Modernity, Globalization and Identity: Towards a Reflexive Quest*, New Delhi: Aakar Books, p. 58.
14. Singh, Ramashankar, *op. cit.*
15. Gandhi, M.K. (1909), *op. cit.*
16. Singh, Ramashankar, *op. cit.*

4

Gandhian Perspectives on Economy and Society

Hetal Mehra and *Kirti M. Vyas*

> "True economics never militates against the highest ethical standard, just as all true ethics, to be worth its name, must at the same time, be also good economics... True economics stands for social justice; it promotes the good of all equally, including the weakest, and is indispensable for decent life..."
>
> —*M.K. Gandhi* in *Harijan*, 9th October, 1937

INGREDIENTS OF GANDHIAN ECONOMICS

Swaraj

One of Gandhi's basic principles underlying Gandhian Economic is: Earth provides enough to satisfy every man's need but not for every man's greed. Whereas mainstream economics makes the common man completely vulnerable in the matter of production and distribution of resources, Gandhi visualized an alternative through the system of *swaraj*. According to Gandhi, every country should stand on its own strength. The components of *swaraj* are based on two independent variables—psychology and ethics. Since resources are scarce, production cannot be increased indefinitely. The psychology of affluence is an irrational phenomenon. The basic principles of economic activity are based on needs and not on affluence. Affluence breeds inequality, as it is based on economic distortion. Greed grows out of the desire to be affluent. Here, psychology can play a crucial role. Values which condition the mind can change human behaviour. The goal of *swaraj* brings limits to human wants. The basic ingredient of economic independence is that Gandhi gave adequate importance to the traditional sector. Highest priority is given to agriculture and agro-centric industries. Gandhi observed that we cannot build non-violence on a factory civilization, but it can be built on self-contained villages. And for that we must have to be rural-minded, and to be rural-minded, we have to have faith in the spinning wheel.

Swadeshi

For Gandhi, the soul and spirit of India rested in its villages. He said that the true India is to be found not in its few cities but in its seven hundred thousand villages. If these villages perish, India will perish too. According to the principle of *swadeshi*, whatever is made or produced in the village must be used, first and foremost, by the members of the village. Mainstream economics believes in centralized, industrialized and mechanized modes of production, whereas Gandhi envisions a decentralized, home-grown, hand-crafted mode of production. Mass production forces people to leave their villages, their land, their crafts, and their homesteads and go to work in city based factories. Instead of dignified human beings and members of self-respecting village communities, villagers become cogs in the wheel. For Gandhi, a machine civilization was no civilization. A society in which workers had to labour at a conveyor belt, in which animals were treated cruelly in factory farms and in which economic activities necessarily lead to ecological devastation, could not be conceived of as a civilization. Its citizens would only end up as neurotics; the natural world would inevitably be transformed into a desert, and its cities into concrete jungles. *Swadeshi*, for Gandhi, was a sacred principle, as sacred as the principles of truth and non-violence.

Trusteeship

Gandhi's idea of Trusteeship arose from his faith in the law of non-possession. It was founded on his religious belief that everything belonged to God and was from God. Therefore, the bounties of the world were for His people, as a whole, not for any particular individual. When an individual had more than his respective portion, he became a trustee of that portion for God's people. If this principle could be imbibed by people in general, Trusteeship would become a legalised institution. Gandhi wished it to become a gift from India to the world. Basically, Gandhi suggested this concept as an answer to the economic inequalities of ownership and income, a kind of non-violent way of resolving all social and economic conflicts prevalent in the world. Therefore, man's dignity, and not his material prosperity, is the centre of Gandhian economics. Gandhian economics aims at a distribution of material prosperity, keeping only human dignity in view. Thus it is dominated more by moral values than by economic ideas. According to Gandhi, Trusteeship is the only ground on which one can work out an ideal combination of economics and morality.

The Gandhian concept of Trusteeship departs significantly from Marxian economic philosophy too. If Marxism is the child of Industrial Revolution, Gandhian theory can be understood only in the context of certain basic spiritual values of the Indian tradition. Marxian socialism aims at the destruction of the class called capitalists, whereas the Gandhian approach is not to destroy the institution, but to reform it. Gandhian socialism, being ethical, is different from Marxian socialism. Man to Gandhi, is an ethical being first and a social being later. The most significant difference between Marxian socialism and Gandhian socialism lies in the method they recommend to achieve it. Whereas Marxian socialism harps on violence, Gandhian socialism aims at a change of heart on the part of the rich. There is no place for violence, but only trust. The common man trusts his trustee and the latter plays the role of a custodian. Though this kind of socialism is difficult to achieve, Gandhi advocated it as he believed in the basic strength of the goodness of man and the value of morals.

Aparigraha

Gandhi has said, "by economic progress, I take it to mean material progress without limit and by real progress we mean moral progress, which again is the same thing as progress of the pre-eminent element in us"[1]. Commenting on the material progress without limit, he said, the society that prospered materialistically experienced a moral fall. Rome suffered a moral fall after it achieved material affluence. The Yadavas ruined themselves morally when they were rolling in riches. Gandhiji thought that an ordinary measure of morality is possessed by most including the very rich, but material gain by them did not ensure moral richness.

Gandhiji then says that Jesus Christ was the greatest economist of his time. Quoting the dialogue between the Christ, a citizen and other disciples described by St. Mark, Gandhiji emphasizes in the lecture the virtue of sharing wealth in the service of the poor and have-nots. The point that he brings out is against amassing wealth. Later he has formulated the idea of *aparigraha* (non-accumulation) as one of the principles he has advocated. It can be readily seen that his reservation was to limitless material prosperity in the society. Gandhiji in *Hind Swaraj* explains the implications of fall in the moral standards in the society following material prosperity.

Non-Violence

Rajmohan Gandhi (1995) quotes Gandhiji on means and ends with respect to violence, which again is a value that was very central to the economic systems propagated by Gandhi. Rajmohan Gandhi says that Gandhi's case on means and ends against violence was compelling. "If I want to cross the ocean, I can do so only by means of a vessel; if I were to use a cart for the purpose, both the cart and I would be at the bottom…. The means may be likened to a seed, the end to a tree; and there is the same inviolable connection between the means and the end as there is between the seed and the tree."[2]

Moral value was extremely important for Mahatma Gandhi. Economics without ethics and ethical consideration was not warranted. Dasgupta in his comprehensive analysis on Gandhi's economic thought had dealt with the subject thoroughly. According to him, Gandhi's approach to economic issues was explicitly based on ethical considerations. Gandhi insisted that the relationship between the economics and ethics works both ways. While economic concepts were laden with ethical implications, ethics too must descend from the clouds and become 'good economics'. Ethics, Gandhi is saying, is not simply an exercise for philosophers, a convenient handle for sharpening their wits on the logic of extreme. It must be relevant to the ordinary business of life where one's options are limited by resource constraints. Ethics by its nature is an enterprise for worldly, a guide to the perplexed; and its answers, to be credible, need to be economically viable. "No person in the world has found to maintain something which is a source of constant economic loss."[3]

From the foregoing analysis it should be clear that Gandhi's economic thought cannot be brought into the framework of the economics discipline as it has emerged. However, it is possible to explain the implications of Gandhi's economic thoughts on the microeconomics and macroeconomics tenets.

Let us first examine the implications for individual behaviour in the microeconomic framework. Edgeworth averred more than a century ago that the first principle of economics was that every agent was actuated only by self-interest.[4] It is here that the 'economic man' was born. This 'economic man' is unacceptable to Gandhiji. It is here that he parts company with the standard economics. According to Dasgupta[5], it is Gandhiji's conviction that one's behaviour as an economic agent cannot be isolated from one's behaviour as an autonomous moral agent. In this context Gandhiji brings in self restraint. Then he talks about limiting wants. In his scheme, wants cannot be unlimited and hence they would have to be controlled. Those who have should not aspire for more and more and more.

Gandhi suggested a consumption behaviour for the economically better off people which was moderated by ascetic and paternalistic values. In modern economics there is no scope to introduce this constraint and then maximise utility. Income is the only constraint that is accepted. On the Macroeconomics front too, Gandhiji was clearly promoting decentralized production systems. Village level self-sufficiency was meant to provide maximum opportunity for production at local level. He preferred simple systems as against modern complicated systems. Lakdawala's assessment on this issue about Gandhi may be seen in the following expression. "Gandhiji instinctively disliked the working of the money or the banking mechanism. The institution of money was too complex in his opinion; transactions in kind were more easily understood and more human. The only types of banks he approved were in the nature of grain banks for safe local storage. Ordinary commercial banks associated with urbanisation were a part of the mechanism of local exploitation."[6] Complicating the production and supply processes or deliberate attempts to make the processes of societies economic functions complex and then looking for smooth devices for solving the complexities that arise in economic transactions needs to be distinguished. The use of science and technology for the latter is also not only useful but desirable too even within the framework of simple living and high thinking. At the time of writing of the *Hind Swaraj* Gandhiji had seen the efforts all over the world and especially in England which was imperial lord of the world then, about complicating the economic activities so that the one who set in complications reaped the maximum benefit by way of profit for the firm and industry and income and employment for the population. The criticism by the advocates of simple and uncomplicated societies for human survival, who also draw their basic strength from the emphasis on spiritual growth and development of the human civilization rather than from the materialistic growth has been that the modernisation of the society with the beginning of the industrialisation has largely implied complicating economic transactions. The main reason for this is the acceptance of the premise that human wants are insatiable. And this has been accepted as such without any serious scrutiny with morals and ethics in the society. In this context Sethi[7] refers to Lionel Robbins's celebrated definition and says that all that economics has been doing is the opposite of what Gandhi had said. Gandhi did not accept the concept of economic man because he refused to recognise the separation of economics from ethics. He denounced the technological determinism because it enslaved man and sanctified only those technologies that conformed to value promises. About all, he struggled against the mightiest imperial power in terms of non-violent theory and order. As he went along with these tasks, he discovered his own science of economics, although he did not analyse it in a very vigorous manner.

IMPACT OF ECONOMIC GROWTH ON NATURE AND MAN

There has been some complications in making the assessment of economic development especially after 1970. Rapid economic growth has created immense pressure on the natural resources base such as land, forest, water and air. Overexploitation and pollution are two menaces in the context of the use of both renewable and non-renewable natural resources. Changing social fabric and moral standards in the society as a result of rapid economic change has been relegated to back stage. A new movement, namely the environment movement has emerged and it is fairly powerful. Morality and values have been brought to the discussion *via* the irreversible damages being caused to the nature. The conventional development models have supposedly led to disaster and destruction. 'Sustainable Development' is the concern of groups spearheading the environmental movement. There is a lot of literature reflecting the views and analysis based on environmental concerns. In this chapter its review is not attempted. But, it is relevant to note that the scholars, activists and practitioners basing their work on Gandhian thought have clearly sided with the environmental movement in the world in general and the country in particular. There have been some serious arguments relating to the present crisis with the Gandhian path, and it is argued that had the society followed the Gandhian path the possibility of achieving sustainable development was high.

GANDHI AND GLOBALISATION

By now thousands of papers and hundreds of books have been written on Globalization. One can be sure that there are many definitions trying to explain globalization. Many see it as a primary economic phenomenon, involving the increasing interaction, or integration, of national economic systems through the growth in international trade, investment and capital flows. One can also point to a rapid increase in cross-border social, cultural and technological exchanges as part of the phenomenon of globalization. Gandhiji in *Hind Swaraj* and subsequent writings and speeches was mainly concerned with questions relating to modernity and global culture. His position on economic philosophy was more fundamentally related to morality and ethics in earning and spending. Similarly, he defined in his own way a modern civilization for Indians and India that had to be different from that of the British and England.

Once we understand these basic tenets in Gandhi's Economic thoughts, it becomes clear that globalisation appears at a fairly late stage. In his writings that are scattered, he has written to the effect that he was not against selling genuine surplus in the local economies. He was not averse to technologies and knowledge that reduced the human misery and drudgery. It did not matter whether it was local or foreign. But it is also very clear that he never was in agreement that the economics should be growing with export as the engine. By promoting that was more local that helped in the generation of dignified livelihood, the cultural onslaught from outside would by itself get minimized. In his scheme globalisation would not enter as it is poised today to influence the developing economies.

This is a very modest attempt to define the Gandhian outlook sharply, however, it is believed that the Gandhian approach is superior because its concepts lie in their in-built dynamics and close relations with praxis implying the once on a Gandhian path, not only the system put on the path of steady growth, its moral legitimacy also does not remain in doubt any longer. He was not interested in the scope of and method of economic science, as we economists naturally understand it. Rather, he worked for a whole lifetime on articulating the principles of an alternative and "more real" human economy centering on the very themes outlined in his lecture: the lack of correlation between material expansion and genuine progress, the need for an economics-cum-ethics that will enable moral growth and dignity for all, the fallacy of seeking happiness in individual acquisitive behaviour, and the need for encouraging people to seek a self-esteem and genuine meaning.

NOTES

1. Government of India (2000), *Collected Works of Mahatma Gandhi*, Volume 15, 4th Revised Edition, New Delhi: Publications Division, Ministry of Information and Broadcasting, Government of India.
2. Gandhi, Rajmohan (1995), *The Good Bantam: A Portrait of Gandhi*, New Delhi: Penguin Books.
3. Dasgupta, Ajit K. (1996), *Gandhiji's Economic Thought*, London: Routledge.
4. Diwan, Romesh and Lutz, Mark, (eds.) (1985), *Essays in Gandhian Economics*, New Delhi: Gandhi Peace Foundation.
5. Dasgupta, *op. cit.*
6. Lakdawala, D.T. (1971), "Gandhiji and Growth Economics", in Raval, M.N., *et al.*, (editors) *Gandhiji's Economic Thought and its Relevance at Present,* Surat: South Gujarat University.
7. Sethi, J.D. (1978), *Gandhiji Today*, New Delhi: Vikas Publishing House.

REFERENCES

Brahmananda, P.R. (1971), "A Theoretical Note on the Economic Foundations of a Gandhi-Type Society", in Raval M.N., *et al.*, (editors) *Gandhiji's Economics Thought and its Relevance at Present*, Surat: South Gujarat University.

Desai, Meghnad (1998), "Development Perspectives: Was there an Alternative to Mahalanobis", in Ahluwalia Isher Judge, Little I.M.D. (Editors), *India's Economic Reforms and Development; Essays for Manmohan Singh*, New Delhi: Oxford University Press.

Guillen, Mauro F., 2001, "Is Globalisation Civilising, Destructive or Feeble? A Critique of Five Key Debates in Social Science Literature", *Annual Review of Sociology*, Vol. 27.

Hanley, Nick, Shogren Jason F. and White Ben (1997), *Environmental Economics in Theory and Practice,* New Delhi: MacMillan India Ltd.

Parel, Anthony J. (ed.) (1997), *Gandhi: Hind Swaraj and Other Writings,* (Foundation Books), New Delhi: Cambridge University Press.

Raval, M.N. (1971), "Contentment and Containment of Wants—A Suggested Interpretation" in Raval M.N., *et al.*, (editors) *Gandhiji's Economic Thought and its Relevance*, Surat: South Gujarat University.

5
Gandhian Idea of Economic Independence

A.N. Panda

Very few individuals are born in this world with the capability to influence the destiny of nations long after they leave this world for their heavenly abode. They put forward such powerful ideas and make such contributions during their lifetime that they continue to motivate the people even after they are no longer there to regulate and direct their followers. Mahatma Gandhi was one of such few great personalities who forwarded ideas which continue to provide guidance to the people of the world in general and those of India in particular for all time to come. His ideas and opinions are still relevant to the people as those continue to create hope in a period in which there is an atmosphere of despair and resentment throughout the world. He still invokes creative and positive thoughts in the minds of people to face various worldly challenges.

Mahatma Gandhi was a multifaceted personality. During his lifetime he has advanced ideas and opinions on multifarious issues and given suggestions on how to deal with heterogeneous questions. He has expressed his opinions on a variety of topics and made recommendations to tackle the prevailing problems faced by mankind. As he has delved into different aspects he has not developed any carefully organized viewpoint which can be presented as Gandhian philosophy and he has been often criticized by his critics that he has not contributed any systematic concept. However, if one goes deeper into his writings and speeches one can find many useful and discernible prescriptions with regard to various difficulties faced in life. More significantly, the most glaring difference Gandhi has from many other great personalities of the world is that he propagated only such opinions which he had already experimented during his lifetime.

Mahatma Gandhi is generally credited with the freedom of India and regarded as the most successful political leader of the country to guide the common mass to their independence. He took charge of the freedom struggle at a critical stage and fruitfully led it to its desirable end. He played an instrumental role to galvanize the passive Indians to a dynamic state and inspired them to actively oppose the colonizers; he was responsible for ultimately driving away the British from India. He was truly a leader of the common men and he was able to dismantle the British rule in India by transforming the elite freedom movement into a mass movement.

Mahatma Gandhi considered the individual as the centre of the social system and the goal of a man was to realize his moral being. Gandhiji laid emphasis on the performance of duty by the individual. He proposed that society should provide maximum opportunity to the individual to attain his personal development which included his ability to perform selfless service for others and willing fulfilment of his social obligations. An individual should be free so that he would carry out his obligations to the best of his ability. Gandhi believed that no country should be subjugated by another because freedom was necessary for the citizens to discharge their duties efficiently.

According to Gandhi, an individual should be free from all limitations to pursue his best personality which was attainment of a moral self. The best moral self could not be achieved if an individual suffered from economic hindrances. Therefore, Gandhi also focused on economic independence of the individual. He was in favour of evolving an economic system which would allow freedom to the individual from economic point of view and would make him economically free by satisfying his basic material needs. As per him, if the bare necessities of an individual remained unfulfilled he could not be in a position to enjoy his political freedom. An economically enslaved man could not be expected to take political decisions independently.

Before going into the economic system as prescribed by Mahatma Gandhi it is necessary to understand the few economic premises on which Gandhi lays specific significance. Gandhi believes that 'increase of material comforts generally does not in any way whatsoever conduce to moral growth.' It means Gandhi attaches priority to the growth of the moral personality of the individual as he regards the individual as a moral being; a moral being does not seek worldly pleasure and is not after the material aggrandizements and possessions, as his aim in life is attaining moral perfection.

Gandhi always gave equal importance both the means and the ends. To him, means was like the root and the goal was the fruit. As said by him, "The means may be likened to a seed, the end to a tree; and there is just the same inviolable connection between the means and the end as there is between the seed and the tree"[1] Therefore, he asserted, "there is no connection between the means and the end is a great mistake."[2] He authoritatively told that if a bad method was applied for a good cause then neither the means could be justified nor the outcome would be a good one and ultimately, the consequence would be dreadful and he said, "We reap exactly as we sow."[3] So, according to him, the means and ends could never be separated from each other like the fruit and the root. Hence, all activities of the individual must have an ethical basis. Unless an action had an ethical foundation it became immoral and undesirable.

The economic activity of a man must have an ethical foundation and without a moral basis it became an undesirable act on the part of the individual. Thus, unlike many economists who gave importance to the increase of production of goods and services so that the profit could be maximized and the possessions of the possessor could be increased, Gandhi laid emphasis on the final utilization of the products for the betterment of humanity. Even he propagated for applying the moral principles in the conduct international relations so that the entire mankind was benefited. In his words, "That economics is untrue which ignores or disregards moral values. The extension of law of non-violence in the domain of economics means nothing less than the introduction of moral values as a factor to be considered in regulating international commerce. And I must confess that my ambition is nothing less than to see international relations placed on a moral basis through India's efforts."[4]

Mahatma Gandhi was against injustice of any kind. He was opposed to the exploitation of one by another. He was a champion of equality of individuals. He considered all human beings as the sons of God and all were entitled to enjoy the basic facilities of life. In the economic field, according to the Mahatma, the bare necessities of all must be fulfilled because without such contentment no individual could lead a life of dignity and self-respect. Hence in the economic field, there should not be a gap between the haves and the have-nots and the haves were only the custodians of the resources of society.

He assumed that the rich were not given the licence to exploit the poor and become richer at the cost of the latter.

Gandhi was out and out a peace loving person and he abhorred violence of any kind. He regarded violence as the weapon of a beast. For him, the display of violence was a demonstration of the destructive nature of an actor. Only when a man became controlled by his animal instincts he became violent. But he had a strong conviction that non-violence was consonant with the true nature of human beings which was basically noble. He strongly affirmed, "It is the only true force of life."[5] He criticized the use of violent means in any human conduct. He did not prescribe for hurting an individual in any manner. It had been commented, "Gandhi's non-violence is based on the higher aspects of human nature, which rebel against tyranny, injustice and authoritarianism."[6] According to the Mahatma, the supreme law of the universe must be respected and he said, "Non-violence is the supreme law"[7] Even in economic activities he did not want an individual to be hurt to the minimum extent. So, to him, the purpose of an economic activity was to fulfil a material need of an individual and that too not at the cost of hurting another individual in any way. Therefore, the economic system should be such that the needs of all would be satisfied but nobody would suffer.

VILLAGE ECONOMY AND RURAL DEVELOPMENT

Mahatma Gandhi had a clear understanding of the Indian economy. He had realized the importance of village in India. While Gandhi advocated for freedom of the country from the foreign rulers he craved for freedom not only in the political sense but also in its totality. He had an integral view of freedom. To Gandhi, every individual and every part of the country must be free from all forms of hindrances and even a unit at the lowest level must have freedom. He said, "Independence must begin at the bottom. Thus every village will be a republic or Panchayat having full powers. It follows, therefore, that every village has to be self-sustained and capable of managing its affairs even to the extent of defending itself against the whole world."[8] He was of the opinion that village was the core unit of Indian democracy and said, "In the true democracy of India, the unit is the village."[9] He continued, "I have believed and repeated times without number that India is to be found not in its few cities, but in its 70,00,000 villages."[10]

As India is a country of villages where 80 per cent of people inhabit in villages, the economy of the country should be so decided that the requirements of the rural people should be met. Underlining the importance of villages in India he said, "if village perishes, India will perish too"[11] The villages should be self-sufficient; to make them self-reliant, it is necessary to produce goods and create services which would be useful for the people of villages. Every village should be a self-contained economic unit where all the basic needs of the people are to be fulfilled by the village itself.

Mahatma Gandhi opposed hegemony of any kind and wanted that people of India must be free; he fought for *swaraj*. He said, "It is *swaraj* when we learn to rule ourselves."[12] He used the term *swaraj* to denote self-government and preferred *swaraj* for everybody; even for the lowest of the low should have *swaraj*. He proclaimed, "the *swaraj* of my dream is the poor man's *swaraj*."[13] Unless the poorest of the poor had access to the highest authority and the right to exercise decision-making power, independence had no value; everybody must have the prerogative to decide for himself. Mahatma Gandhi stated, "That *swaraj* is the poor man's *swaraj* or *Rama-Raj*. Ram symbolized justice and equity, Rama symbolized truth and charity. Justice and equity mean the establishment of just and equitable relations between capital and labour, between the landlord and the tenant. The land and the capitalist will cease to exploit the tenant and the labourer, but studiously protect his interests."[14]

Gandhiji believed that the responsibility of the state was to provide opportunity to the individual to attain perfection in his life; so an individual must be free in the state to develop his moral self. He announced, "The real question is how to bring about man's highest intellectual, economic, political and moral development".[15] All persons residing in the state must have the prospect of leading a life towards their goals and there should not be any discrimination between the people of urban areas and those of rural areas. In his opinion "there should be equality between the town dwellers and villagers in the standard of food and drink, clothing and other living conditions. In order to realize this equality today, people should be able to produce their own necessities of life, i.e., clothing, foodstuffs, dwellings and lighting and water."[16] Therefore, there must be village *swaraj*. He clarified, "My idea of village *swaraj* is that it is a complete republic, independent of its neighbours for its own vital wants and yet interdependent for many others in which dependence is a necessity."[17]

Gandhiji feels that the essential needs of all must be fulfilled by the goods produced in the village itself. The distribution system in the village should be so managed that all get their vital necessities fulfilled. He proposes that if the surplus goods are distributed among the needy and poor villagers there would not be any person in the village who would be hungry and helpless and at the mercy of others. If poverty can be eradicated from the rural areas, there would not be any starvation in the rural areas and in the country. So the prerequisite is to end the problems of the people of rural India and to do so, it is necessary to give importance to the rural economy and remove poverty of the rural people. Therefore, Gandhi gave importance to village economy and enriching the village life.

CONCEPT OF *SWADESHI*

To revitalize the Indian economy Gandhi suggested adoption of *swadeshi*. He narrated that *swadeshi* meant using of locally produced goods and acceptance of the indigenous talent in preference to imported goods and alien genius. In his words, "*swadeshi* is that spirit in us which restricts us of the use and service of our immediate surroundings to the exclusion of the more remote."[18] He observed, "Much of the deep poverty of the masses is due to the ruinous departure from *swadeshi* in the economic and industrial life."[19] He remarked that the departure from traditional economic life was the cause of suffering for the masses in India. Because India had ruined its village economy so the country was on the verge of destruction. To negate the damaging trend of Indian economy the most imperative step was to resuscitate the rural economy in the country. He commented, "Every village in India will almost be a self-supporting and self-contained unit, exchanging only such necessary commodities with other villages where they are not locally producible."[20]

He linked the country's loss of freedom with the ruin of village economy and end of self-sufficiency of the villagers. He firmly believed that the people of India had developed a slave mentality as they were dependent upon the supply from foreign lands and unless this mind set was changed India could not be free in true sense of the term. So he advised, "It is a world-known maxim that the removal of the cause of a disease results in the removal of the disease itself. Similarly if the cause of India's slavery be removed, India can become free."[21]

Explaining the comprehensive meaning of *swadeshi* Gandhiji continued, "I have never considered the exclusion of everything foreign under every conceivable circumstance as a part of *swadeshi*. The broad definition of *swadeshi* is the use of all home-made things to the exclusion of foreign things in so far as such use is necessary for the protection of home-industry, more especially those industries without which India will become pauperized.... *Swadeshi* which excludes the use of everything foreign, no matter how beneficent it may be and irrespective of the fact that it impoverishes nobody, is a narrow interpretation of *swadeshi*."[22] The idea of *swadeshi* was not narrow in its interpretation. It did not mean rejection of anything foreign just for the sake of rejection. It was, for Gandhiji, a justification for survival of the local talent and its growth. But if necessary, something foreign could be utilized for one's own growth and he said, "for I shall buy from every part of world that is needed for my growth. But by the same token, I refuse to buy from anybody anything however nice or beautiful if it interferes with my growth or injures those whom nature has made my first care."[23] He maintained, "I have never considered the exclusion of everything foreign under every conceivable circumstance as a part of *swadeshi*. The broad definition of *swadeshi* is the use of all home-made things to the exclusion of foreign things, insofar as such use is necessary for the protection of some industry."[24] He further stated, "To reject foreign manufacturers because they are foreign and go on wasting national time and money in the promotion in one's country of manufacture for which it is not suited would be a criminal folly and a negation of *swadeshi* spirit."[25]

PROPAGATION OF COTTAGE INDUSTRY

Mahatma Gandhi condemned the predisposition to earn money for the sake of earning it. He criticized the inclination to maximize profit by remaining engaged in different economic activities. He disapproved the profit making tendency of people which was making the people slaves of money and reflected, "Formerly, men were made slaves under physical compulsion. Now they are enslaved by temptation of money and of the luxuries that money can buy."[27]

In Gandhi's view, the goal of economic activities is to fulfil the material needs of mankind and he wants that the basic needs of all should be satisfied and all must lead a life with dignity. All these will be possible only if all are provided with a means of livelihood. To do so, there must be end of unemployment. In a capitalist system, big industries are established for large scale production and to generate wealth for the rich; in this system, the rich become richer as the purpose of all such economic activities is to increase production so that profit can be maximized and the owners of capitalist establishments get scope to increase their property. It also becomes easier for the capitalists to control the workers in a more stringent manner as the industries can be established at limited number of places and very often it leads to exploitation of workers at the hands of the mill owners. Further, due to use of heavy machineries many workers lose their means of livelihood. It results in increasing the number of poor people in the society on the one hand and increasing the degree of their poverty on the other hand.

Gandhiji was against centralized production and he opposed concentration of economic power in the hands of a few persons. He was for intensive, small scale and cooperative farming and development of cottage industry. He propagated for social justice and economic opportunities for all and mentioned, "What do I resent is the wanton and wicked destruction of the one cottage industry of India that kept the wolf from the doors of thousands of homes scattered over a surface 1,900 miles long and 1,500 miles broad."[28] Mahatma Gandhi supported organization of economy through decentralization and village Panchayats. He objected to the use of machines to produce goods which led to destruction of cottage industry. He gave preference to decentralization of economic power of the society because according to him, centralization was generally associated with coercion which was unethical.

Giving the example of weavers and the important role they can play in the economy of the country he presented the view, "If the weavers wake up and decide exclusively to weave hand spun yarn, not only would million earn a little by spinning but, along with them, thousands of others employed in ginning, carding and starching would get more work to do. The daily earnings of thousands of carpenters and blacksmiths would go up."[29]

If cottage industry is given importance then large number of workers can be employed in different economic units. It will not only end concentration of wealth in the hands of fewer individuals and end exploitation of many at the hands of a few but also help ending unemployment problem in the society and transforming the economy into a need based economic system as the people of different parts of the country would produce goods necessary for the people of those areas. Ultimately, it would lead to economic self-reliance of the people.

Rejecting the modern way of industrialization Gandhi gave the opinion that modern form of industrialization was detrimental to the country's economy as it resulted in destroying local talent, creating unemployment and making the people of India poor. So he concluded, "India does not need to be industrialized in the modern sense of the term"[30]

Especially he was in favour of producing cloth by the native weavers and gave his idea in these words, "I have nothing to say against the development of any other industry in India by means of machinery, but I do say that to supply India with cloth, manufactured either outside or inside through gigantic mills, is an economic blunder of the first magnitude, just as it would be to supply cheap bread through huge bakeries established in chief centres of India and to destroy the family stove"[31]

Criticizing the profit motive of the mill owners and advising people not to use mill-made clothes Gandhiji said, "Those of us, therefore, who have accepted *swadeshi* as a religious duty should not use mill-made clothes."[32]

Gandhi knew that Indian economy in the past had a glorious history and it was capable of meeting the needs of all people in the country. Every village in the country was a self-sufficient and self-reliant economic unit. The villagers used to fulfil all their basic needs in the village itself. But when the British came, they changed the need-based economy of India into a profit-based economy as their main motive was to earn profit for themselves and they were concerned neither about the people of India nor about India's working class. As a result, Indian economy got destroyed and was replaced by a system which catered to the desires of the colonizers. The aboriginal talent was ignored and the native workers became unemployed. The people of the country got habituated to use the foreign goods and became party to the destruction of the economy of their own motherland. Gandhiji dreamt of an ideal village and expressed his dream in these words, "It will produce its own grains, vegetables and fruits and its own *khadi*."[33]

Advising the boycott of foreign cloth and engaging the peasants in spinning he said, "The plan, therefore, is not merely to induce the peasant to refuse to buy the cheap and nice-looking foreign fabric but also by teaching him to utilize his spare hours in carding and spinning cotton and getting it woven by the village weavers, to dress himself in *khaddar* so woven and thus to save him the cost of buying foreign and, for that matter, even Indian mill-made cloth. Thus, boycott of foreign cloth by means of hand-spinning and hand-weaving, i.e., *khaddar*, not only saves the peasant's money, but it enables the workers to render social service of a first class order. It brings us into direct touch with the villagers. It enables us to give them real political education and teach them to become self-sustained and self-reliant."[34]

He relied on the premise that *swaraj* was dependent of *swadeshi*. If a country had self-sufficiency to generate and meet its economic needs indigenously and detested using foreign product it was bound to retain its independence. He claimed, "I am convinced that, if the country understands the idea of complete *swadeshi*, she will secure *swaraj* without having to resort to civil disobedience or non-violent revolt."[35]

Rejecting the much quoted economic principle that demand determined supply and controlled the market he strongly contended, "I do not endorse the proposition that supply follows demand. On the contrary, demand is often artificially created by unscrupulous vendors. And if a nation is bound, as I hold it is, like individuals to comply with a code of moral conduct, then it must consider the welfare of those whose wants it seeks to supply. It is wrong and immoral for a nation to supply for instance intoxicating liquor to those who are addicted to drink."[36]

He viewed hand-spinning as an expression of self-reliance and assertion of one's self-dependency. Supporting the use of hand-spinning he firmly believed on the utility of it and opined, "Attacks on hand-spinning notwithstanding, I cling to the belief, that *swaraj* is unattainable without the beautiful art becoming universal in India. The reasoning applied to the proposition is incredibly simple. India cannot live unless her homes become self-supporting. They cannot become so, unless they have a supplementary occupation. It will, therefore, not avail if all our cloth was manufactured in our mills. If hand-spinning became universal, every home would get a share of the crores and without any complicated machinery being necessary. And India is able to manufacture all her cloth. It is understood, that when spinning become universal, the millions of weavers and lakhs of carders will revert to their original occupations."[37]

TRUSTEESHIP SYSTEM

Though Gandhi was not against private property of an individual and did not object to material possessions by individuals after their achievement, he never permitted the possessors to misuse their possessions for private pleasure. He regarded private possessions as the trust of whole society which belonged to the entire humanity and were to be used for the benefit of the needy ones. Mahatma Gandhi was against concentration of wealth in the hands of a few. In his opinion, concentration of economic power in the hands of a few created an economic class and it exploited those who were without material possessions. The rich people, because of their wealth became privileged and got the additional advantages in other fields and tightened their grips in deciding the fates of the unfortunates; as a result, the underprivileged people remained at the mercy of the rich people and became susceptible to be exploited. At the same time, Gandhi believed that the rich people had no right over the property created by the labour of other people and whatever was generated by the society must belong to members of the entire society. Therefore, he thought the owners of property as the custodians of those possessions.

He concurred with the age old Indian precept of renunciation of material possessions and comfort and acknowledged its value in life. According to him, one should lead a simple life and should not be over indulgent in worldly pleasures. He conceded, "The spirit of renunciation should rule all activities of life. A householder does not cease to be one, if he regards life as a duty rather than as indulgence. A merchant, who operates in the sacrificial spirit, will have crores passing through his hands, but he will, if he follows the law, use his abilities for service. He will, therefore, not cheat or speculate, will lead a simple life, will not injure a living soul and will lose millions rather than harm anybody."[38] He further added, "Self indulgence leads to destruction, and renunciation to immortality."[39]

If one was engaged in the futile exercise of creating material possessions, then it was inconsequential for Gandhi. Gandhiji subscribed to the view that the ultimate goal of riches was to serve humanity and if it was not in the interest of the poor then it had no justification. Accumulation of property for self-satisfaction was a criminal act for him and it was a matter of shame and thus, he revolted against the ridiculous yearning to increase material assets and declared, "We should bury our heads in shame if we add to our wealth. Indeed, we may possess wealth for service. But some people accumulate wealth, regarding their greed as their religion. This is not proper."[40]

The Mahatma always highlighted self-control in individual conduct and he emphatically stated all human beings must possess this attribute while dealing with their fellow human beings. According to him, all the capability of an individual was to be utilized for the betterment of society and the ultimate goal of an individual was to serve others by making self-sacrifice. Therefore, the proprietor of material possessions should regard the more unfortunate ones as his brothers and be helpful to them at the time of need. The rich and the poor were not adversaries but partners in the society and both should behave accordingly. If the rich failed in their duty to come to the help of poor they would denigrate themselves before their superior-self, the self which stood for the ultimate moral precept of selfless service. Thus he opined, "If capital is not to fall into utter discredit, it behoves capitalists voluntarily to exercise self restraint and make common cause with labour."[41]

He commended the members of the ancient Indian business class who were known as *Vaisyas*; their profession was production and distribution of material goods for other members of the society. Praising their role in society he recalled, "If we analyze the functions of the *Vaisya* of the ancient times, we find that he was assigned the duty of production and distribution not for personal gain but for common good. All the wealth that he amassed, he held as a trustee for the nation. Capitalists, if they are to fulfil their real function, must exist not as exploiters, but as servants of society."[42] He counselled the rich, "I want the rich to hold their riches in trust for the poor or to give them up for them."[43]

He insisted on the cooperative relationship between the rich and the poor. Unlike other philosophers such as Marx, Mahatma Gandhi did not propagate for a class war between the capitalists and the labourers because he believed a class war perpetuated the differences between the competing groups. He opined in these words, "To inflame labour against moneyed men is to perpetuate class hatred and all the evil consequences flowing from it. The strife is a vicious circle to be avoided at any cost. It is an admission of weakness, a sign of inferiority complex. The moment labour recognizes its dignity, money will find its rightful place, i.e., it will be held in trust for labour. For, labour is more than money."[44] He further explained that the rich should voluntarily relinquish their indulgence on their possessions. He left the choice to the rich to take a voluntary renunciation of their riches and advised them in this manner, "Similarly would all rejoice if a capitalist were to divest himself of exclusive ownership and declare himself to be in possession as a trustee for the people."[45]

He believed that the objective of capital was to serve the interests of the poor and if the worldly possessions were spent otherwise it could be considered as their misuse. Therefore, capital should have the target of fulfilling the interests of the poor in society. In Gandhi's view, "Capital should be labour's servant, not its master."[46] The capitalists must regard themselves as the caretakers of the property they owned and Gandhi advised them to act as the trustees of their worldly possessions. Praising the trusteeship system he opined, "It is an attempt to secure the best use of property for the people by competent hands."[47]

The Gandhian concept of trusteeship was based on the premise that one could not appropriate wealth without violence and Gandhi was against the use of violence for any purpose. But if property was regarded as a trust to be used for the benefit of all then the possessors of property would not misuse their resources to aggrandize more riches by using force and exploiting others; they would not accumulate wealth for the benefit of others through improper methods. Thus, to end the perversities of human beings he did not give them licence to misuse their property for self-appeasement though he gave right to property to private individuals.

The trusteeship system was not based superior-subordinate relationship; neither the rich were superior nor the poor were subordinate. The whole system was based on mutual cooperation and give and take principle. In Gandhi's opinion, "The trusteeship theory is not unilateral, and does not in the least imply superiority of the trustee. It is, as I have shown, a perfectly mutual affair, and each believes that his own interest is best safeguarded by safeguarding the interest of the other."[48]

Mahatma Gandhi was against the use of property as an instrument of exploitation and he favoured the end of exploitation through a non-violent way. He advised those who had property must regard it as a trust and must not use it for oppressing others. All property should be held in trust, no matter who owned it and what its nature or quantity was. No one should have property more than what one needed.

CONCLUSION

According to Gandhi, the economic system should be such that the bare needs of all can be met, economy should grow in a peaceful manner and the means of production and distribution should be based on ethical basis. There should not be paucity of material goods for anybody and the requirements of all should be fulfilled. The economic benefits of the society should be shared by all persons living in the society as the means and production and distribution belong to the society as a whole; whatever things are created by the economic system are the trusts of the entire society put at the trusteeship of the rich people.

Thus, Gandhi visualized an economic system in which there should be no capitalist class with the power to control all economic activities for increasing their wealth at the cost of the economic needs of the needy and poor people. To him, the economic system should be a need based system and all economic activities must be carried on to fulfil the requirements of the people. He asserted this by giving an example, "At one time our national economics was this that just as we produced our own corn and consumed it so did we produce our own cotton, spun it in our homes and wear the clothes spun by our weavers from our own yearn. The first part of this description is still true while the latter part has almost ceased to hold good. A man generally spends upon his clothing a tenth of what he spends upon his food; hence instead of distributing ten per cent of our income among ourselves we now send it to England or to our own mills."[49]

In an ideal economic system, production should not be made for purely profit motive. It has a social purpose and it must serve the interests of the people in society. If anything is created solely to earn profit then, to Gandhi, it was unethical.

Gandhi advocated *swadeshi* should be the principle of economic independence. The people must use whatever was locally available and should not depend on foreign supply. He championed for the cause of the native workers. He propagated for the enhancement of the locally known skill. According to him, the native workers should be encouraged to produce things which were needed for the people of the locality. *Swadeshi* would serve the twin purpose of ending dependence on foreign supply and encouraging the local talents. It would also end the unemployment problem in the country. So, he opposed the use of foreign goods as he was aware that the British had come to India to earn profit and they were keeping the Indians slaves because they wanted to continue increasing their profit. Moreover, they were utilizing that earning to suppress the Indians and colonize the whole country. He propagated for the revival of village economy in India to revive the whole country against the British. Mahatma Gandhi wanted the adoption of *khadi* as a symbol of self-reliance. Therefore, Gandhi pays special importance to the rural economic activities such as *khadi*, handlooms and handicraft. The principles of *swadeshi* and trusteeship, according to Gandhi, would provide economic independence and establish a sound economic system where the needs of all would be fulfilled and all would lead a life of dignity.

NOTES

1. Gandhi, M.K., *Hind Swaraj*, Ahmedabad: Navajivan Publishing House, 1938, p. 51.
2. *Ibid.*
3. *Ibid.*, p. 52.
4. *Collected Works of Mahatma Gandhi*, Vol. XXV, New Delhi: The Publications Division, Ministry of Information and Broadcasting, 1967, p. 475.
5. Gandhi, M.K., (1948), *Non-violence in War and Peace*, Vol. I, Ahmedabad: Navajivan Publishing House, p. 114.
6. Radhakrishnan, S. (ed.) (1968), *Mahatma Gandhi 100 Years*, New Delhi: Gandhi Peace Foundation, p. 9.
7. Gandhi, M.K. (1948), *Non-violence in War and Peace*, Vol. I, Ahmedabad: Navajivan Publishing House, p. 172.
8. Gandhi, M.K., (1966), *The Village Reconstruction*, edited and published by A.T. Hingorani, Bombay: Bharatiya Vidya Bhawan, p. 117.
9. *Ibid*, p. 119.
10. *Ibid*, p. 105.
11. *Ibid*, p. 43.
12. Gandhi, M.K. (1938), *Hind Swaraj*, Ahmedabad: Navajivan Publishing House, p. 47.
13. Gandhi, M.K. (1970), *Capital and Labour*, edited and published by A.T. Hingorani, Bombay: Bharatiya Vidya Bhawan, p. 53.
14. *Young India*, May 28, 1931.
15. Gandhi, M.K. (1966), *The Village Reconstruction*, edited and published by A.T. Hingorani, Bombay: Bharatiya Vidya Bhawan, p. 42.
16. *Ibid.*, p. 42.
17. *Ibid.*, p. 115.

18. Gandhi, M.K. (1967), *The Gospel of Swadeshi*, edited and published by A.T. Hingorani, Bombay: Bharatiya Vidya Bhawan, p. 1.
19. *Ibid.*, p. 4.
20. *Ibid.*, p. 5.
21. Gandhi, M.K. (1938), *Hind Swaraj*, Ahmedabad: Navajivan Publishing House, p. 47.
22. *Young India*, 17.2.1926, p. 218.
23. *Young India*, 12. 3.1925, p. 88.
24. *Young India*, 17. 2.1926, p. 213.
25. Gandhi, M.K. (1957), *From Yervada Mandir*, Ahmedabad: Navajivan Publishing House, p. 51.
26. Gandhi, M.K. (1938), *Hind Swaraj*, Ahmedabad: Navajivan Publishing House, p. 30.
27. *Collected Works of Mahatma Gandhi*, Vol. XXV, *op. cit.*, p. 476.
28. *Ibid.*, p. 476.
29. *Ibid.*, Vol. XXI, 1966, p. 329.
30. Gandhi, M.K., *The Village Reconstruction*, edited and published by A.T. Hingorani, Bombay: Bharatiya Vidya Bhawan, 1966, p.13.
31. *Ibid.*, p. 14.
32. *Collected Works of Mahatma Gandhi*, Vol. XXI, *and op. cit.*, p. 255.
33. Gandhi, M.K., *The Village Reconstruction*, edited and published by A.T. Hingorani, *op. cit.*, p. 111.
34. *Collected Works of Mahatma Gandhi*, Vol. XXV, *op. cit.*, p. 474.
35. *Collected Works of Mahatma Gandhi*, Vol. XXI, *op. cit.*, p. 293.
36. *Collected Works of Mahatma Gandhi*, Vol. XXV, *op. cit.*, p. 474.
37. *Collected Works of Mahatma Gandhi*, Vol. XXI, *op. cit.*, pp. 178-179.
38. Gandhi, M.K., 1971, *Service Before Self*, edited and published by A.T. Hingorani, Bombay: Bharatiya Vidya Bhawan, 1971, pp. 5-6.
39. *Ibid*, p. 6.
40. *Ibid*, p. 95.
41. *Young India*, July 25, 1929.
42. *Young India*, December 19, 1929.
43. *Young India*, April, 2, 1931.
44. *Harijan*, October 19, 1935.
45. *Harijan*, February 20, 1937.
46. Gandhi, M.K., 1970, *Capital and Labour*, edited and published by A.T. Hingorani, Bombay: Bharatiya Vidya Bhawan, p. 79.
47. *Harijan*, February 20, 1937.
48. *Harijan*, June 25, 1938
49. *Collected Works of Mahatma Gandhi*, Vol. XXV, *op. cit.*, p. 556.

6
Five Myths about Gandhian Economics

Koilpillai J. Charles

Gandhi did not receive any formal training in economics; nor did he study much economics on his own. His busy political life left little time for reading, as he notes in his candid autobiography, *The Story of My Experiments with Truth*. He had probably read Adam Smith's *Wealth of Nations*, and he turned to the serious study of Marx only in his 75th year. Since, moral considerations weighed heavily with Gandhi in everything he did, his economic ideas were influenced not so much by economic treatises as by his reading of such books as Tolstoy's *The Kingdom of God is Within*, Ruskin's *Unto This Last*, *The New Testament*, and the *Bhagavad Gita*. They were also distilled from the crucible of experience comprising intense political activity that spanned three continents. In view of these circumstances it is not surprising that his economic ideas are not expressed in the jargon of the economist, nor are they presented in the form of a scientific or scholarly treatise. Nevertheless, it is possible to cull from his scattered writings and pronouncements a consistent body of knowledge in economics, that is as distinctive as to merit the name "Gandhian Economics, and which has contemporary relevance, remarkable originality and the attributes of an analytical contribution of a high order. It is unfortunate that professional economists, with a few notable exceptions, have not given to Gandhian economics the scholarly attention it deserves. Nevertheless, Gandhi's economic ideas are widely known, in a general way, and have become associated in the popular and professional minds with certain definite conceptions. Among these, myths seem to me, to have the widest currency. By and large, in the minds of most people, Gandhian Economics has come to be associated with the advocacy of the following:

1. Acceptance of poverty;
2. Return to the simplicity of India's economic past;
3. Elimination of machinery and large-scale production;
4. Adherence to the social and economic rules and regulations of orthodox Hinduism; and
5. Rejection of communism and acceptance of a modified capitalism.

In spite of the wide popularity of these notions, and the authoritative support that they have sometimes received from scholars and even from some of Gandhi's own disciples, each one of these propositions is basically false, and examination of Gandhi's writings would show that Gandhi did not, in fact, advocate any of these measures.

The rest of this chapter is devoted to such an examination of these five economic myths that have grown around the name of Gandhi. First: Gandhi's advocacy of the acceptance of poverty. In order to show his complete identification with the poor people of India, Gandhi adopted their dress and their simple ways of living at all times. Even when he went to see the British King George V, he wore just a loin cloth like the poor people of India, provoking an outraged Churchill to call him a "half naked fakir".[1]

Nevertheless, Gandhi did not admire poverty, and most emphatically did not see in poverty the virtues that are sometimes claimed for it. He said "No one has ever suggested that grinding pauperism can lead to anything else than moral degradation. Every human being has the right to live and, therefore, to find the wherewithal to feed himself and where necessary to clothe and house himself. Again he said, "If by advance you mean everyone having plenty to eat and drink and to clothe himself with, enough to keep his mind trained and educated, I should be satisfied.[2]

No, Gandhi was not an admirer of poverty. He wanted India to develop herself economically, to make possible a satisfactory life for all. As early as 1928 he wrote, "According to me, the economic constitution of India and for that matter, the world, should be such that no one under it should suffer from want of food and clothing. In other words, everybody should be able to get sufficient work to enable him to make the two ends meet. And this ideal can be universally realized only if the means of production of the elementary necessities of life remain in the control of the masses.[3]

After thirty-five years of planned efforts, Indian economic development has not come anywhere close to fulfilling Gandhi's economic aspirations. In fact, even in the United States of America, universally regarded as the richest nation in the world, suffering from want of food and clothing is the lot of a substantial minority of her people. What Gandhi advocated was not poverty but sufficiency for all. He wanted enough development to enable all people to live in comfort and dignity. But, of course, he was opposed to extreme inequalities and to the pursuit of ever-rising material standards of living, because he realized that such a path would not lead to happiness.

As early as 1908, he wrote in his important book *Hind Swaraj* "We notice that the mind is a restless bird; the more it gets the more it wants, and still remains unsatisfied. The more we indulge our passions the more unbridled they become. Our ancestors, therefore, set a limit to our indulgences. They saw happiness was largely a mental condition. A man is not necessarily happy because he is rich or unhappy because he is poor. The rich are often seen to be unhappy, the poor to be happy. Millions will always be poor. Observing all this, our ancestors dissuaded us from luxuries and pleasures.[4]

Gandhi felt that the solution to the economic problem through continuous increase in material production was a false solution. Ever increasing wealth will not ensure happiness because of the tendency of wants to multiply even faster. This can be called Gandhi's first impossibility theorem. The experience of the rich nations and of rich people in poor nations testify its validity.

Gandhi, however, firmly believed that all human beings should have enough to satisfy their basic needs. In the planning efforts of India and other developing countries, economic growth is the central goal. Under a Gandhian scheme, reduction of inequalities, provision of full employment, and the eradication of poverty would be the dominant goals, and economic growth would not be a separate growth objective. In such a society, economic growth is likely to be the consequence of the pursuit of the other goals mentioned above.

Secondly, many persons think that Gandhi advocated a return to India's economic past. For example, Dr Arthur Lewis, Nobel-laureate in economics, in an otherwise admirable book, observes "Not all nationalist politicians favour economic development. Some like Gandhi have resisted westernism and desire on the contrary to return to old ways."[5] Gandhi called his ideal republic *Ram Rajya*, a throwback to a mythical past where under the rule of God-King Rama perfect justice prevailed. Nevertheless, it is not correct to say that Gandhi advocated a return to India's past. To be sure, there were certain attributes of India's civilization, like the recognition of the dangers of the multiplication of human wants, and the need to exercise restraint, that Gandhi admired, and wished his countrymen not to forsake. But his face and feet were firmly turned toward the future and not toward the past. In an exchange of letters with Nehru, he drew a robust picture of the ideal village of his dreams. "My ideal village will contain intelligent beings. They will not live in dirt and darkness as animals. Men and women will be free and able to hold their own against anyone in the world. There will be neither plague nor cholera, nor small pox; no one will be idle; no one will wallow in luxury…It is possible to envisage railways, post and telegraph…and the like"[6]

It is relevant to note that in that letter Gandhi describes the ideal village as his dream. Since at no time in India's past the village even remotely resembled the ideal portrayed by Gandhi, it would be hard to sustain the claim that he advocated a return to the past. Untouchability, lack of freedom for women, and extreme inequalities have been part of village life in India from time immemorial to the present. Gandhi was uncompromisingly opposed to these. He said "Today, there is gross inequality. The basis of socialism is economic equality. There can be no *Ramarajya* in the present state of iniquitous inequalities in which a few roll in riches and the masses do not get enough to eat.[7] To his radical mind, the present which is a product of the past, was unsatisfactory and needed to be changed in fundamental ways.

He was willing to borrow many bricks from the past, but the edifice itself was new and belonged to the future. On the subject of machinery and large-scale production, Gandhi's views are especially susceptible to misrepresentation because these views evolved over a period of time. As a rule, whenever there seems to be conflicting pronouncements of Gandhi on any subject, the chronologically latest one is the idea that should be attributed to him. Gandhi himself recommended this course to his followers. Another point that should be borne in mind is that Gandhi's economic ideas were evolved in the context of India's fight for independence. Some of the measures he recommended, such as hand-spinning and weaving were designed to weaken the hold of a foreign power over India. Since he died a revolutionary's death at the hands of a reactionary Hindu fanatic soon after independence, he did not have the opportunity to examine adequately the validity of many of his economic ideas to the problems of an independent India. This underscores the need to pay special attention to the context in which his ideas were expressed in assessing their significance.

Gandhi's attitude toward machinery changed considerably with the passage of time. In his book *Hind Swaraj,* written in 1908, he had said, "Machinery is the chief symbol of modern civilization; it represents a great sin. I cannot recall a single good point in connection with machinery. Books can be written to demonstrate its evils. It is necessary to realize that machinery is bad. We shall then be able gradually to do away with it."[8] Again in 1926 he wrote in *Young India,* "The fact is that this industrial civilization is a disease because it is all evil.

Let us not be deceived by catchwords and phrases. Our concern is, therefore, to destroy industrialism at any cost.[9] From this uncompromising opposition to all machinery that he took in the early years, he gradually began to recognize the useful role that machinery can play under proper public control and in th appropriate conditions. Firstly, all machinery is permissible if it does not cause unemployment. In 1934, he wrote "Mechanization is good when the hands are too few for the work intended to be accomplished. It is an evil when there are more hands than required for the work as in India. The problem with us is not how to find leisure for the teeming million inhabitants of our villages. The problem is how to utilize their idle hours, which are equal to the working days of six months in the year."[10]

Increasingly he began to realize that it is not machinery as such that is an evil but the social conditions under which it is used. Four years later, we find him making a still stronger statement in support of machinery under appropriate conditions. He wrote "If I could produce all my country's wants by means of 30,000 people instead of 30 million? I should not mind it, provided that the 30 million are not rendered idle and unemployed."[11]. But even in his early years, he was in favour of simple tools and implements that improved the productivity of labour for he wrote "I am uncompromisingly against all destructive machinery. But simple tools and instruments, and such instruments and machinery as save individual labour and lighten the burden of the millions of cottages I should welcome."[12] But Gandhi began more and more to see that under proper conditions of social control even large-scale machinery could be used in such a way as to serve the villages and their crafts and not destroy them as they did in the past in the absence of social control. He wrote in 1940, "I do visualize electricity, ship-building, ironworks, machine-making and the like existing side by side with village handicrafts. Hitherto industrialization has been so planned as to destroy the village and village crafts. In the state of the future, it will subserve the villages and their crafts".[13] In other words, he wanted mass production to be replaced by production by the masses. Thus, the position that Gandhi came to hold on machinery was quite close to that of Marx. In the absence of social control machinery causes unemployment and leads to exploitation of labour and the destruction of the artisan.

While the indiscriminate proliferation of machinery is harmful, under proper social control, machinery could confer many benefits on society. While Gandhi with the passage of time began to realize that machinery under proper conditions could be a valuable asset to man and society, the views advanced against large-scale industrialization very early in his life are valid to this day. He advances four reasons why it would be impossible for industrialization to provide a satisfactory solution to man's economic problem. This is Gandhi's second impossibility theorem and constitutes at the analytical level, an original and durable economic contribution.

1. First, he noted that industrialization involves exploitation of the underdeveloped countries by the industrializing nations. They require the poor countries as suppliers of raw materials and as buyers of their finished goods. Under these circumstances, if all countries attempted industrialization their efforts must surely fail. Stronger nations would try to prevent the weaker nations from embarking on independent paths of development. Competition and rivalries among the developed countries would lead to war and destruction of human life as well as material resources.
2. Secondly, the wide use of large-scale methods of production would lead to mass unemployment in many countries, especially in labour-abundant countries like India.
3. Thirdly, since industrialization involves a very high cost of investment per worker, to provide employment for all unemployed human resources would involve capital accumulation on such a massive scale that it would be beyond

the investment resource mobilization capacities of most of the poor countries.

4. Fourthly, the industrialized way of life when universally practiced would make such large demands on our non-renewable resources that simply cannot be met by our meagre planet. Gandhi often said that there were enough resources for man's needs but not enough for his greed. Thus, long before all the countries could become industrialized, the process will be brought to a sudden halt by the barrier of resource depletion.[14] It is only in recent years that scientists and scholars in the rich nations are beginning to realize the validity of Gandhi's second impossibility theorem so presciently articulated by him half a century ago.

The fourth myth that Gandhi was an orthodox Hindu who advocated strict adherence to the social and economic institutions and practices of Hinduism will also be shown on closer examination to be lacking in validity. Gandhi was a person with a strong religious motivation and found in each religion something of permanent value. What attracted him to Hinduism was its catholicity and freedom from doctrinal rigidity. It was the only religion which did not forbid him to be also a Muslim, a Christian and a Sikh. But there were many things about Hindu society he passionately disliked, and throughout his life, he carried on an active crusade against such established Hindu practices as untouchability, caste system and inferior status assigned to women. Even to this day in independent India, the caste system is rampant and the Harijans continue to suffer privations and persecutions of various kinds. But Gandhi accepted the Harijans as his equals even at the beginning of the century and would not tolerate his wife washing the commode of a Harijan in their South African home with a sullen face. In the beginning, though always opposed to untouchability, Gandhi saw some merit in the caste system and the practice of hereditary occupations. But these positions he later abandoned, and, in fact, strongly opposed them. There was a time when he was opposed to inter-caste marriage. Later, he withdrew this opposition and would attend only inter-caste weddings. His fight against untouchability is well known, and no individual has done more for the welfare and uplift of the Harijans than Gandhi.

For the cause of emancipation of women and their acceptance as equals, he fought a valiant fight against the citadels of Hindu orthodoxy. Gandhi was a Hindu heretic and a radical Hindu religious reformer whose message and achievements bear comparison with those of Martin Luther and the Buddha.

Lastly, Gandhi's attitude towards capitalism has also been subject to a great deal of misunderstanding. Marxists often portray him as an apologist for capitalism, and conservative Gandhians frequently invoke his name to oppose radical land reforms and other changes in society. Both of these positions are untenable and arise from misinterpretations of Gandhi's ideas and actions.

When Gandhi was engaged in the fight for India's independence, the Indian capitalist class saw in that struggle an opportunity for its self-expansion and growth. It wanted to take the place of the foreign British capitalist class and, therefore, gave its support to the independence struggle. Thus, the historical circumstances conferred on the Indian capitalist class a progressive role, and under these circumstances Gandhi saw no reason to oppose them. Indian capitalists like Birla were his followers, and Gandhi was often a guest in their homes. These were the circumstances that gave rise to the myth that Gandhi was an apologist for capitalism. Actually, Gandhi had a prescient understanding of the progressive role that the Indian capitalist class and the wealthy were playing during the struggle for independence. He knew that in an independent India there would be the need to oppose these people. So we find him as early as 1928 writing to Nehru "I am quite of your opinion that some day we shall have to start a movement without the rich people and without the vocal educated class, but the time is not yet."[15] It is thus evident that Gandhi had an uncanny historical sense of the progressive role that the capitalists were playing during the independence struggle. But he had no great fondness for capitalism and nowhere in his writings or in his speeches can anyone find any support expressed for capitalism or for private property. He was not only a firm believer in socialism, but his socialism is of a very radical kind. He sometimes referred to himself as a foremost communist. His disagreement with the Marxists and communists was not about the end to be sought about which he had no quarrel with them but about the means to be adopted for the attainment of the goals of communism. Gandhi felt that far from the end justifying the means, the means should justify the end. If communists were advocating violence for the attainment of socialism, Gandhi parted company with them at that point. He wanted socialism to be attained through the use of non-violence.

He clearly foresaw the need for change and did not use his dislike of violence to justify the *status quo*. He not only saw the need for fundamental change but even recognized its inevitability. In 1942 he wrote, "I see coming the day of the rule of the poor, whether that rule be through force of arms or of non-violence."[16] He, therefore, urged his countrymen to establish socialism through peaceful means with the utmost dispatch. Gandhi saw with remarkable prescience that communism has not successfully dealt with the problem of power, either in theory or practice. Bringing all the means of production under public ownership creates enormous concentration of power, and the communists have not evolved a satisfactory method of dealing with this situation. The theory of socialism through trusteeship was Gandhi's answer to the problem of power. Unfortunately, his political preoccupations prevented him from elaborating on his theory. Soon after independence was won, his energies had to be given to the cause of the restoration of communal harmony, when his life was brought to an abrupt end by an assassin's bullet. But there is no doubt that Gandhi had great faith in the efficacy of trusteeship.

In a nutshell, the theory holds that all possessions including one's talents and mental excellence belong to society and those who have these possessions should hold them in trust for society. Gandhi said, "the rich man will be left in possession of his wealth, of which he will use what he reasonably requires for his personal needs, and will act as a trustee for the remainder, to be used for society. In this argument, honesty on the part of the trustee is assumed."[17]

Again, Gandhi clearly understood the dependence of the

capitalist on labour. "We invite the capitalist to regard himself as a trustee for those on whom he depends for the making, the retention of, and increase of his capital."[18] A detailed examination of the concept of trusteeship falls outside the scope of this chapter. But two points deserve mention. In the Gandhian social order, when capitalists refuse to act as trustees, there is room for "legislative regulation of the ownership and use of wealth."[19]

Secondly, according to Gandhi all the key industries should be nationalized and labour must be assured a dignified position. Speaking of such industries he said, "But I am socialist enough to say that such factories should be nationalized. They ought only to be working under the most attractive conditions, not for profit, but for the benefit of humanity, love taking the place of greed as the motive power. It is an alteration in the condition of labour that I want." [20] In the light of the above, it should be clear that the Gandhian concept of trusteeship so far has not been tried, though from time to time charlatans have tried to blunt its cutting edge by misrepresenting it to equal something close to a slightly modified *status quo*. Such attempts constitute a travesty of the spirit and letter of Gandhi's concept. If that concept is fully implemented capitalism and private property as we know them today will cease to exist.

Today, we live in a world where the imperfections of both the capitalist and communist paths have become painfully evident. The Gandhian method of transforming *society through state-regulated* trusteeship holds great promise of safely steering the modern state between the Scylla of capitalist chaos and the Charybdis of communist rigidity. A distinguished Indian economist, Dr. V.M. Dandekar delivering the Zakir Hussain Memorial Lecture on March 8, 1978 in New Delhi subjected the Gandhian economic system to a searching examination, and concluded that the Gandhian path "...is a path leading to an alternative goal of human life and existence; a human society which is removed and immovable, unchanged and unchangeable, using the same kind of ploughs that existed a thousand years ago, living in the same kind of cottages as there were in times immemorial and educating its people on the same system as ever before;

resources, preservation of ecology, justice in income distribution and opportunities. Everybody should be given the right to earn according to his capacity using just means. The rich should serve the society after satisfying his needs. Life is not meant for enjoyment only, but it is meant to help others.

For him the means are as important as the aims. The means must be nonviolent, ethical, and truthful in all economic spheres. He provided the new economic system with those means. He advocated trusteeship, decentralization of economic activities, labour intensive technology, and first priority to rural India. He explained that capitalism and mechanization would lead to unemployment, poverty, and inequality. Communism would not survive as it was inhuman. We have seen the collapse of communism and also observed unemployment, inequality of income and instability of common man even in rich and capitalist society.

The contest between Gandhian thought and contemporary historical trends is just another instance of the perennial tension between history and utopia. Forces already at work in the historical process lead it towards a new equilibrium. Gandhi perceived the organic necessities of all parts of social system. Thus, he proposed his own alternatives, to face the challenge coming from modern capitalism and industrialism. It is relevant to summaries his proposal and contrast it with the contemporary trends.

Gandhi's basic conceptions about the ideal economy reveal that their realization would require a reversal of contemporary historical trends. This contradiction is described as follows:

The fundamental problem of global destruction lies in the production. Excessive production to excessive consumerism has given birth to all the problems. A major part of neo-classical economics deals with issues of production: what, why, and how are "goods" produced? The question is: production to meet the minimum need of people but not to use for destructive things?

The following distinctive features of this doctrine are:

1. It accepts the principle of comparative advantage but it rejects it as the sole basis of international trade;
2. It accepts the reciprocal need as the determining factor in trade among nations;
3. It is need of nation-states, not the market that governs the nation-states;

development of agriculture and village industries. This way full employment for 80 per cent of Indian population can be achieved. Even in the world economy nearly 70 per cent of the world's population is rural population. Their development can be made easy by the development of rural economies. There should be small scale and cottage industries in these areas. That will create just distribution of income without special efforts. The agricultural activities should be done with the help of livestock and bio fertilizers. He explained in detail how to produce organic fertilizer without any extra cost and minimum labour. He described the number of benefits which can be achieved from the use of livestock and cooperative farming. Today bio-technological revolution, popularity of organic fertilizer, and awareness against harmfulness of chemicals used in agriculture prove the worth of Gandhi's thinking.

3. The government must give full support regarding finance, technology, and market to village industries. The people of the country must give first priority in purchasing their rural productions. He advocated for *khadi* and all other village industries and worked hard till his end. He even left the Congress to concentrate fully in this activity since 1934.
4. He advocated *swadeshi* and advised boycott of foreign goods, foreign companies, and foreign capital to maximum possible extent. This was not politically motivated. Not to punish the foreign countries but for the economic betterment of our country. If we look into history, George Washington advised his countrymen to throw away European goods in the sea for self development. U.K. had passed laws prohibiting all types of Indian cloths during the time of their industrial revolution. Japan had resolved to consume her rough and inferior rice instead of foreign superior rice. These examples prove the importance of *swadeshi* attitude even if the home made product is inferior for the sake of economic independence. There are several elements in a policy of *swadeshi*, of self-reliance: (a) the society must be capable of satisfying the basic minimum needs of its people without dependence on external sources. This also means that each society will have to define its minimum standards in terms of its economic capacity. They must be attainable within the

borrowed from Gandhi's India and repaid the debt with word that reached Gandhi in South African cell.[2]

Tolstoy immensely influenced Gandhiji. He established 'a farm' of community living, on the lines of his philosophy. Gandhiji has acknowledged his indebtedness to this great Russian writer:

> Russia gave me a Tolstoy, a teacher who furnished a reasoned basis for non-violence. Tolstoy blessed my movement in South Africa when it was still in its infancy and of whose wonderful possibilities I had yet to learn. It was he who had prophesied in his letter to me that I was leading a movement which was destined to bring a message of hope to the downtrodden peoples of the earth.[3]

Gandhiji wrote on Economics in *Hind Swaraj* when he was on his way to South Africa. It was an incisive disparagement of the industrial revolution and its evil effects. Gandhiji's egalitarianism was centred on the preservation of human dignity rather than material advancement. He advocated the principle of paying the highest attention to the prime needs of the weaker sections of society, and he insisted upon raising their quality of life. In his opinion, Economics that hurts the moral well-being of an individual or a nation is immoral and, therefore, he looked upon it as a sinful entity. He pleaded that everyone in the state should have a right to earn according to his capacity, using just means. The rich should serve the society after satisfying their needs. He advocated 'trusteeship' and decentralization of economic activity and the power.

But all these statements deserve to be examined only contextually. He made those statements in the pre-Independence era and when there was a mass movement against colonialism. His main concerns then were unemployment and resistance to the colonial rule. In course of time, he modified his opinions with due recognition to the verified facts. He wrote:

> I am uncompromisingly against all the destructive machinery. But simple tools and instruments, and such instruments that lighten the burden of millions of cottages, I should welcome.[4]

Again in 1940 he wrote:

> I do visualize electricity, ship-building, iron works, machine-making and the like existing side by side with village handicrafts. In the state of the future, it will subserve the villages and their efforts[5].

In this context, it is appropriate to understand even the Gandhian concept of village in the light of what transpired between him and Pandit Nehru:

> My ideal village contains intelligent beings. They will not live in dirt and darkness like animals; men and women will be free and be able to hold their own against anyone in the world. There will be neither plague, nor cholera nor smallpox; no one will be idle; and no one will wallow in luxury...[6]

In Gandhiji's opinion, continuous increase in national production was not a proper solution to the human problems since the tendency of the human wants multiply even faster. Therefore, he insisted on his basic principle of 'plain living' which alone could help the man to cut down luxury and keep the societal needs on priority basis. Thus he made a distinction between 'standard of living' and 'standard of life'—while the former merely states the material and physical standard of food, cloth and housing, and the other comprises cultural and spiritual values which would satisfy human soul.

Gandhiji condemned industrialization on a large scale as it led to passive as well as active exploitation of people since the problem of competition and marketing comes in. But he never opposed industrialization in cases where the aim was to meet societal needs. Therefore, he pleaded that all industries should be nationalized and the labour classes must be assured a dignified position. With reference to such industries he wrote:

> But I am socialist enough to say that such factories should be nationalized. They ought only to be working under the most attractive conditions, not for profit, but for the benefit of humanity, love taking the place of greed as the motive power. It is an alternative in the condition of labour that I want.[7]

Gandhiji read *Das Kapital* in his seventy-fifth year. He admired

He even rejected the idea of 'economic man'. He accepted the average man with all his characteristics. He said that an average man lives a satisfied life with his resources. 'Unlimited demand', 'Dissatisfied man' and 'Limited resources' are wrong concepts. At the same time he explained about the required need. A man should have food worth 3000 calories every day, 15 metres of cloth per year, a house of 100 sq. yards and educational and medical facilities. To satisfy such real need the resources are sufficient. God has given enough to satisfy the need but not the greed.

Eminent western thinkers and economists like Schumacher and Capra were among the earliest to appreciate Gandhi's views on a new economic system which was reflected in their advocacy of Intermediate Technology, Soft Technology, and Technology with a Human Face.

It is high time for the government to focus on *swadeshi* policies that would cut imports drastically limiting the human wants, thereby reducing the economic pitfalls like inflation. Instead, our government thinks *swadeshi* as a tool for living for the poor sections of the society catering to the development of science and technology has surely improved our economic status but to be applied for purposes that would bring about greater indigenous production carried on in peace and harmony. It could be overcome by adding more regulations on foreign investments, cutting more sanctions on foreign trade and granting concessions for indigenous works. It has been a known fact that intellectuals and economists of our country would ever give a thought of doing this in the past. It is true that this kind of reform would be criticized along the lines of putting back the clock of progress of the nation. But, unless we break this trend for a while at the least, it is highly plausible for us to face all sorts of economic evils that put us nowhere except to knock our brains.

Basic Tenets of Gandhian Model

The basic tenets of Gandhian economics model are as follows:

1. To provide full employment for all, particularly for all potential members of the work force, so that these workers can provide for their own necessities by their own efforts, in dignity, without depending on charity.
2. He advocated developing rural economies with the

the government tries to attract direct foreign investment, either through these corporations, or in areas where the government corporations are not the preferred option for some reason. Nevertheless, the government becomes a ruthless promoter of the corporate entities in search of higher growth, irrespective of how it affects the interests of the people.

This is a case of state-led corporatism, and today's China seems to fit this description reasonably well. South Korea, despite the obvious differences in the political and geo-political situations and dependence at an earlier stage on foreign borrowing, might have traversed a similar path. All these variants provide some insight the way world economic is pushing the national boundary of nation-state, where the command and control of national government hardly play any role. As a result rich becomes richer and poor becomes poorer. The same theory is applied to individual also in national stage.

Crisis and its Impact

The present crisis can be stressed to different model used by economist at different points of time. British economist John Maynard Keynes, (considered to be the father of modern macro-economics,) have for long emphasized that state intervention is indispensible to regulate economy in order to avoid destructive cycles of recessions, depressions and booms. After the Great Depression of 1929 and after the Second World War Keynesian theories helped to rebuild the world economy. This worked until the first oil shock of the 1970s after which the Keynesian idea of regulated markets were abandoned and the 'free market' system rapidly came into full play. Now world economy is governed by the neo-liberals principle which advocated that unfettered markets are self-correcting, so governments need not intervene at all.

The global financial crisis of recent decade has led too much introspection and discussion about what is the best way forward in order to rebuild trust and bring growth back into the system. There seems to be unanimity on the need for regulatory reforms in the international banking and financial systems so as to prevent risky financial practices and place strong restraints on the built up of excessive risk. Inadequate competition and inadequate procedures to ensure transparency and accountability have been recognized as among the major causes of the systemic failure.

Market Economy, undoubtedly hampers the development of the working class as a whole.

In this context one should know 'greed and need' in human personality. Every person needs a degree of wealth for his survival; but greed has a strong biological basis. Greed may be defined as an excessive or extreme desire for resources, especially money and all other symbols of wealth. Possessing excessive beyond a certain degree is harmful. For instance, excessive eating or drinking is harmful to one's physical health. Of course, possessing excessive wealth may not be harmful to the individual since his excessive wealth can buy him more comfortable and better life. But the fact is that human beings are gregarious by nature. Greed is good for the individual but not for the social group with which he is associated. Unrestrained greed in an individual leads to callousness, arrogance and megalomania. A person dominated by greed will naturally ignore the harm that he causes others. Unsafe working conditions, destruction of normal livelihood and pollution of natural environment are, in fact, some of the consequences of this callousness among the greedy. The greediness of individuals makes them insensitive to the pricks of human conscience. Yet, society cannot ban individual greed, since it is greed that motivates people to work. It is good to stimulate the incentive in workers but not to kill it.

Albert Camus in *the Rebel* writes that *Man is the only creature who refuses to be what he is.*[13] Man has an abiding relationship with society. All his thoughts and deeds are related to it. A society that has a strong urge to go ahead will not subscribe to the aspect of an unchanging character. Life moves forward. It surmounts all the obstacles with the irrepressible desire to explore new realms. Reason and conscience aids such explosions all through. Man, since the cave age, has passed through so many vicissitudes, reached nuclear age, and has attained supreme power and status. Transformation in human life has become possible, since he or she refuses to remain static. This is not unique to our age but this urge for change happens to be the essential nature of society—past, present and future. Therefore, it is appropriate to restrain greed when its operation adversely affects the basic needs of the common man.

Soon after Independence, leaders of the nation, keeping in view the true spirit of the Constitution of India, introduced 'Mixed Economy' replacing the exploitative economic policy of the British government. Under the Mixed Economy the state controlled the industrialization and all other matters relating to it. Public and private sectors were allowed to function under the legislative control of the state. Of course, our economic growth was very slow but the lowest sections of the people were well protected against exploitation. But this policy was replaced by Market Economy with effect from 1990 on the plea that the growth rate in terms of GDP was not up to the expected levels under the Mixed Economy. The 'Market Economy' with its LPG (Liberalization, Privatization and Globalization) policies, notwithstanding the different political parties in power, continued to be in operation with effect from 1990 onwards.

The very concept of 'Market Economy' is not in any way conducive to our constitutional commitments. But no one ever questioned the same at any stage. Market Economy permits an open exchange of goods and services between producers and consumers. The state cannot control market prices. Market forces decide pricing index and the consumer has no protection against exploitation. Market Economy improved the GDP growth rate but its adverse impact on the common man cannot be borne any more. Market Economy has widened the gap between the haves and the have-nots in their 'standards of living' and continues to deprive the poor of their legitimate basic needs. Therefore, it is the need of the hour to restrain the greediness of a few through a legislative regulatory mechanism in order to protect the common man's interest.

All governments legitimize their survival on the plea that they work for the good of the individual and improve their 'standard of life'. But in fact, there is a general tendency to devour individual freedom, thus subordinating the individual to material gains, and reducing him to be a mere cog in the machine. This tendency appears to be inevitable in the mechanized and consumerist world. No wonder, in this mad pursuit, the valuable aspects of human personality and human spiritual development are totally ignored. Furthermore, we do see a threat of total extinction of human values in our social set-up.

We never feel tired of repeating Gandhiji and his ideology but we have never given a fair trial to its implementation after Independence. Unfortunately, he was shot dead on 30th January, 1948. It was an end of a sage, who died in a violent act for the mission of nonviolence.

In fact, even in his life time, Gandhiji was not allowed adequate time to deal with the problems of the poor in the country. Had he had blown off my feet." India lives in villages; naturally the development of the country depends on the development of villages. All the goods and services necessary for the village members should be grown within the village. In a word, every village should be a self-contained republic. If every village distributes its surplus produce to the poor villagers then there will not be the problem of poverty and starvation in the rural areas. Only this can help eradicating poverty and thus people can be happy and self-reliant. Agricultural sector alone cannot solve the problem of rural poverty and unemployment. That is why Gandhi gives stress on the growth of the rural industries like *khadi*, handlooms, sericulture and handicrafts. Rural industries are the symbols of unity and equality.

Prior to understanding Gandhian concept of economic development, it would be worthwhile to understand a few prominent principles inherent in Gandhi's economic ideals, and their relevance to the future ideologist. The first of these is Gandhiji's outlook on the relationship of man and commodity. Gandhi wrote, "Increase of material comforts, it may be generally laid down, does not in any way whatsoever conduce to moral growth.. Bombay, Calcutta, and the other chief cities of India are the real plague spots….Medical science is the concentrated essence of black magic…."[1] The idea is that man and his all round healthy development of personality is the end, a temporary satisfaction gained from a consumable commodity cannot be the aim of life.

The second principle on which Gandhian economy rests is that all economic functionings and developments should have an ethical base. This view is quite contrary to the view of some western economists that utility which is different from moral obligation being the central concept of economics, this field of study should be developed in isolation from ethics. Gandhi succeeded in his attempt to combine economics with ethics, as in his economic philosophy, from the principle of truth and non-violence, emerged a series of economic ideals like non-exploitation, non-possession, trusteeship, bread-labour and so on. All these ideas, which in fact originated under different contexts, form the basic pillars of his economic thought. Professor Abdul Aziz writes: "From the principle of truth and nonviolence emerged a series of economic ideas like non-exploitation, non-possession, trusteeship, and bread-labour and so on. All these ideas, which in fact having originated under different contexts, formed the founding pillars of Gandhi's economic system."[2]

people, fall into this, and get themselves deeply into debt. This also applies to many developing countries, which acquire debts so horrendous that they can never hope to repay them, and bankrupt themselves just keeping up with interest payments. So the need of the hour is to recast the visionary idea, practice by Gandhi during his life time, not it is just an ideal or utopia but as a guideline to practice in everyday life so that the real development will be achieved and vision of inclusive society can be realized.

NOTES

1. Appadori, A. (1993), *Political Thought in India*, Delhi: Khanna Publisher.
2. Bhaduri, Amit (2010), *Essays in the Reconstruction of Political Economy*, New Delhi: Aakar Books.
3. Bhattacharyya, Buddhadeva, (1969), *The Evolution of Political Philosophy of Gandhi*, Calcutta: Calcutta Book House.
4. Antony Copley (1999), *Gandhi against the Tide*, New Delhi: Oxford University Press.
5. Sandeep Chauhan, (2002), *GATT To WTO: Gandhian Alternative to NEIO*, New Delhi: Deep & Deep Publications.
6. Ghosh, B.N. (2007), *Gandhian Political Economy: Principle, Practice and Policy*, London: Ashgate Publishing Ltd., p. 21.
7. Hanna Newcombe, http://www.peacemagazine.org/archive/v14n2p28.htm
8. Kapoor, A.N.; V.P. Gupta, and Mohini Gupta (2007), *The Gandhian Era*, New Delhi: Radha Publication.
9. Nanda, B.R. (1985), *Gandhi and His Critics*, New Delhi: Oxford University Press, pp. 11-40.
10. Parel, J. Anthony (2006), *Gandhi's Philosophy, and the Quest for Harmony*, Cambridge University Press, p. xiii.
11. Bhikhu Parekh (1989), *Gandhi's Political Philosophy*, London: MacMillan Press, pp.139-140.
12. Roy, Himansu (2001), *Poverty of Gandhian Philosophy*, New Delhi: Concept Publishing Company.
13. Sharma, Anand (ed.) (2007), *Gandhian Way, Peace, Non-Violence and Empowerment*, New Delhi: Academic Foundation.
14. Tripathy, Sridhar (2007): *Gandhi: His Life and View*, New Delhi: Anmol Publication.
15. Wadhwa, Madhuri (1991), *Gandhi between Tradition and Modernity*, New Delhi: Deep & Deep Publications.
16. *Essays on Gandhian Economics*, Part-II, May 2009 http://globalswadeshi.ning.com/forum/topics/essays-in-gandhian-economics-1, 20.
17. Sikri, Veena, The Global Financial Meltdown and Gandhian Philosophy-

and exploitation of Asia, Africa and Latin America and the white colony settlements in North Africa and Australia were all instances of globalization' In other words, globalization was from the outset associated with imperialism (the global linkage was based on European capitalist accumulation through the exploitation of the third World) and its impetus was always centred around imperial state institutions, specific class configurations, extracting resources from the domestic economy to finance overseas conquest and private accumulation, exploitation of the third world, inter-imperial trade, trading companies integrating and appropriating resources and exploiting cheap labour and international exchange (on unequal terms) of commodities. Essentially then, globalization is hardly a new phenomenon: it is merely a new name, a sub code for capitalism that subsumes diverse socio-political and economic processes. The imperial historical origins have remained embedded in a matrix in which new states and actors compete for privileged access to networks and state support. The principal agencies today, the multinational corporations, fulfil the roles played earlier by the trading companies (integrating and appropriating resources and exploiting cheap labour) while the imperial states extract domestic resources to finance overseas expansion and to secure the conditions for the reproduction of global capital accumulation.[3]

In view of the above context, addressing Gandhi in the globalizing ethos which seems to refute all that he stood for, is, indeed, challenging yet compelling. The ethos epitomizes the complexities of 'technicized' developmentalism, enormous acquisitive attainments, spiraling politico-economic ambitions and shrinking space of human and normative concerns. Impressive cumulative accomplishments in all major spheres of human life notwithstanding, it is being gradually realized that the erosion of a sense of a common valued past, ideas about the superiority of the Western civilization, the desirability of the goal of economic growth, faith in scientific reason and knowledge and belief in the intrinsic value of secular, 'this worldly' existence indicate toward the conclusion that the enlightenment idea of progress, on which the current phenomenon of globalization largely rests, is in peril.[4]

In a technological and modern world science and technology play very prominent role in the development of any nation. India is a developing country in the world. Indian economy is the fourth largest economy in the world. According to 2001 Census the literacy rate of India is 64.84 per cent. It is very less when compared to developed country in the world. The Planning Commission made a survey for finding out the number of persons below poverty line and estimated that 18.96 per cent of the total peoples live below poverty line as of the year 1993-94. It is necessary to take care about poor and illiteracy. The time is to give a clarion call for *Sarvodaya*, i.e., 'rising of all'. Sarvodaya a coinage of Gandhian thought. The term *Sarvodaya* commands a two-fold meaning. In one sense, *Sarvodaya* means making all happy by removing suffering and poverty with the help of scientific knowledge. Thus, establishing a world state full with divinity, kindness and equality is called *Sarvodaya*.[5]

IMPACTS OF GLOBALIZATION

Positive

1. Foreign Direct Investment (FDI) has helped to reduce poverty by creating jobs and improving incomes.
2. The expansion of trade and foreign investment has accelerated social mobility and strengthened the middle class.
3. New communications and information technology have helped disseminate knowledge in many fields of study and disciplines.
4. Communication is cheaper and easier.
5. Globalization makes it possible for humanity to have compassion for each other when calamities, natural or man-made, affect others.
6. Issues such as human rights and public accountability are brought to the fore.
7. The rights of women are highlighted and the problems many women face are now addressed.

Negative

1. Environmental degradation due to unrestrained activities of multinational corporations whose sole aim is to multiply profits.
2. Although poverty has been reduced to a certain extent, new economic disparities have been created. There are stark regional disparities in poverty.
3. Basic necessities in life are set aside in favour of profits.

preconditions Gandhi laid down as absolutely necessary for the practice of *satyagraha.*

The above-mentioned economic objectives within the framework of this structure will ultimately contribute to the realization of the goals of the Gandhian system—the welfare of the society as a whole, i.e., *Sarvodaya* including the poorest of the society. This can be achieved through harmonious balance of Gandhian idea of Economics and ethics and politics. The foundation of a good society must rest on fully integrated human persons. To Gandhi, providing a mere economic minimum to the members of society was not the *summum bonum* of existence. A society must follow a norm of life where material well-being is not the only motivating force. So Gandhi talked of the limitation of wants. To quote his famous sentence: "Nature produces enough to meet the needs of all the people but not enough to satisfy the greeds of any man".

CONCLUSION

Gandhi had his original vision in economics He propagated a novel way of thinking in science of economics. He integrated economic aims and activities with morality and nonviolence. He integrated our successful past experiences with the recent development process. He made the use of labour force and livestocks and rural economy for the nation's smooth progress. He was the first thinker from the east who analyzed and rejected mechanization, capitalism and communism. He was the man who took the advantage of science and machine for the benefit of population at large.

He was the first man in the world who provided a practical alternative economic system against the prevailing economic system. The village based economy of China and Israel, the small scale industry based economy of Japan are nearer to Gandhian ideas in some aspects.

A growth model for economic development is shown on the basis of Gandhi economic thoughts. This model is applicable to India and other developing economies. His ideas are helpful for backward and developing economies in the world. His ideas are also useful for solving problems in capitalist economies.

The axiomatic fact is that, capitalist economics does not care about the fate of the unemployed, because they cannot buy the luxury goods being produced anyway. Many, especially inexperienced young

4. The moral purpose embodied in the notion of service to govern the flow of trade among nations;
5. The philosophical principle of *ahimsa* must be the guiding principle; and
6. Protection against unequal distribution of gains from trade among nations.

The Gandhian concept of man is one of an integral man, who is a part of an integral society. The Gandhian concept is one of an integral transformation of man and society. In the Gandhian conception, the processes of individual (spiritual) transformation and political transformation are inevitably interconnected. The Gandhian concept basically pursues the unity of the individual and the social order. Gandhi stresses the unity of the private and public life. It is the Gandhian view that private life must be transparent and in that transparency, we can see the public life too. In the Gandhian thought, the stress is on the unity of the individual and social praxis. The Gandhian conception may be termed as the "Unity of Existence". Which is in total negation to modern economic model which stress men to excessive individualism and market the sole guiding force, which deals with man in relation to society? Hence Gandhi's idea of economic and ethics are important while analyzing his economic methods to realize the vision of good society.

Gandhi on Economics and Ethics: His Vision of an Inclusive Society

Gandhi said economics and ethics were not unrelated areas of human endeavour: 'I must confess that I do not draw any distinction between economics and ethics. Economics that hurt the moral well-being of an individual or a nation are immoral and, therefore, sinful. Thus, the economics that permit one country to prey upon another are immoral.' There are several issues involved in this assertion and too many of the votaries of unlimited growth words like morality or ethics do not mean anything. And even if they matter it might be just as inconvenient irritants. Gandhi strove for the spiritualization of politics so that politics would free itself from the stranglehold of power brokers. The economics that disregard moral and sentimental considerations are like the wax works, that being life still lacks the life of the living flesh'.

and wrong. Such individuals are the real antidotes to the bad effects of globalization.

GANDHI'S PRESCRIPTION TO COMBAT THREATS OF GLOBALIZATION

An interesting and significant aspect of the freedom movement in India was that along with the struggle against colonial rule, vigorous efforts were made to find an alternative path of development. While several people in India were eager to 'develop' as much as the British and later some others wanted to industrialize as rapidly as the Soviets, there were others who kept alive the concept of small and cottage scale development to be based in largely self-reliant rural communities.

This viewpoint was most vigorously articulated by Mahatma Gandhi who popularized the spinning wheel or *charkha* to symbolize this aspect of self-rule or *swaraj*. Gandhi's early experiences with the *charkha* are still significant in the context of the 'large *vs*. small, global *vs*. local' debate.[7]

In *Hind Swaraj* or 'Indian Home Rule' he wrote in 1908: "It is difficult to measure the harm that Manchester has done to us. It is due to Manchester that Indian handicraft has all but disappeared. But I make a mistake. How can Manchester be blamed? We wore Manchester cloth and this is why Manchester wove it." So Gandhi argued strongly in favour of going back to the self-reliant production of clothes in villages, a task in which *charkha* will have the crucial role of spinning the yarn, which will be used further by the handloom weavers to produce entirely hand-made cloth, called *khadi* or *khaddar* (hand-spun, hand-woven cloth)."

Mahatma Gandhi recognized that given the low per capita land availability in villages, the Indian peasant needed some additional craft work that could be pursued easily by the family without much capital investment. He wrote quite clearly in 1919: "Without a cottage industry the Indian peasant is doomed. He cannot maintain himself from the produce of the land."

In 1921, he wrote: "I have seen women beaming with joy to see the spinning wheel work, for they know that they can through that rustic instrument both feed and clothe themselves. I swear by this form of *swadeshi*, because through it I can provide work to the semi-starved, semi-employed women of India. My idea is to get these women to spin yarn, and to clothe the people of India with *khadi* woven out of it."

It is clear from this episode that Gandhi's concern was not confined to reducing the dependence on foreign mills, he was equally eager to reduce the villagers' dependence on domestic mills in the context of that produce which could be made by villagers themselves.

Gandhi was well aware how hidden state subsidies help the big industry and hinder the cottage industry: "In the open market a more organized industry will always be able to drive out a less organized one, much more so when the former is assisted by bounties and can command unlimited capital and can, therefore, afford to sell its manufactures at a temporary loss. Such has been the tragic fate of many enterprises in this country."

Therefore he asked for a different type of socio-economic evaluation: "I therefore maintain that, though yard per yard *khadi* may be dearer than mill-made cloth, in its totality and in terms of the villagers it is the most economic and practical proposition without a rival. *Khadi* may be interpreted to include other village industries for the purpose of a thorough examination of the proposition."

Gandhi linked economics closely to moral and ethical principles. In 1924 he wrote: "That economics is untrue which ignores or disregards moral values. The extension of the law of non-violence in the domain of economics means nothing less than the introduction of moral values as a factor to be considered in regulating international commerce."

These views were reflected increasingly in Mahatma Gandhi's perception of the role of a consumer or a buyer. For Gandhi a buyer in need of a product should not enter the market merely to maximize his satisfaction. Instead he should be guided to a large extent by social responsibility. He unhesitatingly exhorted people again and again to buy *khadi* and support it, ignoring questions such as coarseness or unevenness of the fabric.

Closely linked to this is the concept of *Swadeshi*. Literally this means 'my country' but Gandhi used the word in a much broader sense. Explaining this concept he wrote in 1916: "*Swadeshi* is that spirit in us which restricts us to the use and service of our immediate surroundings to the exclusion of the more remote. In the domain of economics I should use only things that are produced by my immediate neighbours and serve those industries by making them efficient and complete where they might be found wanting."

Gandhi's dream was that every village of India will almost be a self-supporting and self-contained unit, exchanging only such necessary commodities with other villages as are not locally producible."

In 1931, he declared: "A votary of *swadeshi* will carefully study his environment and try to help his neighbours wherever possible by giving preference to local manufactures even if they are of an inferior grade or dearer in price than things manufactured elsewhere. He will try to remedy their defects, but will not give them up, because of their defects and take to foreign manufactures."

Gandhi explained that the concept of *swadeshi* did not involve any ill feeling towards foreigners or other related narrow feelings. He wrote in 1923: "My definition of *swadeshi* is well known—(a) I must not serve my distant neighbour at the expense of the nearest. (b) It is never vindictive or punitive. (c) It is in no sense narrow, for I buy from every part of the world what is needed for my growth. I refuse to buy from anybody anything however nice or beautiful, if it interferes with my growth or injures those whom nature has made my first care. (d) I buy useful healthy literature from every part of the world. I buy surgical instruments from England, pins and pencils from Austria, and watches from Switzerland. But I will not buy an inch of the finest cotton fabric from England or Japan, or any other part of the world, because it has injured and increasingly injures millions of inhabitants of India. (e) I hold it to be sinful for me to refuse to buy the cloth spun and woven by the needy millions of India's paupers and to buy foreign cloth although it may be superior in quality to the Indian hand-spun."

In 1931, he wrote "But even *swadeshi* like any other good thing can be ridden to death if it is made a fetish. That is a danger that must be guarded against. To reject foreign manufactures merely because they are foreign and to go on wasting national time and money to promote manufactures in one's country for which it is not suited, would be criminal folly and a negation of the *swadeshi* spirit. A true votary of *swadeshi* will never harbour ill-will towards the foreigner; he will not be moved by antagonism towards anybody on earth. *Swadeshism* is not a cult of hatred. It is a doctrine of selfless service that has its roots in the purest *ahimsa*, that is, love."

Swadeshi should be used to support not the products of local mills but that of village industry. In 1926, Gandhi said clearly: "The test of *swadeshi* is not the universality of the use of an article which goes under the name of *swadeshi*, but the universality of participation in the production or manufacture of such an article. Thus, considered mill-made cloth is *swadeshi* only in a restricted sense. For in its manufacture only an infinitesimal number of India's millions can take part. But in the manufacture of *khaddar*, millions can take part."

He also emphasized the voluntary aspect of *swadeshi*: "It is believed by some that *swadeshi* could be affected by an embargo on foreign imports after the attainment of *swaraj*. But that *swadeshi* will be no *swadeshi*. It will be a virtue practiced under compulsion. True *swadeshi* is the invulnerable bulwark of the nation and it can only be said to be accomplished if it is practiced as a national duty."

Thus Gandhian economics is a school of economic thought based on the socio-economic principles expounded by Indian leader Mohandas Gandhi. It is largely characterized by its affinity to the principles and objectives of nonviolent humanistic socialism, but with a rejection of violent class war and promotion of socio-economic harmony. Gandhi's economic ideas also aim to promote spiritual development and harmony with a rejection of materialism. The term "Gandhian economics" was coined by J.C. Kumarappa, a close supporter of Gandhi.[8]

GANDHIAN ETHICS

Now, there are three ways in which ethics enters economics. First, economists have ethical values that help shape the way they do economics. This builds into the core of economic theory a particular view of how the economy does work and how it should work. Second, economic actors (consumers, workers, business owners) have ethical values that help shape their behaviour. Third, economic institutions and policies impact people differentially and thus ethical evaluations, in addition to economic evaluations, are important.[9]

Gandhi's thinking on socio-economic issues was greatly influenced by Henry David Thoreau. Throughout his life, Gandhi sought to develop ways to fight India's extreme poverty, backwardness and socio-economic challenges as a part of his wider involvement in the Indian independence movement. Gandhi's championing of *swadeshi* and non-cooperation were centred on the principles of economic self-sufficiency. Gandhi sought to target European-made clothing and other products as not only a symbol of British colonialism but also the source of mass unemployment and poverty, as European industrial goods had left many millions of India's workers, craftsmen and women without a means of living. By championing homespun *khadi* clothing and Indian-made goods, Gandhi sought to incorporate peaceful civil resistance as a means of promoting national self-sufficiency. Gandhi led farmers of Champaran and Kheda in a *satyagraha* (civil disobedience and tax resistance) against the mill owners and landlords supported by the British government in an effort to end oppressive taxation and other policies that forced the farmers and workers and defend their economic rights. A major part of this rebellion was a commitment from the farmers to end caste discrimination and oppressive social practices against women while launching a co-operative effort to promote education, health care and self-sufficiency by producing their own clothes and food.

Gandhi and his followers also founded numerous *ashrams* in India (Gandhi had pioneered the *ashram* settlement in South Africa). The concept of an *ashram* has been compared with the commune, where its inhabitants would seek to produce their own food, clothing and means of living, while promoting a lifestyle of self-sufficiency, personal and spiritual development and working for wider social development. The *ashrams* included small farms and houses constructed by the inhabitants themselves. All inhabitants were expected to help in any task necessary, promoting the values of equality. Gandhi also espoused the notion of "trusteeship," which centred on denying material pursuits and coveting of wealth, with practitioners acting as "trustees" of other individuals and the community in their management of economic resources and property. Contrary to many Indian socialists and communists, Gandhi was averse to all notions of class warfare and concepts of class-based revolution, which he saw as causes of social violence and disharmony. Gandhi's concept of egalitarianism was centred on the preservation of human dignity rather than material development. Some of Gandhi's closest supporters and admirers included industrialists such as Ghanshyamdas Birla, Ambalal Sarabhai, Jamnalal Bajaj and J.R.D. Tata, who adopted several of Gandhi's progressive ideas in managing labour relations while also personally participating in Gandhi's *ashrams* and socio-political work.

GANDHIAN ECONOMICS

Gandhian economics do not draw a distinction between economics and ethics. Economics that hurts the moral well-being of an individual or a nation is immoral and, therefore, sinful. The value of an industry should be gauged less by the dividends it pays to shareholders than by its effect on the bodies, soul and spirits of the people employed in it. In essence, supreme consideration is to be given to man than to money. In fact, the first basic principle of Gandhi's economic thought is a special emphasis on 'plain living' which helps in cutting down your wants and being self-reliant. Accordingly, increasing consumer appetite is likened to animal appetite which goes the end of earth in search of their satisfaction. Thus a distinction is to be made between 'Standard of Living' and 'Standard of Life', where the former merely states the material and physical standard of food, cloth and housing. A higher standard of life, on the other hand could be attained only if, along with material advancement, there was a serious attempt to imbibe cultural and spiritual values and qualities.

SOCIAL JUSTICE AND EQUALITY

Gandhi has often said that if mankind was to progress and to realize the ideals of equality and brotherhood, it must act on the principle of paying the highest attention to the prime needs of the weakest sections of the population. Therefore, any exercise on economic planning on a national scale would be futile without uplifting these most vulnerable sections of the society in a direct manner. In the ultimate analysis, it is the quality of the human being that has to be raised, refined and consolidated. In other words, economic planning is for the citizen, and not the citizen for national planning. Everybody should be given the right to earn according to his capacity using just means. The rich should serve the society after satisfying his needs and not merely enjoy his life.

GANDHIAN CONCEPT OF GLOBAL GROWTH

Gandhian economics brings a socialist perspective of overall development and tries to redefine the outlook of socialism. Gandhi espoused the notion of "trusteeship" which centred on denying material pursuits and coveting of wealth, with practitioners acting as "trustees" of other individuals and the community in their management of economic resources and property. Under the Gandhian economic order, the character of production will be determined by social necessity and not by personal greed. The path of socialism should only be through non-violence and democratic method and any recourse to class-war and mutual hatred would prove to be suicidal.

Modern Interpretations

The proximity of Gandhian economic thought to socialism has also evoked criticism from the advocates of free-market economics. To many, Gandhian economics represent an alternative to mainstream economic ideologies as a way to promote economic productivity without an emphasis on material pursuits or compromising human development. Gandhi's emphasis on peace, "trusteeship" and co-operation has been touted as an alternative to competition as well as conflict between different economic and income classes in societies. Gandhian focus on human development is also seen as an effective emphasis on the eradication of poverty, social conflict and backwardness in developing nations. Gandhian socio-economic ideas have gained the interest and attention of an increasing number of people across the world.

Gandhian ethics *versus* western technology is a solution to questions of climate change and economic disorder. Gandhi believed that rapid industrialization and craze for mass production causes unemployment and imbalance in the eco-system. His economic school of thought is characterized by its affinity to the principles and objectives of socialism, but with a rejection of class war and promotion of socio-economic harmony. Gandhi's economic ideas also aim to promote spiritual development and harmony with a rejection of materialism. Gandhian views on ethics and technology is that they need to go hand in hand. He believed in technology as a tool for transformation, not as a destination in itself. Technology without ethics will destroy the planet while ethics without technology might create dangerous situations such as ecomentalism. So, to combat the threat of globalization and its associated dangers we need a much more holistic approach and people from multidisciplinary backgrounds working together in mixed teams to really create sustainable solutions.[10]

WHAT IS UNETHICAL?

1. Economic institutions, rules, practices which disadvantage

the poor will be viewed as unethical.

2. Ethical behaviour requires "progressivity": the poor should benefit disproportionately, and
3. Hypocritical behaviour viewed as unethical.

Ethics through Education

Value education means inculcating in the children a sense of humanism, a deep concern for the well-being of others and the nation. This can be accomplished only when we instil in the children a deep feeling of commitment to values that would build this country and bring back to the people pride in work that brings order, security and assured progress.[11]

Value education has the capacity to transform a diseased mind into a very young, fresh, healthy, natural and attentive mind. The transformed mind is capable of higher sensitivity and a heightened level of perception this leads to fulfilment of the evolutionary role in man and in life.

In order to create new social order Gandhiji introduced Nai Talim in the year 1937, which is popularly known as Basic Education[12]-

1. Truth,
2. Non-violence,
3. Freedom,
4. Democracy,
5. *Sarva Dharma Samabhava*,
6. Equality,
7. Self-realization,
8. Purity of ends and means,
9. Self-discipline, and
10. *Suddhi*.

CONCLUSIONS

It is the duty of the Government to give such type of education for each and every student in the country. Through education only we can solve all types of problems. Through education it is easy to motivate people about ethical value and moral values and human rights. Education gives knowledge, strength and creativity. India is a fourth largest economy in the world. The youth population is also very high. By proper using of science and technology and human and natural resources India will become developed country in the world.

"We must protect the forests for our children, grandchildren and children yet to be born. We must protect the forests for those who can't speak for themselves such as the birds, animals, fish and trees."

NOTES

1. Asha Kaushik, 2002, *Globalization, Democracy and Culture* (Jaipur: Pointers Publishers), p. 1.
2. Ronald Robertson, 1992, *Globalization* (London: Sage), pp. 58-60.
3. James Petras and Chronis Polychronius, Capital Reflections on Globalization (*Economic and Political Weekly*, Sept. 6, 1997), p. 2249.
4. See Robert A. Nisbet, 1980, *A History of the Idea of Progress* (New York: Basic Books), p. 329.
5. Anil Dutt Mishra, *Fundamentals of Gandhism* (New Delhi: Mittal Publication, 1995), pp. 5-6.
6. *Journal of Gandhian Studies*, Vol. VII, No. 1, 2009, p 105.
7. Bharat Dogra-http://www. vedamsbooks.in/no29346.htm,
8. Kumarappa, Joseph Cornelius (1951). *Gandhian Economic Thought.* (Bombay, India: Library of Indian Economics (1st ed.). August 2009) http://en.wikipedia.org/wiki/Gandhian_economics
9. Amartya Sen. *On Ethics and Economics.*
10. Kim Poldner Saturday, 06 March, 2010, http://www.ecofashionworld.com/kin/gandhian-economics.html
11. Dr. Venkataiah (ed.), 1998, *Value Education*, (New Delhi: APH Publishing Corporation, first edition).
12. Usha Rai Negi (ed.), 2000. *Value Education in India*, (New Delhi: Association of Indian Universities).

9

Gandhian Economics in the Context of Emerging Rural Scenario

G.K. Singh

In his book *Hind Swaraj* (1909), Gandhi was emphatic that *swaraj* was "*much more than simply wanting (the systems of) English rule without the Englishman; the tiger's nature but not the tiger.*"[1] His argument centred on the belief that the socio-spiritual underpinnings of British political, economic, bureaucratic, legal, military, and educational institutions were inherently unjust, exploitative and alienating. As Pinto explicates, "The principal theme of *Hind Swaraj* is the moral inadequacy of western civilization, especially its industrialism, as the model for free India." Gandhi was particularly critical of the deeply embedded principles of *might is right* and *survival of the fittest*. On another level, the call for *swaraj* represents a genuine attempt to regain control of the 'self'—our self-respect, self-responsibility, and capacities for self-realization—from institutions of dehumanization. As Gandhi states, "It is *swaraj* when we learn to rule ourselves." The real goal of the freedom struggle was not only to secure political *azadi* (freedom) from Britain, but rather to gain true *swaraj* (liberation and self-rule).

Swadeshi, *swaraj* and *satyagraha* were central to India's freedom movement. *Swadeshi* movement as economic battle was necessary adjunct to *swaraj* the political battle for freedom. Economic freedom, according to *swadeshi*, is based on endogenously managed development rather than exogenously controlled development. The word *swadeshi* has an appeal to sections of Indians and perhaps has appeal to all Indians. *Swadeshi* to many means, "what we can do, let us do". *Swadeshi* to me means a set of policies that are good for the economic development of the country, not for some sections of

Indians, be it labour or capital. It gives us a sense of pride. No one will be against foreign collaborations in those areas in which we lack the expertise.

India's long-term economic prospects depend mainly on agricultural sector, which contributes a quarter of gross domestic product, and provides livelihood to two-thirds of the population.[2] It is, therefore, imperative that highest priority is accorded to agriculture. In India, 70 per cent of our population is involved in agriculture and only 7 per cent in processing, transportation, storage and marketing. On the other hand, in advanced countries only 4 to 7 per cent population lives on agriculture and 40 to 45 per cent are involved in grading, processing storage, marketing, transportation, retailing and in exports.

In order to ensure that Indian economy grows at 8 per cent every year on sustainable basis, it requires more focused and determined approach by the Government, industry and society at large.[3] With our strengths and resources both natural and human such as largest cultivable land with diversified agro-climatic zones, large industrial and commercial base and supplemented by large pool of intellectuals, it would not be difficult to achieve faster economic growth. In the last few years, Indian citizens have been demanding faster economic development and transparency and there is growing importance among the masses specially those who are living in rural semi or urban areas. The rural demand for manufactured goods and services also depend on the expansion of the agricultural economy and are essentially due to robust performance of agricultural sector.[4]

In a typical Indian village, economic activities were and, to a considerable extent, even today are generally associated with a particular 'caste' and community, which has practiced a particular profession for generations[5]. The nature of activity undertaken was, in general, hereditary and occupational mobility within the village nearly non-existent.[6] Generally, each village had at least one household each of blacksmiths, carpenters, weavers, potters and those engaged in oilseed crushing. Agricultural and non-agricultural activities had direct and strong organic links within the village. Landowners needed manpower to cultivate their lands and help them in the household. They also needed professionals to take care of their ploughs and other agricultural implements; in return, the village artisans were paid in the form of grains and other farm produce each season.[7] The relationships, sanctified by socio-economic traditions, were thus institutionalized. A typical Indian village in this sense was an organic whole, in which, while each activity had its own distinct identity, there was a considerable degree of inter-dependence.

Under the inspiration of Mahatma Gandhi, the national struggle for India's political independence witnessed a concomitant struggle for the preservation, protection and encouragement of rural industries. The Gandhian strategy for rural development was linked to enhanced utilization of the vast mass of surplus manpower and its active involvement in production processes. The Gandhian ideology was not only economic but also social and political. In the Gandhian idiom, cottage and village industries represent a support structure to a life style that is more moral than economic. Villages keep the workers in close touch with balmy open spaces and nature in all its peace and pleasantness. The unequal competition from cheap mill-made products threatened employment and livelihood of the rural artisans and craftsmen.[8] The preference for *khadi vis-à-vis* mill cloth, and cottage and village industry products *vis-à-vis* the urban and mill-made products was motivated from a realization that the experience of urban handicraft centers might also get extended to rural non-agricultural activity and the cottage and village industries.[9] Gandhi put a premium on simplicity in life style and consumption.

The view, that village industries and crafts are an important part of rural life and should be vigorously protected to ensure sustenance to a self-reliant village, is essentially an outcome of the traditionalist philosophy, articulated so forcefully by Gandhi. It was in fact a reactive approach—a defence mechanism against the onslaught of the British industry. Completing the first stage of industrialization, the British industry was then looking for new markets in the British colonies for its products along with linkages for obtaining raw materials. India was a good opportunity on both counts. The task became easier with improvements in roads, introduction of railways and use of rivers as navigational channels. India's population was large and it had a rich tradition of crafts and village industries. A variety of industrial products were already in use. Low priced substitutes could find ready markets here. On the other hand, India's agricultural base was vast and land was not fully exploited. With a little effort, India could be developed as a dependable source of raw materials. The face of rural India is changing. With the government increasing budget of rural development and other ministries extending their shares of schemes and also with the large-scale intervention of

Public Sector Undertakings as a part of their social obligation in the field of rural development.[10]

Gandhi had an innate sympathy for the poor and deprived. This coupled with a direct observation of the predicament of the poor and the oppressed both in India and in South Africa led him to design an economic model that would alleviate the condition of the poor and the deprived. Gandhi believed that the high capitalist endeavours were at the root of all sufferings. He believed that business without ethical considerations was fundamentally evil. This led to discrimination, oppression and exploitation. Gandhi also held that there is enough in this world to feed and clothe all. However, there is poverty and deprivation because one group of people thrives on the labour put in by others. Gandhi strongly believed in the ethics of hard work and that one is entitled to take from the system only as much as he is capable of producing. This, according to Gandhi, was the only way to fight poverty and to disarm the world of all its economic woes.

Gandhi also strongly believed that laziness and lack of work can cause immense physical and spiritual deprivation among the populace. It is impossible to ignite the masses towards a revolution leading to a bigger political or ideological goal if they are weak, both physically and morally. He understood that the new industrial modes of mass and large scale productions that have been ousting the age-old indigenous village techniques are ultimately leading towards unemployment and laziness. Therefore, he worked hard for a resurrection of the village modes of production.[11]

The most unique feature of Gandhi's economic model was that he wanted to turn the entire flow of profits from the pockets of the big industrialists to the workers. The consumer should, he believed, not only be concerned with acquiring high quality, inexpensive products, but also consider which sections of society are profited by his investment. Foreign clothes may be better and cheaper than the home-spun *khadi*, but the relentless use of the imported fabric would lead to unemployment of thousands of villagers who have traditionally earned a living by spinning and weaving home-made cloths. The same logic extends to agro-based products as well. Choosing such imported goods would lead to a degeneration of the entire village economy, which was the backbone of Indian economy, Gandhi believed.

But at the same time, Gandhi knew the actual implications of an aggressive capitalism: no such humanitarian economic considerations can possibly curb the relentless advance of the big mechanizations initiated by high capitalist agencies. Therefore, he devised a scheme to suit one and all. A nation low on man-power can well use mechanization to enhance its agricultural and mechanical production. But for a nation with a teeming population like India, it would augur no good. Secondly, he thought that a nation should produce only as much as it needs to produce. Extra production, resulting in the beginning of international economic race, would only lead to exploitation. The condition in India, for Gandhi, was ultimately a manifestation of the aggressive mechanization promoted by the British colonialists.

Gandhi's views on economics were simple and straightforward at the outset. They have even been criticized at various levels from being utopian to regressive. But it had deep political connotations. He understood economic motives to be the basic principle of imperialism and colonialism. And he, therefore, understood that the only way to attack and weaken the colonial forces would be to attack the basic economic profits that the British gained from the colonies. This coupled with his actual understanding of the Indian condition led to the development of a unique brand of economic reorientation of the Indian society that he propagated throughout his life. However, it will be erroneous to consider his economic model to be merely a political tool shrouded in spiritual rhetoric. His concern for the predicament of the Indian villagers was genuine, as was his concern for a heartless mechanization of the world economy sans ethical considerations. In his time, the influence of his economic model was immense and has been dutifully followed in various parts of the world as well as in India, with varied degrees of success.

To Gandhi, social emancipation was as critical as political emancipation. Gandhi throughout his life waged a crusade for the upliftment of the socially downtrodden, making significant contributions for the enhancement of the status of women in India. Women under his aegis took a milestone step towards re-establishing their identity in the society. Gandhi's inspiring ideologies boosted their morale and helped them to rediscover their self esteem. Not only there was a general awakening among the women, but under Gandhi's leadership, they entered into the national mainstream, taking parts in the National Movements. In Gandhi's words, "To call women the weaker sex is a libel; it is man's injustice to women." Gandhi's reformist spirit seasoned the role that he played in uplifting the status of women in India.

According to the Mahatma, social reforms were essential for the restructuring of the societal values that had so far dominated the perception of Indian women. Although, he had great reverence for the traditions of the country, he also realized that certain customs and traditions of the Indian society were antithetical to the spirit of development of the women of the nation. To quote Gandhi, 'It is good to swim in the waters of tradition, but to sink in them is suicide.' The custom of child marriage became a target of his criticisms. In his opinion, child marriage is a source of physical degeneration as much as a moral evil. The system of dowry could not pass unnoticed from his critical eyes. He defined dowry marriages as 'heartless'. He opined that girls should never marry men who demand dowry, at the cost of their self respect and dignity. As Gandhi believed that the basis of marriage is mutual love and respect, he urged people to solemnize inter-communal marriages between the Harijans and caste Hindus. Gandhi was extremely perturbed by the plight of the widows, particularly child widows. He put forth an earnest appeal to the young generation of the country to marry the widows. He was also quite hopeful about the immense potentials of the widows in furthering national issues. The system of *purdah* also came under Gandhi's attacks and he questioned the very foundation of this practice. For him, the *purdah* system was no less than a "vicious, brutal and barbarous" practice. The predicaments of the *devadasis*, a part of the lower, untouchable segment of the society, had an indelible effect on the sensitive mind of the Mahatma. The pathetic conditions of the child prostitutes disturbed him immensely. He left no stone unturned for rehabilitating this segment of the society, as for him guarding the honour of women was no less than protecting cows.

Gandhian thought in the area of religious harmony is centrally based on tolerance and respect for all religious systems, while retaining one's own faith. With the kind of communal riots the country faced before, during, and immediately after Partition, and the convulsive violence gripping the society during frequent intervals thereafter, Gandhiji's relevance in this area becomes all the more well-etched. Even when the average citizen rues the fact that Gandhian ideals haven't gained enough ground so as to obviate the recurrence of such violence, the image of Gandhiji once again looms large on the scenario in other ways.

"Gandhi was in reality a man of information age. He knew the power of information and how to utilize it in the most effective manner.

Gandhi may mean different things to different people. Throughout his life he firmly stood for certain deep values, such as, simplicity, sacrifice, truth and love for all. These values helped him get rid of all the impulses of instant gratification and provided him immense courage of conviction." Gandhi was an incredible communicator and a leader, who stripped the larger issues and ideas to a down-to-earth level in order to make it more compatible.

The face of rural India is changing. With the government increasing budget of rural development and other ministries extending their shares of schemes and also with the large-scale interventions of Public Sector Undertakings as a part of their social obligation in the field of rural development, the job opportunities at various levels are also increasing.[12] The new concept is "instead of handling out fish, impart the training of fishing", i.e., make people self-reliant through their capacity building; make them healthy by educating them about health precautions. So the Gandhian concept still exists in the present rural development scenario. It is very necessary to revive the policy and plans as per thought of Gandhi and follow their thought for sustainable development.[13]

NOTES

1. M.K. Gandhi (1909), *Hind Swaraj,* Ahmedabad: Navjivan.
2. *Report of the Backward Classes Commission (1956)*, New Delhi: Government of India Publication.
3. Gadgil, D.R. (1971), *Industrial Evolution of India in Recent Times: 1860-1939*, London: Oxford University Press, fifth edition.
4. Gandhi, M.K. (1952) *Rebuilding Our Villages*, Ahmedabad: Navjivan, p. 4.
5. Kidron, M. (1965), *Foreign Investments in India*, London. Oxford University.
6. Myrdal, G. (1968), *Asian Drama: An Inquiry into the Poverty of Nations*, New York: Pantheon.
7. Bagchi, Amiya Kumar (1972), *Private Investment in India: 1900-1939*, London: Orient Longman.
8. Rao, V.K.R.V. (1979), Industrialization and Integrated Rural Development, *Man and Development*, Vol. I, No. 2, July.
9. B. Shiva Rao (1968), *The Framing of India's Constitution: A Study*, New Delhi: Indian Institute of Public Administration, p. 331.
10. Mahalanobis, P.C. *Approach to Planning in India*, as quoted in G. Myrdal *op. cit.*, pp. 12-19.

11. Planning Commission, (Rural Industries Planning Committee 1962), *Project for Intensive Development of Small Industries in Rural Areas*, July, pp. 28-30.
12. *INDIA*, Planning Commission (1988), *Village and Small Industries Sector Framework: Policy Issues and Perspectives*, p. 71.
13. Singh, Dalbir (2003), *Conference on Indian Banking: Global Benchmark*, Sept. 25-27, Mumbai.

10

Hind Swaraj: A Source Book for Corporate and Business Ethics

Anurag Gangal

Mahatma Gandhi's *Hind Swaraj* or *Indian Home Rule* is a treasure of practical ethics for the growth of the corporate world and business community not only in India but on a larger global plane and intercontinental ethos. World is peaceful, growing and moving towards beneficial and fulsome development only when ethics and values operate and sustain the society and community where we live in.

INTRODUCTION

Every activity in this world, relating to an individual and a nation, moves on the basis of fundamental ethics, values and policy guidelines without which it is difficult to stand on one's feet and grow sensibly and meaningfully any further. In this matter, just see how really modern is Gandhi even in the opening statement of his *Hind Swaraj* about his perspective on the question of 'contradiction' in human affairs:

> I would like to say to the diligent reader of my writings and to others who are interested in them that *I am not at all concerned with appearing to be consistent.*
> In my search after Truth *I have discarded many Ideas and learnt many new things.*
> Old as I am in age, *I have no feeling that I have ceased to grow inwardly or that my growth will stop at the dissolution of the flesh.*
> *What I am concerned with is my readiness to obey the call*

> *of Truth, my God, from moment to moment*, and, therefore, *when anybody finds any inconsistency between any two writings* of mine, ... he would do well to *choose the latter of the two on the same subject.*[1]

A *fundamental continuity of courage of conviction* is apparent in this explanation of Mahatma Gandhi about finding certain inherent contradictions in his writings and views from time to time.

After reading Gandhi's *Hind Swaraj* and *My Experiments with Truth or An Autobiography*, another essential *practical* principle is to be found in his stress on setting standards about *when to* go for compromise and *when not to* compromise in diverse human affairs. It is advisable, as such, for instance, *never to compromise in matters of basic and fundamental principles relating to Truth* while always remaining *eager to compromise and adjust in matters of detail and daily routine,* etc.

Gandhi's *Panch Yama* – from Patanjali's *Yogapradeepta*—such as truth, non-violence, non-stealing, non-possession and *brahmcharya* or celibacy constitute the elementary requirement for any business and community to sustain and develop through the ages. Otherwise, the only alternative that remains is merely chaos and anarchy.

BUSINESS AND ETHICS LINKAGE

Even after reading a few opening pages of *Hind Swaraj*—written in 1908[2]—what surprises most in this booklet is that it appears so deeply belonging to present day age and contemporary challenges of global society, politics and varied economic and professional concerns. What an element of visionary timelessness has Gandhi put into *Hind Swaraj* !

> "Values of truth, courage of conviction, paradigmatic growth of human vision and understanding and development in a self-respecting global civil society are very much an integral part of Gandhi's *Hind Swaraj.* No society can prosper without elementary values of nonviolence and peace combined with a number of other practical requirements of ethics and morals. Any type of social, political and economic activity needs basic and lasting support of ethical practices for growth and prosperity. Otherwise, what follows is widespread chaos,

> anarchism and massive violence leading to gross social misbehaviour, misconduct and massive violence. Such a situation is always highly detrimental not only to society in general but also to business and corporate world in particular."[2]

Corporate and business world grow and prosper only in a primarily peaceful, nonviolent socio-political and economic set-up. Truthfulness, honesty, efficiency, loyalty, determination, self-reliance, discipline and professional dedication are also practical *a priori* values necessary for a successful business and corporate activity and establishment.

It is common knowledge that development and prosperity is possible only in a nonviolent and ordered economic and political system. Peace is also a prerequisite of the process of globalization in the twenty-first century.

The Gandhian values in *Hind Swaraj* are such that they only help build a truly equitable, egalitarian and self-respecting world through real globalization based on good governance and e-governance, global civil society and e-business and commerce.

Despite utter condemnation of industrialisation and mechanisation in *Hind Swaraj,* Mahatma Gandhi has expressed umpteenth time that he is mainly against such industrialisation, mechanisation and technologicalisation which is harmful to ever expanding opportunities for livelihood, humanitarian concerns and ecologically balanced life styles.[3]

Indeed, business prospers when peace prevails. What type of peace and what type of the corporate world for Mahatma Gandhi? In "A Word of Explanation" in *Hind Swaraj* Gandhi says:

> It [*Hind Swaraj*] was written in 1908 during my return voyage from London to South Africa in answer to the Indian school of violence and its prototype in South Africa. I came into contact with every known Indian anarchist in London. Their bravery impressed me, but I felt that their zeal was misguided. I felt that violence was no remedy for India's ills, and that her civilization required the use of a different and higher weapon for self-protection. The *Satyagraha* of South Africa was still an infant hardly two years old. But it had developed sufficiently to permit me to write of it with some degree of

> confidence. What I wrote was so much appreciated that it was published as a booklet. It attracted some attention in India [too]. The Bombay Government prohibited its circulation. I replied by publishing its translation. I thought that it was due to my English friends [prohibition or ban on the circulation of [*Hind Swaraj*] that they should know its contents.
>
> In my opinion it is a book which can be put into the hands of a child. It teaches the gospel of love in place of that of hate. It replaces violence with self-sacrifice. It puts soul force against brute force. It has gone through several editions and I commend it to those who would care to read it. I withdraw nothing but one word of it, and that in difference to a lady friend.
>
> *The booklet is a severe condemnation of 'modern civilization'. It was written in 1908.* My conviction is deeper today than ever. I feel that if India will discard 'modern civilization', she can only gain by doing so.
>
> *But I would warn the reader against thinking that I am today aiming at the Swaraj described therein* [*in Hind Swaraj*]. I know that India is not ripe for it. It may seem impertinent to say so. But such is my conviction. I am individually working for self-rule pictured therein. But today my corporate activity is undoubtedly devoted to the attainment of Parliamentary *swaraj* in accordance with the wishes of the people of India. *I am not aiming at destroying railways or hospitals, though I would certainly welcome their natural destruction. Neither railways nor hospitals are a test of a high and pure civilization. At best they are a necessary evil. Neither adds one inch to the moral stature of a nation. Nor am I aiming at a permanent destruction of law courts, much as I regard it as 'consummation devoutly to be wished'. Still less am I trying to destroy all machinery and mills. It requires a higher simplicity and renunciation than people are today prepared for.*[4]

Gandhi is for fully applying his philosophy of non-violence and *satyagraha* to our modern life styles. It is necessary for *swaraj* and higher fulfilment of the aspirations of the people of India. Gandhi further says in his *Hind Swaraj*:

> I have even seen writings suggesting that I am playing a deep game, that I am using the present turmoil to foist my fads on India, and am making religious experiments at India's expense. I can only answer that *satyagraha* is made of sterner stuff. There is nothing reserved and nothing secret in it. A portion of the whole theory of life described in *Hind Swaraj* is undoubtedly being carried into practice. There is no danger attendant upon the whole of it being practiced. But it is not right to scare away people by reproducing from my writings passages that are irrelevant to the issue before the country.[5]

CORPORATE BUSINESS AND DEMOCRACY

Corporate business works its way up the ladder of growth in a given social and political set-up. This must be recognised in any given situation in order to realise the necessity for needed community action programmes on the part of the business community and the corporate world as a part of their social and political and economic responsibility to the people amongst whom the business of the corporate world is flourishing.

Such functioning and performance on the part of the corporate world is needed for commitment and dedication to the cause of the people in general and challenges of India's poor population in particular. One's presence and continued business at a given socio-geographical area puts a corporate unit and even the elected government into a relationship of Trust to the people. Whenever this sense of responsibility and trust to the concerned people and population inhabiting a particular area is broken by the relevant corporate or business unit then it must be the business of the government and the people to see that such a corporate and governmental existence does not remain a source to fleece any common citizen or person.[6] As such, corporate business and democracy stand and work as repository of *trust* of the people in them—either formally through a legal contract or informally and tacitly through inherent sense of responsibility to those upon whom the growth, development and future of a company or corporation and government depends.

GANDHI'S TALISMAN AND CORPORATE WORLD

It is a common knowledge that Gandhi has given to the world a "Talisman" for showing the path of truth and practical direction to those who face a situation of doubt and difficulty in dealing with taking a decision for taking a decision to act in a particular way at a given point of time. Gandhi's "Talisman" is as follows:

> I will give you a talisman. Whenever you are in doubt, or when the self becomes too much with you, apply the following test. Recall the face of the poorest and the weakest man [woman] whom you may have seen, and ask yourself, if the step you contemplate is going to be of any use to him [her]. Will he [she] gain anything by it? Will it restore him [her] to a control over his [her] own life and destiny? In other words, will it lead to *swaraj* [freedom] for the hungry and spiritually starving millions?
> Then you will find your doubts and your self melt away.[7]

For the corporate world, this talisman may be paraphrased as:

> Whenever a decision needs to be made, or a policy needs to be created, apply the following test. Recall the face of the lowest grade employee who works for you, and ask yourself, if the step you contemplate is going to be of any use to him [her]. Will he [she] gain anything by it? Will it restore him [her] to a control over his [her] own life and destiny? Then you will find your doubts and your self melt away.[8]

It is interesting to know how a top and successful corporate giant of India worked with Gandhi while reposing full trust in him for the upliftment of the poor population of India. This corporate magnate is none other than Jamnalal Bajaj—the founder of the successful Bajaj industries in India. Gandhi was not yet a politician upon his return from South Africa to India in 1915. Jamnalal was first attracted to Gandhi's reformist trait and his achievement in South Africa. What impressed him most was that Gandhi practiced what he preached. By late 1915, Gandhi's austerity, self-discipline, and self-imposed poverty had cast a spell on Jamnalal. He began to visit Gandhi's *ashram* (ascetic's abode) regularly and donated generously towards building the *ashram*. He became a devoted follower and worked to take care of all his worldly needs. When Gandhi shaped his passive resistance movement as a tool for achieving justice for the poor and disaffected, Jamnalal and his followers were inspired. For them Gandhi was a social reformer more than anything else. Inevitably, Gandhi became drawn into Indian politics. Although some criticized Gandhi's methods as well, the British government became increasingly concerned as Gandhi's popularity with the masses grew and his ability to mobilize them with words and deeds took force. Jamnalal was unwittingly drawn into politics through his proximity to Gandhi, despite his lack of interest. When the government official who administered Wardha called Jamnalal and asked him to stay away from Gandhi, Jamnalal refused. He maintained that he was neither responsible for his friends' views nor would he abandon them for holding views contrary to his own. When Gandhi called for sacrifice for the sake of the nation, Jamnalal was the first one to jump in. Gandhi called for renunciation and in response Jamnalal gave up all associations with the British government, including a title that had been conferred upon him, and began focusing on how to make rural India robust.[9]

MANAGEMENT AND PROBLEM SOLVING

Modern corporate industrial houses are—among other things related to Gandhian ethics depicted in *Hind Swaraj*—also dependent on the communication channels and their process of solving organizational problems either through top to bottom system or its opposite. Although Gandhi does not write directly on the importance of "communication" in the corporate world, he has indicated in chapters XIII, XIV and XVI of his *Hind Swaraj* on how corporate world—and rich and poor constituents of such a unit and industry—must act for its own benefit.

As such it may be said that the leadership in the corporate and business units need to turn over the pages of Gandhi's *Hind Swaraj* not only for day to day functioning, managerial approach, communication patterns but also for policy making and honest quality assurance while working in line with their employees and workers at every level of corporate behaviour.

Organisational behaviour is indeed a very significant part of modern corporate world. In this organisational behaviour perspective, communication, its nature and its line of flow become highly important for the sake of larger health of working environment of an industrial unit. However, upward communication is generally a neglected sphere of research in the area of leadership in organisational behaviour and functioning.

Communication from senior managerial officers to non-managerial staff is mostly considered to be the cornerstone of successful running of an organisation. This, however, is not a reality because history is replete with examples of the most powerful organisations and chief executives perishing completely when adopting this one-sided for top-to-bottom technique of communication alone. Leadership does not mean merely giving commands and rendering orders.

Effective line of authority and meaningful leadership evolve in an organisation when there are multiple types of information channels— even going much beyond the "two way flow" of information within an organisation. There are at least seven 'models' and six types of "tactics and techniques". Apart from all these, there have to be informal, non-formal and natural processes of feedback from non-managerial staff to managerial executives, which are necessary for ensuring a healthy and efficient work ethos and conditions.

Therefore, what organisations require is the 'learning' type of communication environment where there is not only upward information flow but also a critical upward communication (CUC) and feedback system—both formal and informal. There must also be a professional analysis unit for upward and downward communication from a 'learning' perspective. All communications must be professionally weighed at all levels of the organisation.

If, for instance, an educational organisation is devoid of this learning outlook, then neither teachers, nor the administration or students can ever be benefited. Multiple types of upward feedback are indeed a must for any organisation. Even one of the most powerful dictators like Adolph Hitler failed miserably, in the ultimate analysis, just because he did not bother to use this learning perspective of organisation while dealing with the problems of the state and politics.

A relatively young organisation like Microsoft has been so successful because it uses this 'learning' module of communication in running its business affairs. Therefore, Lord Acton's phrase must always be kept in mind while running an organisation. For him, "Power corrupts and absolute power corrupts absolutely". Lack of proper feedback also leads to disruption. Hence, for the sake of success, efficiency, healthy working conditions and the continued existence of an organisation, upward influences and communication are necessary.

CONCLUSION

For Gandhi, learning and education throughout life is necessary. But one must not make a fetish out of it.[10] Corporate world must, for the sake of its own prosperity and growth, also keep away from corrupt practices, bribery, use of brute force and exploitation of its employees and general public. Principles of loyalty and devotion to one's own duty are the most important themes for success of any type of business and corporate giants. Otherwise none can prosper perennially.

That is why Gandhi concludes his *Hind Swaraj* with the following words:

Let each do his duty. If I do my duty, that is, serve myself, I shall be able to serve others....

1. Real home-rule is self-rule or self-control.
2. The way to it is passive resistance [*Satyagraha*]: that is soul-force or love-force.
3. In order to exert this force, *swadeshi* in every sense is necessary.[11]

The Gandhian principle of *swadeshi* has now changed its perspective especially after India's independence and her emergence as an industrial giant in the larger global economy. Gandhi has expressed very interesting views in this context. He has said on different occasions about the need of engaging in foreign trade and export of various goods when necessary in the process of India entering into international economic activities and global trade.[12]

NOTES

1. M.K. Gandhi, *Hind Swaraj* or *Indian Home Rule*, Ahmedabad: Navajivan, 1939 (revised new edition nineteenth reprint), p. 4. Emphasis added through italics and paragraphing.
2. M.K. Gandhi, *op. cit.*, p.15 (last but one paragraph).
3. *Hind Swaraj*, *op. cit.*, pp. 15-16. *Young India,* 17 June 1926; *Harijan*, 22 June, 1935 and 15 September, 1946; M.K. Gandhi, *Hind Swaraj or Indian*

Home Rule, Ahmedabad: Navajivan Publishing House, 1938, p. 08, Preface by Mahadev Desai. See also Raghavan Iyer (ed.), *The Moral and Political Writings of Mahatma Gandhi: Truth and Non-violence*, Volume-II, London: Oxford, 1986, p. 181. Gandhi is against "destructive" and "exploitative" mechanisation only. *Harijan*, 16 November, 1939. Ram K. Vepa: 1975. *New Technology: A Gandhian Concept* (New Delhi), p. 170.

4. M.K. Gandhi, *op. cit.*, pp. 15-16. Emphasis added.
5. *Ibid.*, p. 16.
6. Gandhi's idea of trusteeship. Any work on the political philosophy of Mahatma Gandhi can be consulted in this matter. See also Anurag Gangal. *New International Economic Order: A Gandhian Perspective*, Chanakya Publishers, Delhi, 1985.
7. Tendulkar, *Mahatma*, Vol. VII, pp. 89 and 08-47. http://www.mkgandhi.org/gquots1.htm, http://www.mkgandhi-sarvodaya.org/gandhi%27s_talisman.htm
8. http://blog.emptyhead.in/2008/01/20/gandhis-talismantranslated-for-corporate-world/
9. B.R. Nanda, 2003, *In Gandhi's Footsteps: The Life and Times of Jamnalal Bajaj,* New York: Oxford University Press. pp. 34, 37, 49.
10. M.K. Gandhi, *op. cit.*, p. 77.
11. M.K. Gandhi, *op. cit.*, p. 90.
12. S.C. Gangal, *The Gandhian Way to World Peace*, Bombay: Vora, 1960, pp. 90, 100–101. G.N. Dhawan, *The Political Philosophy of Mahatma Gandhi*, Ahmedabad: Navajivan Publishing House, 1957, pp. 96, 284, 34i. Emphasis added. M.K. Gandhi, *Non-violence in Peace and War*, Ahmedabad: Navajivan Publishing House, 1948, Volume II, pp. 163-164. Emphasis added. *Harijan*, 16 November, 1939. Quoted in Ram K. Vepa, *New Technology: A Gandhian Concept*, New Delhi, 1975, p. 170. S.C. Gangal, "Gandhian Approach to Disarmament" paper presented at a seminar on "Perspectives on Disarmament" held under the auspices of *Gandhi Peace Forum* (GPF), New Delhi: Jawaharlal Nehru University, 11 April, 1978. M.K. Gandhi, *From Yervada Mandir*, Ahmedabad: Navajivan Publishing House, 1933, pp. 96-97. Anurag Gangal, *New International Economic Order: A Gandhian Perspective*, Delhi: Chanakya, 1985, pp. 29-30. N.K. Bose, 1948, *Selections from Gandhi*, Ahmedabad: Navajivan Publishing House, p. 42. M.K. Gandhi, *Non-violence in Peace and War*, Ahmedabad: Navajivan, 1948, Volume I, Chapter II and pp. 145, 324. *Encyclopaedia of Pacifism*, London, 1937, p. 100.

PART II
Gandhian Model of Economic Development

11
Gandhian Model of Economic Development: A Vision for an Inclusive Society

Rudra Prasad Sahoo

Capitalism and socialism are the two dominant models of economic systems, accepted today by most of the nation-states. The pure "socialism model" which communist countries has followed, ceased after the disintegration of U.S.S.R. The same fate may soon be met with "existing capitalism,", if they do not address the issue of suffering and deprivation in which many people are languishing, both in developing and developed countries. Even some country like India followed middle path by adopting dual economy.

Now in the age of globalization, the whole world economy is based on with the idea of, free flow of capital, especially financial capital. In the present model we find that all that comes across in terms of trade, commerce, financial arrangements are regulated in centralized manner at the top decision making level. In such situation the policy space of nation-state in the sphere of economic is shrinking and in its place the emerging rule of globalization is dominating day-by-day. The dissatisfaction arising between developing nation is that, the rule of globalization favouring rich nation especially United States. The developing countries imaginations are trapped with idea of TINA Syndromes (There Is No Alternative) in a unipolar world dominated by US on the one hand and at the same time they know that they can rely hardly on the current rules of globalization to further their developmental objectives, on the other. But both developing and developed nations have faced economic crisis one way or other within their respective national boundary. Then question frequently come to one's mind, why such problem is raised and faced by both developing and developed nations in their respective sphere of economy. What are the asymmetric structure and institution responsible for this cause and how to overcome this problem?

This chapter will seek to answer the aforesaid question. To make the chapter easier and in its logical best, the chapter is divided into four main parts. Part one will deal with the structural and institutional arrangement of world economy. Part second will deal with the lacuna and bias responsible for today crisis. Third part deals with, what are alternative models—Is it Gandhian model alone can solve this problem. Fourth part deals with Gandhian vision of Inclusive society—a happy Balance between ethical value and economic activity can only save the future generation from this crisis. Last one is conclusion.

INSTITUTIONAL ARRANGEMENT OF WORLD ECONOMY

The global financial meltdown of recent time has already ignited heated debates about the nature of the 'free market', its relationship with democratic governments, the institutional arrangement of world economy and its impact on developing nations and its common man. To know in detail about the practice of modern economy then we must have to explore, how the structure and institution of world economy shape in a particular juncture of history and how it became an unavoidable phenomenon.

Genesis of World Economic Institution: From GATT to WTO

Long back in 1945, over 50 countries participated in negotiations to create an International Trade Organization (ITO) as a specialized agency of the United Nations. Its first session of preparatory committee held in London. It extended to 17 member countries to negotiate on tariff and trade of all kinds. The original intention was to create a third institution to handle the trade side of international economic cooperation, joining the two "Bretton Woods" institutions, the World Bank and the International Monetary Fund.

But the original idea of ITO Charter which was discussed in different plenary session of UN was finally agreed in Havana in March 1948, but ratification in some national legislatures proved impossible. Even though the US government had been one of the driving forces, but the most serious opposition was found in the US Congress, which opposed the idea in Congress and kill the bill in the house itself.

During this period, the idea of General Agreement of Trade and Tariffs (GATT) was merely a temporary trading agreement among 23 countries.But in April 1947, the tariff negotiation was started in UN and in December 1947 GATT was signed by 23 countries. When the idea of ITO could not materialize, GATT was transformed from a temporary agreement to become the only multilateral instrument governing international trade from 1948 to 1995.

As time passed new problems arose. The Tokyo Round in the 1970s was an attempt to tackle some of these but its achievements were limited. GATT's success in reducing tariffs to such a low level, combined with a series of economic recessions in the 1970s and early 1980s, drove governments to devise other forms of protection for sectors facing increased foreign competition. High rates of unemployment and constant factory closures led governments in Western Europe and North America to seek bilateral market-sharing arrangements with competitors and to embark on a subsidies rate to maintain their holds on agricultural trade. Both these changes undermined GATT's credibility and effectiveness.

The problem was not just a deteriorating trade policy environment. In the early 1980s, it was realized that the General Agreement (GATT) was no longer as relevant as to the realities of world trade as it had been in the 1940s because of its evolving complex business.

So it was in the eighth round of GATT held in 1993 known as Uruguay round talk, some major change was brought at the institutional level... The Director-General of GATT Arthur Dunked came out with fresh reform proposal which was popularly known as Drunkal proposal.

The broad structural projection of GATT of 1994 and subsequent transformation to the WTO provide some insight about the change of world trade in particular and world economy in general. World Trade Organization was created on 1st January, 1995.

In this institutional change, the possibilities of cross-sectoral retaliation was the WTO weapon to keep the South in line to introduce intellectual property law in the hands of TRIPs and to liberalize service and foreign investment.

The WTO is certain to coordinate its programme and policies with the World Bank and IMF, and which may results in "cross-institutional conditionality" in which for instance World Bank loans to a developing country may be made condition to its having a good report from the WTO, that it has followed the rule adequately.

Due to this institutional bias, all the developing countries are forced to change their domestic law to suit to the North. In case the developing countries are not following the practices of developed nation, then countervailing duties will be applied on the south in case of non-compliance. In such a situation the big Multi National Corporation plunder the resources of third world which brought a great divide in world economy.

Globalization and Three Variants Form of Economic Transaction

This arrival of Multinational Corporation (MNC) process signals the arrival of globalization. Looking into the experience of world economic transaction, here we can be identified their ideology and divided it into three different variants In the first variant, some countries with significant deposits of valuable natural resources like oil enter into an implicit political arrangement with the United States. They ensure the supply of oil, receive petrodollars in return, and recycle them through multinational banks to engage multinational corporations for the development and modernization of their economies. Saudi Arabia and many other Gulf states are the prototypes of this model. Understandably, the US gets worried when this model is rejected by Hugo Chavez in Venezuela, and now by Bolivia, Argentina and to a lesser extent in Brazil.

In the second variant, massive commercial borrowing from international banks is done by a willing national government for the purpose of development. This is encouraged and usually coordinated by the IMF and the World Bank by engaging multinational corporations, leading to various expensive, ambitious giant projects, typically according to rules of consultancy and contract fixed by the World Bank. Almost inevitably the country is caught in a debt trap. Many countries of central and Latin America, with Argentina as a prime case, have been examples of this variant of the development model against which they are now reacting.

On the surface the first and the second variants differ because in the former case the country is usually a net international lender, while in the latter it becomes a net international borrower. However, there is a third variant state—led or state-sponsored corporation. These are created and nurtured to compete with multinationals under active government support, especially in the world market. At the same time the government tries to attract direct foreign investment, either through these corporations, or in areas where the government corporations are not the preferred option for some reason. Nevertheless, the government becomes a ruthless promoter of the corporate entities in search of higher growth, irrespective of how it affects the interests of the people.

This is a case of state-led corporatism, and today's China seems to fit this description reasonably well. South Korea, despite the obvious differences in the political and geo-political situations and dependence at an earlier stage on foreign borrowing, might have traversed a similar path. All these variants provide some insight the way world economic is pushing the national boundary of nation-state, where the command and control of national government hardly play any role. As a result rich becomes richer and poor becomes poorer. The same theory is applied to individual also in national stage.

Crisis and its Impact

The present crisis can be stressed to different model used by economist at different points of time. British economist John Maynard Keynes, (considered to be the father of modern macro-economics,) have for long emphasized that state intervention is indispensible to regulate economy in order to avoid destructive cycles of recessions, depressions and booms. After the Great Depression of 1929 and after the Second World War Keynesian theories helped to rebuild the world economy. This worked until the first oil shock of the 1970s after which the Keynesian idea of regulated markets were abandoned and the 'free market' system rapidly came into full play. Now world economy is governed by the neo-liberals principle which advocated that unfettered markets are self-correcting, so governments need not intervene at all.

The global financial crisis of recent decade has led too much introspection and discussion about what is the best way forward in order to rebuild trust and bring growth back into the system. There seems to be unanimity on the need for regulatory reforms in the international banking and financial systems so as to prevent risky financial practices and place strong restraints on the built up of excessive risk. Inadequate competition and inadequate procedures to ensure transparency and accountability have been recognized as among the major causes of the systemic failure.

This systemic failure coincides with several other major crises facing the world, today. There is the environmental crisis caused due to over-exploitation and pollution of the world's water and other natural resources. Then there is the cultural crisis brought on by intolerance and the sharp rise in violent clashes. As a result traditional life-styles and value systems is disappearing and in this place growing religious fundamentalism has showing its ugly face in different patches of globe. There is also the crisis of security brought on by the alarming rise in extremist and terrorist activities. The capitalist mode of economic operation is acting as a boomerang, whose reflection found in the form of different crisis.

As a concerned individual citizen of our respective countries, how we will overcome these daunting challenges? These present attitudes, structures and arrangements of world economy do not provide long-term solution to the problems of mankind. So we must search an alternative model, which will bring desirable result.

The need of the hour is to first effort should be to imbue the younger generation with the Gandhian ethic, to convince them that there is something beyond the profit motive and the monetary incentive. Maximizing Gross National Happiness or discipline happiness should be considered as desirable an objective as maximizing Gross National Product (GNP). This should be the people's contribution, as distinct from whatever policies the government-of-the-day in our respective countries is implementing.

TOWARDS AN ALTERNATIVE MODEL

In the opinion of Alvin Toffler the author of *Future Shocks* and the *Third Wave*, 'Gandhian model is the best and next best alternative to the whole of the world'. He mentions three waves. One is the wave of capitalism; another is the Marxian wave and third is the Gandhian wave. Gandhian wave builds a desirable ideal society, in which social change is possible through non-violence means. In capitalist, model there is a place for exploitation and in Marxian model there is a place for violence and conflict. But Gandhian model helps individuals to lead a harmonious life. Without violence social change is possible. It provides better quality of life.

It is in this background that recasting Gandhian model to economic development can be shown to have its relevance in solving the basic problems of mankind. It is because of this that economic and social policies, attitudes and structures are being revised in almost all countries of the world to make the efforts of economic development more meaningful.

Gandhi did not apply rigorous economic theory to give structure to his thought; he formulated very clearly the basic principles. Amritananda Das in his book *Foundations of Gandhian Economics* expressed how Gandhi offered an alternative model of economic development.

On Gandhian Economic Model

Before explaining Gandhian economic model, it is in fact essential to shed some light on Gandhi's view on modern civilization because this is the gateway to realize the whole vision of Gandhian economic thought.

In his early work *Hind Swaraj*, Gandhiji said "The true test of modern civilization lies in the fact that people living in it, make bodily welfare the object of life". Such people are called by *Gita* as Demoniacal. He explained that economy did not mean the production and consumption of those who have the right use the living and non-living natural resources of the country. It also includes those who are deprived of these resources and have the right to survive and coexistence. Gandhi was the first man to lay emphasis on ecology and human development. He was a strong critique of modern economics where opulence and poverty co-exist and economic progress leads to environmental crisis.

In a speech at Muir College, Economic Society, Allahabad, he said:

> "By economic progress, I take it, we mean material advancement without limit, and by real progress we mean moral progress, which again is the same thing as progress of the permanent element in us. The subject may, therefore, be stated thus dies not moral progress? I know that this is wider proposition than the one before us. But I venture to think that we always mean the large one even when we lay down the smaller.... I venture to think that the scriptures of the world are safer and sounder treatises on the laws of economics than many modern textbooks. He (Jesus) is Himself the greatest economist of his time".

He even rejected the idea of 'economic man'. He accepted the average man with all his characteristics. He said that an average man lives a satisfied life with his resources. 'Unlimited demand', 'Dissatisfied man' and 'Limited resources' are wrong concepts. At the same time he explained about the required need. A man should have food worth 3000 calories every day, 15 metres of cloth per year, a house of 100 sq. yards and educational and medical facilities. To satisfy such real need the resources are sufficient. God has given enough to satisfy the need but not the greed.

Eminent western thinkers and economists like Schumacher and Capra were among the earliest to appreciate Gandhi's views on a new economic system which was reflected in their advocacy of Intermediate Technology, Soft Technology, and Technology with a Human Face.

It is high time for the government to focus on *swadeshi* policies that would cut imports drastically limiting the human wants, thereby reducing the economic pitfalls like inflation. Instead, our government thinks *swadeshi* as a tool for living for the poor sections of the society catering to the development of science and technology has surely improved our economic status but to be applied for purposes that would bring about greater indigenous production carried on in peace and harmony. It could be overcome by adding more regulations on foreign investments, cutting more sanctions on foreign trade and granting concessions for indigenous works. It has been a known fact that intellectuals and economists of our country would ever give a thought of doing this in the past. It is true that this kind of reform would be criticized along the lines of putting back the clock of progress of the nation. But, unless we break this trend for a while at the least, it is highly plausible for us to face all sorts of economic evils that put us nowhere except to knock our brains.

Basic Tenets of Gandhian Model

The basic tenets of Gandhian economics model are as follows:

1. To provide full employment for all, particularly for all potential members of the work force, so that these workers can provide for their own necessities by their own efforts, in dignity, without depending on charity.
2. He advocated developing rural economies with the

development of agriculture and village industries. This way full employment for 80 per cent of Indian population can be achieved. Even in the world economy nearly 70 per cent of the world's population is rural population. Their development can be made easy by the development of rural economies. There should be small scale and cottage industries in these areas. That will create just distribution of income without special efforts. The agricultural activities should be done with the help of livestock and bio fertilizers. He explained in detail how to produce organic fertilizer without any extra cost and minimum labour. He described the number of benefits which can be achieved from the use of livestock and cooperative farming. Today bio-technological revolution, popularity of organic fertilizer, and awareness against harmfulness of chemicals used in agriculture prove the worth of Gandhi's thinking.

3. The government must give full support regarding finance, technology, and market to village industries. The people of the country must give first priority in purchasing their rural productions. He advocated for *khadi* and all other village industries and worked hard till his end. He even left the Congress to concentrate fully in this activity since 1934.
4. He advocated *swadeshi* and advised boycott of foreign goods, foreign companies, and foreign capital to maximum possible extent. This was not politically motivated. Not to punish the foreign countries but for the economic betterment of our country. If we look into history, George Washington advised his countrymen to throw away European goods in the sea for self development. U.K. had passed laws prohibiting all types of Indian cloths during the time of their industrial revolution. Japan had resolved to consume her rough and inferior rice instead of foreign superior rice. These examples prove the importance of *swadeshi* attitude even if the home made product is inferior for the sake of economic independence. There are several elements in a policy of *swadeshi*, of self-reliance: (a) the society must be capable of satisfying the basic minimum needs of its people without dependence on external sources. This also means that each society will have to define its minimum standards in terms of its economic capacity. They must be attainable within the

productive limits of the society. (b) Self-reliance also means the maximum use of indigenous resources and technology. (c) *swadeshi* or self-reliance does not mean absence of trade with other societies, although foreign imports have to be discouraged if, as Gandhi believed, they injure the millions of India. A self-reliant economy will buy only those goods that meet the following conditions: (i) they are essential for the growth of its people; and (ii) they are not produced locally.

5. Gandhi was not opposed to technology, but advocated a proper mix (depending on prevailing conditions) of technology-intensive and labour-intensive production. The economist's task should be to determine what the proper mix is; econometric calculations based on facts can help determine this. In short, the amount of available investible resources must keep pace with the population increase of employable workers. This is the basic principle, on which the economist must base his/her other recommendations, e.g., how much external trade the country should engage in. Gandhi's basic advice was "don't rush into technologically oriented development; first make sure what impact it will have on employment and through this on the well-being of the poor people." This principle completely stands on its head the usual assumption of capitalist economics, namely that the primary aim is to maximize the efficiency of the production of goods, almost regardless of whether the goods produced are basic necessities for the poor or luxury goods for the rich. The basic principle of Stalinist economics was to maximize the production of capital goods, such as heavy machinery, so that future generations could enjoy a plenitude of consumer goods. Both capitalist and socialist economies were based on technology-intensive rather than labour-intensive production. Gandhian economics reverses this preference. (Incidentally, technology also tends to increase environmental damage.). He was a practical thinker. He accepted the foreign economic relation for unavoidable useful things which could not be produced in the country. He also accepted some basic industry on large scale like mines, cement, electricity, etc.
6. He also encouraged big industrialists and big farmers with the expectation that they will develop the attitude of trusteeship.

He warned them, that if they fail to accept trusteeship they will have to face bloody revolution. He also explained, with a real experience, about ideal labour union activities.

7. His economic model link to methods of education. He said present method of education imparted the importance of information only, and less importance had given to practical activity and ethical living of life. He suggested work oriented, skill oriented and nationality oriented basic education. He said that there should be a sufficiently big group of translators to translate important useful knowledge of the world in Indian languages. He advised the development of research and science for helping the country and population at large and not to help a few rich. He also declared a prize for every such useful research. So, he introduced the community-based *Nai Talim* (Basic Education). It was aiming at developing a social order where nobody could be an exploiter or exploited and which would ensure the equitable distribution of wealth and justice.
8. Effect of Advertisements: Gandhi was aware of the effects of advertisements which misguided and attracted the people for useless and even harmful things in the life. In the context of such advertisements and created demands, the resources are felt limited.
9. Gandhi had advocated an economic organization that can be characterized as a decentralized, market-negotiated economic system. He postulates participatory democracy in all institutions and emphasizes that economic decisions should be group-negotiated rather than individually-managed decision. His economic system can be characterized by some income differentials that are functional in the sense that they are necessary for ensuring the growth of the individuals concerned.

Gandhian economy thus ensured full employment and providing minimum standards of consumption to all.

THE CONTESTED TERRAIN: GANDHIAN *VERSUS* THE PRESENT MODEL

His economic aims were different from conventional economics. His aims were *sarvodaya*, full employment, use of country's own resources, preservation of ecology, justice in income distribution and opportunities. Everybody should be given the right to earn according to his capacity using just means. The rich should serve the society after satisfying his needs. Life is not meant for enjoyment only, but it is meant to help others.

For him the means are as important as the aims. The means must be nonviolent, ethical, and truthful in all economic spheres. He provided the new economic system with those means. He advocated trusteeship, decentralization of economic activities, labour intensive technology, and first priority to rural India. He explained that capitalism and mechanization would lead to unemployment, poverty, and inequality. Communism would not survive as it was inhuman. We have seen the collapse of communism and also observed unemployment, inequality of income and instability of common man even in rich and capitalist society.

The contest between Gandhian thought and contemporary historical trends is just another instance of the perennial tension between history and utopia. Forces already at work in the historical process lead it towards a new equilibrium. Gandhi perceived the organic necessities of all parts of social system. Thus, he proposed his own alternatives, to face the challenge coming from modern capitalism and industrialism. It is relevant to summaries his proposal and contrast it with the contemporary trends.

Gandhi's basic conceptions about the ideal economy reveal that their realization would require a reversal of contemporary historical trends. This contradiction is described as follows:

The fundamental problem of global destruction lies in the production. Excessive production to excessive consumerism has given birth to all the problems. A major part of neo-classical economics deals with issues of production: what, why, and how are "goods" produced? The question is: production to meet the minimum need of people but not to use for destructive things?

The following distinctive features of this doctrine are:

1. It accepts the principle of comparative advantage but it rejects it as the sole basis of international trade;
2. It accepts the reciprocal need as the determining factor in trade among nations;
3. It is need of nation-states, not the market that governs the nation-states;

4. The moral purpose embodied in the notion of service to govern the flow of trade among nations;
5. The philosophical principle of *ahimsa* must be the guiding principle; and
6. Protection against unequal distribution of gains from trade among nations.

The Gandhian concept of man is one of an integral man, who is a part of an integral society. The Gandhian concept is one of an integral transformation of man and society. In the Gandhian conception, the processes of individual (spiritual) transformation and political transformation are inevitably interconnected. The Gandhian concept basically pursues the unity of the individual and the social order. Gandhi stresses the unity of the private and public life. It is the Gandhian view that private life must be transparent and in that transparency, we can see the public life too. In the Gandhian thought, the stress is on the unity of the individual and social praxis. The Gandhian conception may be termed as the "Unity of Existence". Which is in total negation to modern economic model which stress men to excessive individualism and market the sole guiding force, which deals with man in relation to society? Hence Gandhi's idea of economic and ethics are important while analyzing his economic methods to realize the vision of good society.

Gandhi on Economics and Ethics: His Vision of an Inclusive Society

Gandhi said economics and ethics were not unrelated areas of human endeavour: 'I must confess that I do not draw any distinction between economics and ethics. Economics that hurt the moral well-being of an individual or a nation are immoral and, therefore, sinful. Thus, the economics that permit one country to prey upon another are immoral.' There are several issues involved in this assertion and too many of the votaries of unlimited growth words like morality or ethics do not mean anything. And even if they matter it might be just as inconvenient irritants. Gandhi strove for the spiritualization of politics so that politics would free itself from the stranglehold of power brokers. The economics that disregard moral and sentimental considerations are like the wax works, that being life still lacks the life of the living flesh'.

At the base of Gandhi's vision of life there lies contentment and simplicity. To Gandhi 'life is more than money'. He said, 'It is cheaper to kill our aged parents who can do no work and who are a drag on our slender resources. It is also cheaper to kill our children whom we have to maintain, no matter what their maintenance costs us'.

In a remarkable essay *Gandhian Economy and the Way to Realise It*, J.C. Kumarappa summarized the salient difference between the 'artificial adjustment of demand to supply and the "natural economy" geared to the satisfaction of the primary needs of the largest number'. Kumarappa succinctly pointed out:

> Our life is something higher than material possessions and our life is also to be looked at from the possibilities of development of personality. The personality of an individual does not require for its development the satisfaction of a multiplicity of wants. In fact the simpler the life the more conducive it is exercising the higher faculties.

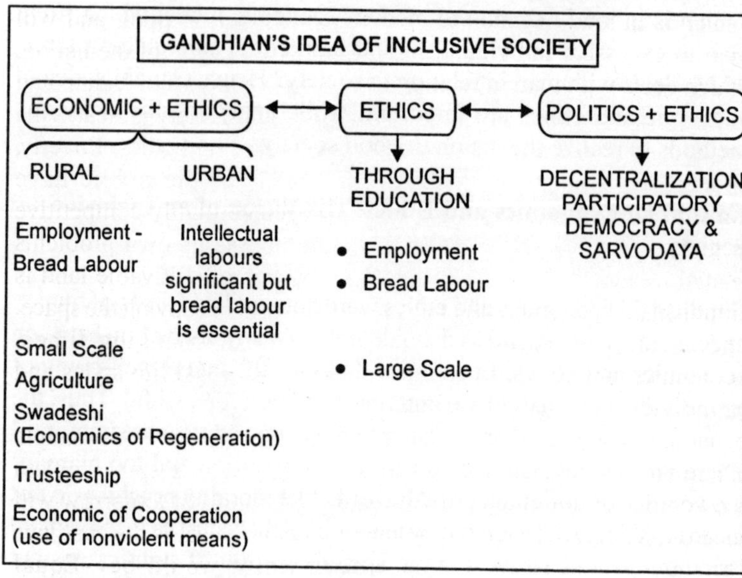

Fig. 11.1: Gandhian's Idea of Inclusive Society

What J.D. Sethi pointed out in this connection deserves attention: What Gandhi did was to lay down principles and methods of practice by which the individual and social utility functions were jointly determined. A non-violent economic society and the replacement of demand-oriented production by need-oriented production are two principles out of the many he put forward. The introduction of such principles makes an entirely new approach to the subject necessary and the methodology a social scientist must follow consequently becomes entirely different from that of modern social sciences.

To Gandhi true economics is the economics of justice. People will be happy insofar as they learn to do justice and be righteous. All else is not only vain but leads to destruction.

When the rich gets richer and richer becomes richest, poor becomes poorer and the poorer becomes the poorest. "No one has ever suggested that grinding pauperism can lead to anything else than moral degradation. Every human being has the right to live and, therefore, to find the wherewithal to feed himself and where necessary to clothe and house himself. But for this simple performance, we need no assistance from economists or their laws." Gandhiji said this long ago. The current trend of governance adopted by politicians in power would broaden the gap between the rich and poor, and will have serious effects on the social and cultural aspects of the nation. The issue of exploitation of the poor by the capitalists of Indian and foreign origin meted out by some sections of the society indicates the pervasive and nonchalant attitude of the governing bodies. Poverty, unemployment, education and basic needs of the public have transformed into everlasting issues and become highly competitive in terms of world standards. Rural India too has its own problems related to agriculture and farming and the size of cultivable land is diminishing with builders from all over the world occupying the space. The rural population is under the swing of changing times, psychologically moving from and to their traditional life styles and modern livings.

It is in this context, Gandhi was strict to its objective of principle of non-violence and life of simplicity, where half of the present problem is over. In addition, Gandhi once wrote: "The world of tomorrow will be and must be a society based on non-violence. That is the first law. The second great law of tomorrow's world would be—Equal distribution. It implies not that the world's goods shall be arbitrarily divided up but that each man shall have the wherewithal to supply his natural needs, no more." But it would be necessary to understand the preconditions Gandhi laid down as absolutely necessary for the practice of *satyagraha.*

The above-mentioned economic objectives within the framework of this structure will ultimately contribute to the realization of the goals of the Gandhian system—the welfare of the society as a whole, i.e., *Sarvodaya* including the poorest of the society. This can be achieved through harmonious balance of Gandhian idea of Economics and ethics and politics. The foundation of a good society must rest on fully integrated human persons. To Gandhi, providing a mere economic minimum to the members of society was not the *summum bonum* of existence. A society must follow a norm of life where material well-being is not the only motivating force. So Gandhi talked of the limitation of wants. To quote his famous sentence: "Nature produces enough to meet the needs of all the people but not enough to satisfy the greeds of any man".

CONCLUSION

Gandhi had his original vision in economics. He propagated a novel way of thinking in science of economics. He integrated economic aims and activities with morality and nonviolence. He integrated our successful past experiences with the recent development process. He made the use of labour force and livestocks and rural economy for the nation's smooth progress. He was the first thinker from the east who analyzed and rejected mechanization, capitalism and communism. He was the man who took the advantage of science and machine for the benefit of population at large.

He was the first man in the world who provided a practical alternative economic system against the prevailing economic system. The village based economy of China and Israel, the small scale industry based economy of Japan are nearer to Gandhian ideas in some aspects.

A growth model for economic development is shown on the basis of Gandhi economic thoughts. This model is applicable to India and other developing economies. His ideas are helpful for backward and developing economies in the world. His ideas are also useful for solving problems in capitalist economies.

The axiomatic fact is that, capitalist economics does not care about the fate of the unemployed, because they cannot buy the luxury goods being produced anyway. Many, especially inexperienced young people, fall into this, and get themselves deeply into debt. This also applies to many developing countries, which acquire debts so horrendous that they can never hope to repay them, and bankrupt themselves just keeping up with interest payments. So the need of the hour is to recast the visionary idea, practice by Gandhi during his life time, not it is just an ideal or utopia but as a guideline to practice in everyday life so that the real development will be achieved and vision of inclusive society can be realized.

NOTES

1. Appadori, A. (1993), *Political Thought in India*, Delhi: Khanna Publisher.
2. Bhaduri, Amit (2010), *Essays in the Reconstruction of Political Economy,* New Delhi: Aakar Books.
3. Bhattacharyya, Buddhadeva, (1969), *The Evolution of Political Philosophy of Gandhi*, Calcutta: Calcutta Book House.
4. Antony Copley (1999), *Gandhi against the Tide*, New Delhi: Oxford University Press.
5. Sandeep Chauhan, (2002), *GATT To WTO: Gandhian Alternative to NEIO*, New Delhi: Deep & Deep Publications.
6. Ghosh, B.N. (2007), *Gandhian Political Economy: Principle, Practice and Policy*, London: Ashgate Publishing Ltd., p. 21.
7. Hanna Newcombe, http://www.peacemagazine.org/archive/v14n2p28.htm
8. Kapoor, A.N.; V.P. Gupta, and Mohini Gupta (2007), *The Gandhian Era*, New Delhi: Radha Publication.
9. Nanda, B.R. (1985), *Gandhi and His Critics*, New Delhi: Oxford University Press, pp. 11-40.
10. Parel, J. Anthony (2006), *Gandhi's Philosophy, and the Quest for Harmony*, Cambridge University Press, p. xiii.
11. Bhikhu Parekh (1989), *Gandhi's Political Philosophy*, London: MacMillan Press, pp.139-140.
12. Roy, Himansu (2001), *Poverty of Gandhian Philosophy*, New Delhi: Concept Publishing Company.
13. Sharma, Anand (ed.) (2007), *Gandhian Way, Peace, Non-Violence and Empowerment*, New Delhi: Academic Foundation.
14. Tripathy, Sridhar (2007): *Gandhi: His Life and View*, New Delhi: Anmol Publication.
15. Wadhwa, Madhuri (1991), *Gandhi between Tradition and Modernity*, New Delhi: Deep & Deep Publications.
16. *Essays on Gandhian Economics*, Part-II, May 2009 http://globalswadeshi.ning.com/forum/topics/essays-in-gandhian-economics-1, 20.
17. Sikri, Veena, The Global Financial Meltdown and Gandhian Philosophy-

11, http://www.gandhiswaraj.com/the-global-financial-meltdown-and-gandhian-philosophy-ii/24 August 2009.

18. N. Radhakrishnan, *The Culture of Peace versus Materialism and Consumerism*, http://www.ignca.nic.in/cd_09023.htm
19. Balaji, Balmurli (June 2008), *Applying Gandhian Thought of Economics*, http://www.merinews.com/article/applying-gandhian-thoughts-of-economics/136295.shtml,24

12
Economic Development: The Gandhian Way

Ashutosh Pandey

This article gives an insight about Gandhian concept of economic development. Gandhi holds the view of the maximization of social welfare and for this he gives prime importance to the welfare of the individuals by reducing inequalities in income and wealth. According to Gandhi every person should be provided with bare minimum necessities, i.e., food, shelter, and clothing. Concentration of wealth to a few groups of people certainly will shatter the dream of a society which will be socialist in nature. Gandhi is in favour of the self-sufficient village economy where the villages will be the independent economic units. In this chapter an attempt has been made to analyse the relevance of Gandhian concept of Economic Development in this age of globalization. For the purpose, the chapter has three parts as follows: (i) Nature of economic development and challenges to human society, (ii) Relevance of Gandhian concept of economic development in this age of globalization, and (iii) concluding remark to follow Gandhism for all future practical purposes.

I

Globalization raises certain questions that will be central for understanding the ensuing developments in the twentyfirst century. Every nation has to introduce it with human face. Even Gandhiji, the Father of the Nation, who was fond of and always emphasized for *swadeshi* set tone of globalization as early as in *Young India*, June 1, 1921, when he said, "I do not want my house to be walled in on all sides and my window to be stuffed. I want the cultures of all lands to be blown about my house as freely as possible. But I refuse to be blown off my feet." India lives in villages; naturally the development of the country depends on the development of villages. All the goods and services necessary for the village members should be grown within the village. In a word, every village should be a self-contained republic. If every village distributes its surplus produce to the poor villagers then there will not be the problem of poverty and starvation in the rural areas. Only this can help eradicating poverty and thus people can be happy and self-reliant. Agricultural sector alone cannot solve the problem of rural poverty and unemployment. That is why Gandhi gives stress on the growth of the rural industries like *khadi*, handlooms, sericulture and handicrafts. Rural industries are the symbols of unity and equality.

Prior to understanding Gandhian concept of economic development, it would be worthwhile to understand a few prominent principles inherent in Gandhi's economic ideals, and their relevance to the future ideologist. The first of these is Gandhiji's outlook on the relationship of man and commodity. Gandhi wrote, "Increase of material comforts, it may be generally laid down, does not in any way whatsoever conduce to moral growth.. Bombay, Calcutta, and the other chief cities of India are the real plague spots....Medical science is the concentrated essence of black magic...."[1] The idea is that man and his all round healthy development of personality is the end, a temporary satisfaction gained from a consumable commodity cannot be the aim of life.

The second principle on which Gandhian economy rests is that all economic functionings and developments should have an ethical base. This view is quite contrary to the view of some western economists that utility which is different from moral obligation being the central concept of economics, this field of study should be developed in isolation from ethics. Gandhi succeeded in his attempt to combine economics with ethics, as in his economic philosophy, from the principle of truth and non-violence, emerged a series of economic ideals like non-exploitation, non-possession, trusteeship, bread-labour and so on. All these ideas, which in fact originated under different contexts, form the basic pillars of his economic thought. Professor Abdul Aziz writes: "From the principle of truth and nonviolence emerged a series of economic ideas like non-exploitation, non-possession, trusteeship, and bread-labour and so on. All these ideas, which in fact having originated under different contexts, formed the founding pillars of Gandhi's economic system."[2]

The third principle of Gandhian economy is its emphasis on cultivating a totally nonviolent economy. According to this principle all sorts of violence included every kind of economic activity should be minimized. G.N. Dhawan writes that in *Satya* and *Ahimsa* are also implicit the vows of *asteya* (non-stealing) as well as *aparigraha* (non-possession) which follows logically from *asteya*. The two along with the vows of bread-labour and *swadeshi* determine the economic aspect of Gandhiji's philosophy. Obviously one wedded to truth and universal love should not steal. But to Gandhiji non-stealing means much more than what it parlance does in common. According to him acquisitiveness divorced from need is theft. Gandhiji's economy is the economy of needs and welfare and not that of acquisitiveness which is the characteristic of capitalism. The concept of non-violence in economics has mainly three dimensions—The life force dimension, the non-acquisitive dimension, and the self-sufficiency dimension. First is the life force dimension, which consists in causing minimum damage or injury to any form of life human, animal or microbial, while producing commodities. Second is the non-acquisitive dimension, which means wealth can be amassed only by violence. G.N. Dhawan opines that people cannot amass wealth without violence and without the co-operation and help of other members of society. They have, therefore, according to Gandhi, no moral right to use any of it for personal advantage and to exploit others. So long as they are not prepared to give up possessions beyond their immediate needs they should change their attitude and act not as proprietors but as trustees, utilizing the property for the benefit of the community.

The fourth important principle of Gandhian economic theory is that of basic economic rights. According to Gandhi one has the right to possess commodities for any type of use if and only if all poor men are fed and clothed. This principle follows from the principle of unity of all lives. Unity of life entails non-possession or a curtailment of possession by the rich. Non-possession is the extension of the meaning of stealing to the possession of things we do not need in the immediate present. Absolute non-possession, which is the corollary of absolute love, would mean total renunciation. This would demand that man should have no house, no clothing and no stock of food for the morrow, depending on God for his daily bread. The body too is a possession and man should learn to use it for the purpose of service so long as it exists, so much so that service, and not bread, becomes the staff of life. As applied to thought non-possession implies that the so-called knowledge which turns us away from the values of inner life and from the service of mankind, is ignorance pure and simple and should be eschewed. Non-possession thus means non-dependence on material things. It implies total abolition of private property in all kinds of belongings, a view more radical than that of extreme communists.

The fifth principle is the principle of 'adjustment of wants'. This principle upholds economics to be a normative science. The aim of economics is to remove all poverty, and to realize non-violence as far as possible. The adjustment of wants' would fulfil three objectives: Firstly, we all know that in the present stage of human and economic development, it is not possible to immediately boost up economic production to the extent, and to achieve redistribution of wealth in such a way, that all economic disparity and poverty is eliminated at once. Therefore, instead of forcibly abducting the wealth of the rich by law it is more germane to establish the ideal that everyone, the rich and the poor alike, should cut down his wants and needs to the bare subsistence level, and though the rich may have more money, since he would live as simple a life as the poor, there would not be the paucity of consumable goods and items for anyone in the whole society. The extent to which this ideal is cultivated, there would be the immediate solution to the problem of poverty, malnutrition, etc. Abdul Aziz observes that it was Gandhi's desire that the good should percolate even to the last of the socio-economic ladder—the poorest of the poor. This principle originated out of his reading of Ruskin's *Unto This Last* which held that the good of individual contained in the good of all.

II

Gandhi took the position that concentration of economic power created the capitalist class. This class was exploitative of the talent and resources available in the society. According to him concentration of economic power created a gulf between the privileged few and the under-privileged majority. Concentration of economic power went hand in hand with concentration of political power. Gandhi held that decentralization of economic power could fruitfully serve the interest of the community. This can bring about rapid development of industries. Gandhi advocated universal use of *khadi*. He wanted to attain this aim by fostering the patriotic spirit for *swadeshi*. It was a part and parcel of his comprehensive programme of decentralization through dispersal of economic power. Gandhi's concept of village *swaraj* was in conformity, with full self-sufficiency in economic matters of every village. He visualized a communitarian village society. This society had to look after food, clothing, shelter and educational needs of every individual in the rural area. In such a village of Gandhi's conception, consumption would be regulated by minimization of wants. It aimed at simplicity in life. There were three reasons of Gandhi's advocacy of economic decentralization. First, through his concept of decentralization Gandhi wanted to find solutions to certain basic issues like arbitrary state power, unlimited violence, economic exploitation of man by man, removal of poverty and socio-economic inequalities. Secondly, centralization, according to Gandhiji, by its very nature implied application of force upon smaller unit by the central or higher unit. Thirdly, macro-distribution of commodities by macro enterprises might involve fraud and speculative activities in a roundabout way, to which Gandhiji was deadly opposed.

Gandhiji held that small scale production at peoples home should be encouraged. According to Gandhi there should be no privilege or monopoly for any economic organization: Because, Gandhiji believed that whatever that cannot be shared with the masses should be a taboo. In general, heavy industry should be cultivated only in so far as it does not interfere with cottage industry, and even this should not contain elements of centralization. Moreover, we know that if there is only small scale decentralized mode of production, it is very unlikely that problems of monopoly would arise.

The use of machines leads to mass production. It causes concentration of production at one place. The distribution centres; become located at far distant places. In the Gandhian system a balance between production and distribution is a sufficient condition to generate a healthy economy. The forces of fraud and speculation found in traditional economy must not be given an opportunity to rise. Gandhiji disapproved the use of machines. He disapproved the production of modern goods and amenities. Gandhi held: "India's salvation consists in unlearning what she has learnt during the past fifty years or so. The railways, telegraphs, hospitals, lawyers, doctors, and such like have all to go, and the so-called upper classes have to learn to live consciously and religiously and deliberately the simple life of a peasant knowing it to be a life giving true happiness."[3] Professor Abdul Aziz observes that Gandhi's disapproval of modern goods and amenities again originates out of his fear that production and distribution of such goods and amenities would sow the seeds of exploitation. Gandhi was not against big machines *per se*. But he was against the use of machines to exploit individuals. He did not want the machine to cripple the life of man. Gandhi did not oppose mass scale production as such. He opposed mass scale production by factories because he wanted mass scale production by the masses.

It is interesting to note that from the angle of psychoanalysis all economic activities that were advocated by Gandhi were in fact identity giving activities. Any economic activity and especially bread labour was an identity-giving activity. It could give a person a sense of control not only over the enterprise but also over some of his basic needs. Ronald Terchek opines whether it was spinning or agriculture, the products were an extension of self and gave the worker a sense of accomplishment and independence. Hannah Arendt makes a useful distinction between machinery and tools which helps to clarify Gandhi's reasoning here. The machine determines worker responses; but when he uses a tool, he is the originator of the activity. Gandhi believed that it was unlikely that an individual would develop a strong ego in any social structure in which he were part of a stimulus response organism, conditioned to react to external forces.

In a complex industrial environment, central direction is augmented by centres of industry or the seats of political power. As the domain of social co-ordination expands, the range of control an individual exercises over his own life contracts. For Gandhi, the "advance of technology has thus actually resulted in the decline of individual liberty and a terrific concentration of power in the hands of small groups or bodies of men." To enforce a harmony required for the complex society, Gandhi believed, decision-makers pandered to mass fear and greed. But threats and rewards distributed by the dominant system only actualize order. These do not generate self-respect, nor do they foster co-operation, and purposefulness.

The Gandhian philosophy of balanced regional economic development does not favour the operation of a large scale industrial production. It favours the expansion of village and small scale agro-industries. This may help create decentralization of wealth and economic power. It may provide employment opportunities to million of Indians who are poor and without work and employment. He has opposed industrialization, for this leads to concentration of wealth and economic power. However, he believes that some key industries are necessary. Thoughtless industrial development leads to moral degradation and degeneration of moral and human values. That is why Gandhi wanted the *swadeshi* pattern of production process.

Gandhi pondered over the problem how an effective equitable distribution system could be made operational. In this connection the Gandhian approach of development has also suggested two things more: (a) foreign markets should not be tapped in order to dispose of domestic goods; and (b) the rich should act as trustees so that their excess wealth may be used for the benefit of the society as a whole. If the rich failed to behave as trustees of their wealth for social ends, the methods of non-violence, non-co-operation and civil disobedience should be used against them. The Gandhian idea of trusteeship is advanced to take out the sting of capitalism in order to yoke the same to the service of the society as a whole.

As the metaphysical basis of his economic philosophy Gandhiji used concept of 'Metaphysical Idealism' which implied his living faith in the omnipresent and differentiated existence theory of God. That is why Gandhi has treated all human beings as the embodiment of God. Philosophisation of spiritualism negates the existence of conflicts between the individual and social interests. This is actually based on the practice of self-realization. As a consequence, the concept of 'Universalism' is co-existent with that of 'Individualism'. Given the complex of above ideas, the Gandhian approach to development is based on the goal of *Sarvepi Sukhinah Santu*. This ideal is akin to that of Ruskin's *Unto the Last* and Bentham's *Utilitarianism*. The attainment of this goal partly depended on the nature of politico-economic order of the society which had to be changed.

The Gandhian concept of economic development is a combination of economic and real progress. By economic progress Gandhi meant material advancement. His concept of real progress is referred to as moral progress which is the same thing as progress of the permanent element in us. To Gandhi, material progress must accompany moral progress otherwise the economic development of society will break and stagnate leading to its decay. His contention was that grinding pauperism could lead to anything else than moral degradation. So the objective of material progress should be to curb poverty, that there may not be moral degradation. This implies that material progress should combine moral values with development process. Gandhi has cited the historical examples of Rome, Britain, the Dwapar

(India), Egypt, etc., that faced their downfall due to the fast deterioration in moral values with high material affluence.

Gandhi advocated that the production should be localized (i.e., regionalized). Therefore, this approach laid stress on the growth and expansion of indigenous industries. Thus the Gandhian model of development is basically an ideological alternative. The purpose of this strategy is to present comprehensive politico-economic programmes for providing social justice and equity to the million poor Indians who laıgely live in villages.

This shows that the remedies of poverty and unemployment lay, according to Gandhi in (a) creating a self propelling and self-sustaining process of production in the villages; (b) decentralization of production system, wealth and economic power; and (c) formation of trusteeship for social ends.

Swadeshi demanded the exclusion of all foreign cloth. India could, as she once did, manufacture all the cloths of her requirement. Besides, in an agricultural country like India *Khadi* was a universal subsidiary industry. On this the semi-starved and semi-employed peasants could depend to increase their scanty income. Besides, Khadi was the symbol of decentralized economy. That is why Gandhiji considered *Khadi* a necessary and the most important corollary of the principle of *swadeshi*. It was an indispensable step towards the discharge of *swadeshi dharma* towards society. He observed in 1947, "Immediately after my return to India in 1915, I discovered that the centre of *swadeshi* lay in *Khadi*. If *Khadi* goes, I contended even then, there is no *swadeshi* the manufactures in Indian mills do not constitute *swadeshi*. To that belief I cling even today." Moreover, the economic aspect of *swadeshi* did not end but began with *Khadi*. *Swadeshi* implied a comprehensive preference to local manufacture, and the boycott of all foreign cloths and articles which could be manufactured in one's own country.

Gandhi believed that the capitalists were thief. But there would be no lasting solution to this problem if wealthy persons are expropriated of their wealth by force because in that case the urge to amass wealth shall not die with the act of confiscation. However, Gandhi was one with Marx in believing that capital was the fruit of labour of other persons. Therefore, rich men should be made the trustees of wealth, and they should take only that much as is required by their basic need. Social necessity, not the personal whim of entrepreneur should determine the nature and amount of production.

Concept of Trusteeship rests on the belief that people cannot amass wealth without violence and without the co-operation and help of other members of society. They have, therefore, no moral right to use any of it for personal advantage and to exploit others. So long as they are not prepared to give up possessions beyond their immediate needs they should change their attitude and act not as proprietors but as trustees, utilizing the property for the benefit of the community, the original trustee should have the right to nominate his successor but the choice must be finalized by the state—an arrangement which Gandhiji expected to put a check on the state as well as the individual. Thus he was against inherited riches and unearned income. According to him, "A trustee has no heir except the public." The misuse of the trust property should be set right by the state confiscating it with the minimum use of violence. He was also in favour of death duties and of riches being heavily taxed.

To bring about trusteeship he would depend on the effect of the example set by the *satyagrahi*, persuasion, creating a general atmosphere in favour of trusteeship and non-violent non-co-operation. He expected that "If this truth was imbibed by the people generally, it would become legalized and trusteeship would become a legalized institution." As pointed out above he was not against the state resorting to confiscation with the minimum use of coercion when necessary. He, however, distrusted the state and preferred voluntary non-violent action.

Critics often demur to the conception of trusteeship of which, they think, the capitalists take advantage in relation to their workers. To Gandhiji, however, the theory was a necessary corollary of non-violence; for "It was in order to avoid confiscation that the doctrine of trusteeship came into play, retaining for society the ability of the original owner in his own right."[4]

Gandhiji remarked, "My theory of 'trusteeship' is no makeshift, certainly no camouflage. I am confident that it will survive all other theories. It has the sanction of philosophy and religion behind it. That possessors of wealth have not acted up to the theory does not prove its falsity; it proves the weakness of the wealthy. No other theory is compatible with non-violence".[5] He wished the ideal of trusteeship becomes a gift from India to the world. If accepted by the world, he felt sure it would remove exploitation and causes of wars from international relations.

G.N. Dhawan observes that the conception of trusteeship seems to be implicit in the communist ideal also. In the classless society, when violence and profit motive are eliminated, those in charge of productive and other activities of society will not be salaried civil servants, for the state it will wither away. He further says that they will need for their upkeep some money or its equivalent and unless, in the management of activities entrusted to their charge, they are inspired by the, ideal of selfless service and act as trustees, the very existence of the classless and stateless society will the endangered.

Commenting on his ideas of Trusteeship V.P. Patil and I.A. Lokopur writes, "The world will not implement his ideas for the simple reason that it is too late to change the path it has bestowed upon itself. When the world has reached a high state of industrialization, how can it put the clock back and embrace industrial primitivism? Moreover, there are many inconsistencies and gaps in his theory of trusteeship, and it would require a great deal of expertise and thought on the part of contemporary scholars to develop a viable and relevant theory of trusteeship applicable to the modem period."[6]

According to the followers of Gandhi, though Gandhi was not a socialist in the conventional sense of the term, in his idealism in many respects he went far ahead of all socialists. Gandhi equated private property, in excess of the basic needs of human existence with exploitation. He proclaimed his profound belief in the rightness of economic equality. Once he clearly said, "My ideal of socialism is that everyone should get the same wages. A lawyer, a physician, a teacher, a labourer or a sweeper—all should get equal wages."[7] Gandhi only differed from the traditional socialists about the means of how to bring in socialism. He said, "This I do say fearlessly and firmly, that every worthy object can be achieved by the use of *satyagraha*... socialism will not be reached by any other means."[8] Yet some of Gandhi's beliefs like his faith in *varnashram vayavastha* and trusteeship were such that with these no traditional socialist would agree. Today in the last decade of twentieth century when Gandhian Ideology has but very few followers, and Marxian socialism has also declined, the future ideologist will have to think anew on Gandhism and socialism.

Bread-labour is a corollary of the principle of non-stealing. It is a means of realizing non-possession. The economics of bread-labour, which Gandhiji calls "the living way of life," means that every man has to labour with his body for his food and clothing. 'Bread' is symbolic of the unavoidabie primary necessities of life, these require productive labour. One who enjoys them without properly sharing in the labour is a thief the so-called civilized but really depraved people multiply wants and free themselves from manual labour. These men really exploit the labour of the poor people. They use the latter as mere means for their gratification. Gandhiji felt that if people had been convinced of the value and necessity of bread-labour there never would be any want of bread and cloth.

Food is the first among these primary necessities. The ideal form of body-labour, therefore, should be related to agriculture. If that is not possible, body-labour should take the form of any other productive manual work. It should be connected with some primary need, e.g., spinning, weaving, carpentry, smithy, etc. Gandhiji's great love for the spinning wheel is due to the fact that spinning, even more than 'agriculture, deserves to become the universal form of bread-labour. He writes, 'A *satyagrahi* occupies him in productive work. There is no easier and better productive work for millions than spinning." Besides, "No other village craft has the capacity that spinning and its auxiliary process have for putting so much money into the pockets of the largest number of villagers with minimum of capital outlay and organizational effort."[9]

Bread-labour, however, does not include intellectual labour for "The need of the body must be supplied by the body.. Mere mental, that is, intellectual labour is for the soul. It is its own satisfaction. It should never demand payment." Physical labour over and above that for earning bread as well as intellectual labour should be the labour of love done solely for the benefit of society. "Intellectual work has an undoubted place in the scheme of life. But what I insist upon is the necessity of physical labour for all. No man ought to be free from that obligation. It would serve to improve even the quality of his intellectual output."[10]

But bread-labour according to Gandhi should be voluntary and not compulsory. India's millions today undoubtedly obey the law of bread-labour for half the year. But they would shirk the law if they could. Theirs is a compulsory obedience. For them bread-labour is a drudgery that deadens their finer feelings and breeds poverty, disease and discontent.

It may be difficult to practice the ideal in its entirety. But even if without fulfilling the whole law people performed physical labour enough for their daily bread, society should go a long way towards the ideal. Even if people earn through intellectual labour, their remuneration should be equal to that of manual workers. Those who earn more than necessary for their requirement must use the bulk of their greater earning, for the good of the community. In other words, over-possession should go with trusteeship.

If generally accepted this law will simplify life. It would facilitate the observance of non-violent values. It would "co-ordinate the vision of the inward eye with the work of the hands." It will make men able-bodied and minimize disease. Educational psychology has for long recognized that the use of hands profoundly helps mental growth. It will eliminate large-scale production. It will end profit-motive. It shall bring about virtual self-sufficiency of the village and the country. It will be at once a levelling up and a levelling down. Bread-labour will work as a remedy for the exploitation of the poor and the swelled head of the rich. Everybody will be his own master and class distinctions will disappear.

Universally practiced, non-possession and bread-labour would lead to economic equality. Even if they were partially observed and if people who earned more than their immediate needs adopted the attitude of trustees, equitable distribution would be brought about. Hence, Gandhiji remarked. "My ideal is equal distribution, but so far as I can see it cannot be realized. I, therefore, work for equitable distribution."[11]

The developing countries had started realizing by the beginning of seventies that the strategy of development they had been following was leading them nowhere. The western writers now began to think of "a drastic transvaluation of values." They felt the "need for a wholly new doctrine that would emphasize income distribution, employment and self-reliance."

Writers and scholars like Johan Galtung in the Western world and Samir Amin, Abdelatif, Benachenau, Fernando Henrigue Cardoso, Godfrey Gunatillake, Theotonio Dos Santos, Osvaldo Sunkel, Rajni Kothari and others in the Third World emphasized the concepts of self-reliance and decentralization. Galtung, like Gandhi, believes that it is not only the developing world which has to become independent of the developed world but the developed world also has to become independent of the developing world. He advocated the maximum degree of decentralization. He opined that the existing international problems like violence, poverty, repression and environmental deterioration could not be eliminated without decentralization. Thinking on development at the world level as such has reached a full circle and come back or gone forward, to the line of development which Gandhi had advocated. It would, therefore, be difficult to challenge the statement that Gandhi is more relevant today to the developing countries. It also is difficult to deny that we have yet no other clear alternative policy. "If we feel desperate these days in the matter of our social problems." Writes I.P. Vidyarthi, "it is because we have not so far tried to give a practical shape to the ideas of one whom in the manner of scientist carried on his experiments on truth"[12] on many points", to quote Hettne, "Gandhi appears strikingly modern. His approach may be described as action-oriented (the oppressive environment was his laboratory), normative (his view point was that of the poorest of the poor), and global (the ultimate goal was a non-violent world order). These same, principles may be found in current ideas on problem oriented social science research."[13]

III

Elaborating his superstructure of rural development, he said, "Independence must begin at the bottom. Thus every village will be a republic or village Panchayat will have power of self-governance. It thus follows, that every village will be self-sustaining and capable of managing its affairs even to the extent of defending itself against the whole world. It will be prepared to perish while defending itself against any onslaught from without. Thus, ultimately, it is the individual who is the unit. This does not exclude dependence on and willing help from neighbours or from the world....in this structure composed of Innu arable village, there will be ever widening, never ascending circles. Life will not be a pyramid with the apex sustained by the bottom. But it will be an oceanic circle whose centre will be the individual always ready to perish for the village, the latter ready to perish for the circle of villages, till at last the whole becomes one life composed of individuals, never aggressive in there arrogance but ever humble, sharing the majesty of oceanic circle of which they are integral units."[14] while addressing the students at Vidyamandir training school at Wardha are asked them to drive away illiteracy from these villages......cast of the cloak of foreign thoughts and ideals, and identify yourselves with the villagers."[15]He desired to exploit the inventive skills of the villages, said he "We will by concentrating on the villages see that the inventive skill that an intensive learning of the craft will stimulate and will subserve the needs of the villagers as a whole."[16] Thus, he wanted to "resuscitate the villages, to spearhead a "silent social revolution."[17] Removal of illiteracy and intensive learning crafts were the keys to this revolution. Gandhi emphasized, "A village unit as conceived by me is as strong as the strongest. My imaginary village consists of one thousand souls. Such a unit can give good account of itself, if it is well organized on a basis of self-sufficiency."[18] Gandhi wrote, "The people of India are found to remain idle at least four months in a year. People who are thus forced to remain idle cannot be revived. For crores of people the spinning wheel is the only occupation which can supplement their income for the fields, most emphatically, they have no other one."[19] Similarly, he regarded *swadeshi* as "*dharma*" and "*artha*" and stressed its economic importance and vehemently asked the nation to adopt the slogan of *swadeshi* and to effectively implement it. It is in this context that Gandhi had expressed: "If the villages perish, India will perish too. It will be no more India. Her own missions in the world will get lost.[20]

In Gandhi's scheme, the foundation of rural development is based on the solid work of workers. He prescribed 'Eleven Vows,' *viz.*, "non-violence, truth, non-stealing, celibacy, non-possession, manual or body-labour, control of the palate, fearlessness, equal respect for all religions, *swadeshi* and spirit of exclusive brotherhood.[21] It must be noted here that Gandhian concept of rural development is certainly multi-dimensional encompassing the total development of man with stress on quality of development. With this conception of rural society, national reconstruction was envisaged by Gandhi. He initiated some earlier works of rural reconstruction at Champaran in 1917 and he took his constructive programme at Sevagram in 1920 and at Wardha in 1938 which was an elaborate programme of rural development in an entirely different fashion and termed it as an instrument of permanent value. He clarified to Nehru "man is not born to live in jungle, he is born to live in society......this conception will bring about a change in human relationship all over the world."[22]

Gandhi while drafting his constructive programme took care of social, economic, political and moral aspects of development. His approach to constructive programme can be classified into five segments, viz., economic, educational, social, environmental and political. The constructive programme as revised has eighteen items with one more addition, i.e., improvement of livestock. These include (i) communal unity, (ii) removal of untouchability, (iii) prohibition,

(iv) *Khadi*, (v) other village industries, (vi) village sanitation, (vii) new or basic education, (viii) adult education, (ix) women, (x) education in health and hygiene, (xi) provincial language, (xii) national language, (xiii) economic equality, (xiv) *kisans*, (xv) labour, (xvi) *adivasis*, (xvii) lepers, (xviii) students, and one more to be included (xix) improvement of livestock.[23]

Gandhi felt the hunger of masses that are to be provided with work for winning bread. He wrote "to those who are hungry and unemployed, God can dare reveal himself only as work and wages as the assurance of food."[24] But he was against giving "free food to these poor people" that are capable of earning their livelihood provided they are given work. One must do "Honest labour"[25] to earn his livelihood. Wrote Gandhi, 'if I had my say I would close down all charitable institutions and alms houses.'[26]

Therefore, he was advocating opening of self employment avenues based on local skills, technical knowledge and raw materials. Wrote he, "I feel convinced that the revival of hand-spinning and hand weaving will make the largest contribution to the economic and the moral regeneration of India. The millions must have a simple industry to supplement agriculture. Spinning was the cottage industry years ago and if the millions are to be saved from starvation, they must be enabled to reintroduce spinning in their homes and every village must repossess its own weaver.[27] Gandhi himself wrote, "the revival of the village is possible only when it is no more exploited industrialization on a mass scale will necessarily lead to passive or active exploitation of the villagers as the problems of competition, and marketing come in. Therefore, we have to concentrate on the village being self-contained manufacturing mainly for use. Provided this character of the village industry is maintained, there would be no objection to villagers using even the modern machines and tools that they can make and can afford to use. Only they should not be used as a means of exploitation of others."[28]

Gandhi sincerely felt that a strengthened and economically sound rural economy would revitalize Indian economy because India lives in villages, where 75 per cent of the population is agriculturalists. He preached, hence "The gospel of rural mindedness."[29] A rural economy of self contained villages alone could be the basis of a non-violent, and to be rural minded you have to have faith in the spinning wheel."[30]

To sum up one may observe: Gandhi believed that modern industry and modern technology resulted in mass frustration, violence and war. It was from it the phenomenon of amassing of wealth and uneven distribution arose. Mechanization, according to Gandhiji, should be on a small scale, and it should be cultivated only to that extent that it did not create unemployment, substitution of labour by machine, and accumulation of wealth and commodities in few hands. Machines or tools such as spinning wheel, tooth pick or plough should be encouraged; labour saving, machines should be discouraged. Capital goods industry, producing tools or small machines like sewing machine or spinning wheel should be nationalized or state controlled. We know Marx and Lenin using complicated socio-economic analysis and reasoning related the phenomenon of modern capitalism and industrialization with imperialism. Gandhi, too, perhaps using a somewhat different logic, related the economic role of big industry with the phenomenon of imperialistic exploitation of third world countries by imperial countries. The future ideologist will have to keep in view the distinctions discussed above between machine and tools while he draws the outlines of his ideal economic system. The distinction between machine and tools as suggested by Hannah Arendt is of primary importance in deciding what should be the proportion of automatic machines and man governed tools in material and mechanical aspect of an economic system. The future ideologist must synthesise Gandhian non-violence with an altruistic and harmless use of automatic machines in such a manner that on the one hand every individual may have optimum creativity and the consequent self-identity, on the other hand for the sake of moral progress; the progress in the field of scientific knowledge may not get unnecessarily thwarted. The writer feels that the ill effects of automation can be avoided even without giving up all advantages of modern science. Anyway the future ideologist shall have to find a way out of this problem.

NOTES

1. D.G. Tendulkar, *Mahatma,* Vol. I, pp. 129-132.
2. Prof. Abdul Aziz, Gandhian Economic System, Quoted from, V.T. Patil, *Studies on Gandhi,* New Delhi: Sterling Publisher, p.87.
3. See. N.K. Bose (1948), *Selections from Gandhi*, Ahmedabad: Navajivan Publishing House.
4. References to Gandhiji's views on Trusteeship are: *Yeravada Mandir*, pp. 45-49; *Nations Voice*, pp. 170-72: *Young India*, III, p. 124: March 31

1937, p. 197; Dec. 16, 1939, p. 376; Aug. 25, 1940, p. 260; Feb. 22, 1942, p. 49; March 8, 1942, p. 67; April 12, 1942, p. 116; March 31, 1946. p. 67; Feb. 16, 1947, p. 25; Feb 23. 1947, p. 39; March 2, 1947, p. 47; and N.K. Bose, *Studies in Gandhism: The Theory of Trusteeship.*

5. See, the references above.
6. V.P. Patil, I.A. Lokopur, *Studies on Gandhi*, New Delhi: Sterling Publishers, p. 104.
7. *Harijan,* October 24, 1948.
8. *Ibid.* July 20, 1947.
9. *Harijan*, December 2, 1939, p. 366 and *Harijan*, December, 16, 1939, p. 376.
10. See, *Harijan*, June 20, 1935, p. 156; June 1, 1935; and Feb. 23, 1947, p. 36.
11. *Young India*, III, p. 124.
12. L.P. Vidyarthi, *et al.*, (eds.) (1970), *Gandhi and Social Sciences*, New Delhi, p. 9171.
13. Bjorm Heline, Saric Report (August, 1978), *Current Issues in Development Theory*, Swedish Agency for Research Cooperation with Developing Countries.
14. *CWMG*, Vol. 85, p. 79.
15. *CWMG*, Vol. 67, pp. 35-36.
16. *CWMG*, Vol. 67, p. 139.
17. *CWMG*, Vol. 67, p. 169.
18. *Harijan*, 04.08.1946, pp. 251-52
19. *CWMG*, Vol. 23, p. 12
20. *Harijan*, 29.08.1936, p. 12.
21. *Harijan*, 31.08.1934 p. 229.
22. *CWMG*, Vol. 82, p. 72.
23. Gandhi M.K. (1986), *Constructive Programme: Its Meaning and Place*, Ahmedabad: Navajivan Publishing House.
24. *CWMG*, Vol. 68, p. 447.
25. *Ibid.*
26. *Ibid.*, p. 447
27. *Young India*, 21.07.1920, p. 4.
28. *Harijan*, 25.08.1946, p. 281.
29. *Ibid.*, 16.05.1936, pp. 107-111.
30. Pyare Lal (1965), *The Last Phase*, Vol. II, Ahmedabad: Navajivan Publishing House, p. 545.

13

Bridging the Development Gap: The Gandhian Way

Ramdas Bhatkal

Market economy is, in simplistic terms, based on the relationship of demand and supply. Though Adam Smith, the founder of modern economics, had recognized the relationship between ethics and economics, over the years the discipline has seemingly taken pride in its scientific, technical nature and maintained that "value" judgments are beyond its scope. In a speech given in 1918 at Allahabad, Gandhi raised precisely this issue, *viz.*, Does economic progress clash with real progress? By real progress he meant moral progress. The parameters of demand and supply are determined by a complex of economic factors, but largely the basis is the so-called rational behaviour of 'an economic man'. No doubt, in any polity the interplay of demand and supply are not unbridled and social and political forces modify these. Yet this is largely an amoral approach. As Gandhi mentioned so simply yet effectively in *Hind Swaraj*, "...people sell out their grain and it is sent to the nearest markets." Utilitarian and later welfare economists aimed at 'the greatest good of the largest numbers'. This objective, they believed, would provide the moral basis to economic policies. With 'market economy' it was necessary to seek justice through intervention by the State. Gandhi had two problems with this. Inspired by John Ruskin's *Unio This Last*, Gandhi wanted 'the good of all' and not just 'the good of the largest number', to be the basis of economic activity. The word *Sarvodaya* that he used for his Gujarati adaptation of *Unto This Last* emphasized the paradigm shift in his thinking. Thus, he had reservations about the very objectives. Secondly, for many years, he had little faith in the institution of state. He looked at the state as an instrument of oppression and since it depended ultimately on the coercive power, it was not acceptable to him as a moral force.

The alternative to Market economy was the Marxist model. As late as 1943, while in detention in the Aga Khan Palace, Gandhi pointed out to his secretary Pyarelal, how his ideas were very close to the Marxian model; but the major difference was his own insistence on pure or nonviolent means as against the strategy of dictatorship of the proletariat advocated by Marx.

A way had to be found out to achieve *sarvodaya* through non-violent means.

BIOGRAPHICAL BACKGROUND

Barrister M.K. Gandhi made most of his discoveries during his two-decade work in South Africa (1893-1914). The distinguishing features were his passion for inclusivity and a holistic approach. Though he himself would refer to 'Truth, Non-violence' and all his discoveries to be 'as old as the hills', he gave them new significance so as to have a deep impact on future generations. *Sarvadharma samabhava*, *Sarvodaya* and *Satyagraha* were prominent among these. Of these, *sarvodaya* was directly linked to economic issues.

The Phoenix settlement established in 1904 was a human laboratory that tried several experiments—consciously or otherwise. It was an experiment in living together by people of different races, religions and nationalities; it was an experiment in practical implementation of the theory of 'bread labour' that Gandhi picked from Bondareff and Tolstoy; and more importantly, it was an experiment in practical working out of the Marxian doctrine of 'from each according to his ability and to each according to his needs'.

> If the means had to be non-violent then the coercive power as indicated by the concept of 'dictatorship of the proletariat' had to be replaced by a new concept. The concept of 'Trusteeship' was the answer suggested. This required a change in human behaviour. Gandhi's *ashrams* attempted to bring about a change in motivations. In his lifetime, the progress in fine-tuning this concept into an effective instrument was slow, but he laid down a different approach to economic issues than the rules of market economy.

Gandhi's thinking was based on ethical considerations. Not just religion, but also all aspects of human behaviour, individual as well as collective, was based on morality.

While in South Africa, Gandhi was not faced with the economic issues at the macro level. His thoughts were on social and political issues. His Sarvodaya objectives were in a nascent state and his efforts were directed more towards changing human nature. For him voluntary poverty and seeking individual good in collective good was the virtue to be developed.

While returning to India after a long period of absence, Gandhi had promised his mentor Gopal Krishna Gokhale that he would get acquainted with India before undertaking any political work. Gokhale was a product of elitist middle class city life. His home was in Pune and his alternate homes were Calcutta and London. But his *chela* went round four corners of the country and realized the significance of villages in India's life.

Decentralization

Gandhi realized that the economic development of India has to be village based. Village self-sufficiency was one of the methods of controlling the injustice that can be caused by the vagaries of market forces. This is not the place to discuss the viability of this approach or its merits and demerits. But its role in understanding Gandhian ethics is very important.

During the South African struggle, Gandhi had made a special mention of Henry Maine's *Village Communities* to justify granting of civic rights to the Indian population. With his holistic approach, Gandhi could relate a self-sufficient village with democratic participation of villagers in ruling themselves. This scheme was far more consistent with his concept of *swaraj*, as against just 'liberation from the British rule' that was implicit in the freedom movement.

Gandhi's concept of Oceanic circles had family and a village at its centre. Growing outward to a group of villages, communities, states, nation and ultimately the international community, this concept avoided confrontation between these entities.

The reason for referring cursorily to Gandhi's various other concepts is to point out that it is necessary to keep in mind his holistic approach to life, even though, at this stage, we want to point out just how decentralization could provide the necessary cushion against tyranny of market forces.

Trusteeship

When Gandhi arrived in India, his effort was to extend the 'inclusive' principle he had adhered to in South Africa to this vast subcontinent. He needed to include all castes, religions and classes in his vision of his *praja*. Thus the class of entrepreneurs and industrialists was also to be an important part of his India. If interest, rent, wages and profit were to be the returns on various inputs, he had to find a moral justification to integrate these into his system.

At a psychological level, he found an answer in the concept of 'Trusteeship'. The industrialists and entrepreneurs could make their millions by using their skill. "The rich would still be there but they would deem themselves to be only trustees of their property and would use it mainly in the public interest." Thus he equated 'profit' with 'wages'. The next important step was that the profit was to be used by them not as their own property, but as something that belonged to society and the earners were to be only the trustees. In his own lifetime some of his followers among the entrepreneurs (Birlas, Tatas and Bajajs) made efforts in this direction. Though he preferred this change be brought about by a change of heart (*hriday parivartan*), he was looking for institutional methods of implementing the concept, may be through legislation. Gandhi himself was not satisfied with progress in this field, but one can take consolation in the fact that the concept has not remained an idle dream, and that we can see its acceptance, however marginal, in the present day world. In fact, these points to Gandhi's unique method of bringing about change through creation of alternate norms.

A passing reference may be made to observations made by the present author in another chapter 'Trusteeship and Non-violence' read at a Seminar held at Indian Institute of Advanced Studies, Shimla, where it is pointed out that while the concept of trusteeship was mentioned by Gandhi in the context of economic activities, he himself applied this principle to all areas. Anything that one had in excess—education, so-called superiority based on nationality, religion, caste, or power arising out of adulthood or male domination—all these were to be utilized for the less endowed or less privileged.

Apart from some propositions of deep significance, the Gandhian approach also called for some practical devices.

Constructive Programme

Gandhi first defined the need for the Congress party to take up 'constructive programme' as early as 1920 after withdrawing the Non-cooperation movement. One of the main items was *Khadi*. The significance of *Khadi* in Gandhi's economic thought is too wide to be discussed here. But he used *Khadi* to counter some of the tenets of market economy. *Khadi* had to be used not as a viable economic proposition but for other human considerations, such as providing employment to *daridranarayan*. Introduction of non-economic factors in market economy was a great contribution. As Schumacher pointed out, Gandhi "highlighted the importance of non-economic goals in human life, inadequacy of market mechanism to deal with non-renewable sources and raises the question of appropriate (or intermediate) technology wherein Gandhi's preference for labour intensive technology is developed to a great extent." That Gandhi's efforts were not utopian was proved by the fact that *Khadi* had a major impact on the textile industry in England. The introduction of 'human development index' as a parameter more important than the purely economic parameters such as GNP and GDP is indicative of this change.

Civil Society

The normal solution considered by socialist, Marxist or even welfare protagonists, was intervention of the welfare state. Gandhi believed that state was largely an instrument of oppression and he wanted civil society to exercise its beneficial influence in modifying the effects of large economic realities.

Cooperatives

In practical terms, Gandhi found in cooperatives a method of mitigating hardships covered by strict adherence to the rules of market economy under his influence, cooperatives and what are now known as NGOs were the institutional forms of this amorphous civil society. Theoretically, producers and consumers' cooperatives could protect their interests and both in conjunction could provide judicious balance to society at large.

Cooperatives struck root in India in various sectors even before independence. While the Company structure gave leverage to large shareholders, the cooperative structure emphasized the equality among all the members irrespective of their shareholding. Cooperatives started in India in various sectors including consumer, producer and housing. A large number of Gandhian and Congress leaders developed cooperative societies, at least some of these in the true spirit of cooperation. After independence (and after Gandhi's death) cooperatives got a fillip from government policies, largely initiated by politicians influenced by Gandhi.

The Gujarat Milk producer's story is a case in point. The Gujarat farmer's cooperative was started by Tribhuvandas Patel, who was directly influenced by Vallabhbhai Patel. Morarji Desai, in his capacity as a Minister of Bombay Presidency encouraged and helped the cooperative in spite of the Government itself getting involved in Dairying. The farmers benefited greatly and the advantages were not restricted to economic factors, but had other benefits such as creating a new leadership, empowerment of women, and development of a scientific approach to dairying and rural development. The farmers' Cooperative was able to get a remunerative price for milk and pass on the benefit to the farmers by eliminating the middlemen.

The model was applied to other products, sometimes not so successfully. If this system was to be followed without any counter forces, the result could be a producers' monopoly. The answer to this was consumer's cooperatives. a number of Sahakar Bhandars came up for the requirements of the consumers and the benefit would be passed onto its members.

That in later years, cooperatives got entangled in feudal mentality to the neglect of the welfare of its members is a sad commentary on our present day acquisitive society. But if we are seeking a way out of the not so happy experience of unbridled free economy and corrupt state control, cooperatives provide a structure that can be fine tuned, not by the government but by its members themselves.

Mixed Economy

One of the baffling questions about Gandhi is why he nominated Nehru as his successor even though their differences on economic issues were known to both. They had discussed these candidly as late as 1945 and had agreed to differ. The socialist ideas based on state ownership of industries to keep pace with the western world were the keystones of Nehru's economic thinking. Industrialization, modernization and urbanization were dear to his heart. On the other hand, Gandhi believed in India's development based on self-sufficient villages and 'small is beautiful'. In spite of this Gandhi's choice was clear and Nehru undoubtedly rode on his shoulders.

A possible explanation is that Gandhi believed in accepting the present situation and then trying to remove what was undesirable in it. Gandhi conceded that 'it is no easy task to do away with a thing that is established'. The most obvious example is that of Hinduism. He was disturbed at the cancer of untouchability in Hindu social life. His solution was to call himself a Sanatani, if you wish, but to find ways of eliminating the disease. So also, he could not wish away the existence of market economy. Perhaps he had faith that Nehru would find practical ways of modifying the extremes of unfettered market economy and rigid state control. Probably, mixed economy was a sincere attempt on the part of Nehru to achieve a seemingly impossible objective. Whether he succeeded or not is not a subject of this chapter.

LARGER ISSUES

In a larger context, Gandhi had some unconventional answers to basic issues of conflicts, particularly in the economic field. They were based on a change in human nature by concentrating on nobler aspects of human nature that, broadly, he called 'Love'. His advocacy of voluntary poverty, his insistence that the good of the individual lies in the good of all, his concept of oceanic circles as a person grows outwards rather than accepting pyramidal structure and his constant effort to develop non-coercive plural civil society indicate the direction in which his thinking needs to be pursued. All these have dimensions that are far beyond the scope of this chapter.

This is, indeed, a simplistic analysis, but further investigation into these basics is avoided at this stage, as the principal effort in this chapter is to identify a few theoretical and a few empirical methods by which the wide gulf between ethics and Market economy was sought to be bridged.

14
Relevance of the Concept of *Swadeshi* in the Era of Globalization

P.L. Devaraj

> *"My ideal is equal distribution, but so far as I can see, it is not to be realized. I, therefore, work for equitable distribution".*

The world has travelled a long way on the path of development. During the march of life human beings have changed much and their life patterns have undergone remarkable changes. In almost every walk of life there have been significant developments which have made the world very prosperous. On the economic front also things have improved a lot. Technological developments have facilitated greater material prosperity and material progress. Economic development implies the growth of economic wealth of a nation. It is a process through which a nation improves the economic, political and social well-being of its people. It can be defined as the efforts to improve the economic well-being and quality of life of a community. Hence, economic development may be described as a process whereby simple, low income national economies are transformed into modern industrial economies. The dominant development model of our times is economic globalization.

Globalization has created a serious social crisis affecting wage workers, farmers and employees everywhere. The march of globalization adversely affected agriculture, the backbone of Indian economy. Unemployment and poverty shot up as a result of the decline of indigenous cottage and small-scale industries. A huge number of workers lost their jobs. The quality of life, especially in the rural areas declined with a steady decline of social services mainly in education and health. In this system, the government will have not much to invest in the schemes favouring the weaker sections of the society since its reliance in necessarily on market and market can never be a benefactor of the deprived classes. All these point to the fact that the world in the twentyfirst century witnesses the global triumph of market economics, the retreat of the state, and the generation of unprecedented wealth. The need of the hour is that kind of policy that can ensure the availability of basic amenities and equal opportunities to the poorest and deprived classes also so that social equality and rights could be enjoyed by all. The benefits of development should reach the poor and all the hurdles in the path of their emancipation should be removed. Here lies the relevance of Gandhian principles. Gandhi's relevance is perhaps even greater to this century than to the one in which he lived. In this chapter an attempt is made to show how Gandhian economic ideals based on ethical principles can prove to be a solution to the current market economic problems faced by India.

GANDHIAN ECONOMIC IDEALS

Mahatma Gandhi was not an economist in the academic sense of the term and he did not produce a treatise or some such thing on economic system which he visualized for India. In some of his general works, lectures, letters written to, or editorials in *Young India* and *Harijan*, he made references to the kind of economic system which according to him was ideal for the country. Gandhian economic ideals were in a sense a logical corollary of his political and moral principles such as '*Swaraj*', '*Sarvodaya*', Truth and Non-violence, etc. To an extent, we can say that his entire life and philosophy were based on Truth, Non-violence, and Dignity of Labour and Simplicity. Based on these wider social principles, Gandhi derived his economic ideas which if brought together would give a picture of the economic system that he visualized.

Gandhi's economics did not aspire to growth and accumulation, but instead to people's *swaraj* or control over their own destinies. He opposed the deployment of machines if people were out of work. He did not believe in unlimited wants, but instead reminded us that the world produces enough for the needs but not the greed of every human being. His economics was not founded on assumption of self-seeking accumulation being central to human nature; instead he was convinced that human beings were essentially altruistic. From the idea of *swaraj* emerged the ideas of *swadeshi* and self-sufficiency. And from the principle of Truth and Non-violence emerged a series of economic ideas like non-exploitation, non-possession, trusteeship, bread labour and so on. All these ideas, which in fact having originated under different contexts, formed the founding pillars of Gandhian economic system.

An important ideal on which Gandhi based his economic programme was the ideal of *swadeshi*. *Swadeshi* is a central concept in Gandhi's economic thought. It is an eternal principle. It has emerged out of his idea of *swaraj*. It is in conformity with the goal of *sarvodaya*. It has both individual and group application. Literally, the term *swadeshi* means "one's own country". Gandhi notices that the deep rooted poverty of the Indian masses is due to their departure from the *swadeshi* principles in the economic sphere. As a remedial measure, he asks every Indian to invite the spirit of *swadeshi* and help his neighbours in their needs as he helps himself. With such self-supporting and serving nature, every Indian village will become an autonomous unit.

'Simple living and high thinking', was a principle that played a significant part in Gandhi's life. He adopted this principle much to the advantage of the nation. As a practical idealist, he found that it was in this ideal that the remedy of the ills of modern civilization lies. Modern industrialism creates in man, according to him, the desire to increase wants and acquire material wealth at the cost of human values. He suggests that simple life is the only means of attaining eternal happiness. It is because of his infallible faith in simplicity he advocated decentralization of economy.

ECONOMIC DECENTRALIZATION

In matters of economics and politics, Gandhi wanted India to become a network of self-governing and self-sustaining village republics, each one of them leading an autonomous existence. Decentralization in both, politics and economics was the key word for Gandhi. He was basically a ruralite. He saw that India lived in villages. Hence, his slogan was 'back to villages'. In fact, he wanted to revitalize the village economy. He suggested that all persons should be supplied with the basic necessities to satisfy their natural needs. The constituent's elements of economic equality include a balanced diet, a decent house, medical relief and education facilities.

ATTITUDE TOWARDS INDUSTRIALISM

As Gandhiji was in favour of economic decentralization, he was a sharp critic of large scale industrialization. According to him, mechanical devices led to drudgery and monotony. He opposed industrial economy because he believed that it created violence. He thought the large scale production was responsible for many socio-economic evils. As stated by Romain Rolland, "He (Gandhi) moved the world with his own example that human ingenuity can be superior to the most complex technology; that human initiative is at its best when it dissolves among the mass of people."[1] His objection to the use of machine arose on account of its abuses such as labour displacement and more importantly, the possibility of the producers growing into monopolists with control over production and distribution.

But Gandhi was not altogether against the use of machines. He said, "Machinery has its place, it has come to stay. But it must not be allowed to displace human labour..."[2] He was not opposed to the establishment of few large scale industries which are essential for the development of the nation. He was against it only because he thought it would give rise to the growth of managerial bureaucracy and unemployment. Thus Gandhi really wanted the establishment of heavy industries to take place in such a way that it does not hamper the growth of cottage industries and that it forms only a small part of the national activity. He believed that greater industrialization may provide more goods but does not necessarily leads to moral progress.

DEPARTURE FROM GANDHIAN ECONOMIC IDEALS AND THE RESULT

Inspired by the ideas of Gandhi, Nehru emphasized the need for a rapid and radical but peaceful socio-economic transition. Through economic planning, Nehru wanted to establish a strong and self-reliant India with a just and social order. He adopted planning not as an end, but as a means at the "well-being and advancement of the people as a whole, at the opening out of opportunity to all and the growth of freedom and the method of co-operative organization and action".[3]

Though Nehru gave enough attention to decentralization in the different Five Year Plans, his successors could not keep his tradition. They gradually left his way and by the time of the current Five Year Plan, we were very much diverted from the concept of decentralization. This led to an economic crisis because we were not able to achieve what we aimed through planning, i.e., eradication of poverty and unemployment. The over-centralization also resulted in the inefficiency of political power and corruption.

The new economic policy of 1991 kick started the unbalanced phase in India's economic development. Through this policy, globalization has led to the emergence and growth of a new rich class with its love for dispensation of wealth, social power and luxuries. Multinational and transnational companies have become the major actors in international politics and economics. Prices of essential commodities, lives saving medicines and other necessities have shot up. Today, everything is for sale; Privatization has become a tool for exploiting the nature without constraint degrading the environment.

We see that the new economic policy of neo-liberalization resulted in the concentration of wealth in the hands of a selected few, keeping the majority out of the development. It has created two sections within the nation. One is the liberalized India of the billionaires and the booming middle class and the other is that of the common man, helpless farmers committing suicides, disposed tribals and other marginalized folks. Liberalization has also created an unstable economy which is evident from the current turmoil ruling the markets the world over. Altogether we can say that it is not at all an ideal model of development. Above all, the industrialization with its mechanization took away from men initiative for work and changed them into nothing but machines. It made life mechanical and artificial. The result is that man lost the zest for life. He seeks an escape by indulging in purely sensuous pursuits like drinking, gambling and the like.

Gandhian Concept of *Swadeshi* as a Solution to the Economic Crisis in the Market Economy

Having outlined the ailment of Indian economy, we can now look how Gandhian developmental strategy can help us to solve this crisis to some extent. Gandhi held that economics and ethics cannot be separated from each other and must be studied as a whole. In the opinion of Anthony. J. Parel "Gandhi, in his turn, re-emphasized this meaning: a sound economy is one that empowered the last and the least of society, and helped to create and develop in them the necessary capacities and moral dispositions".[4] The principle of buying in the cheapest and selling in the dearest market was the most inhuman law of economics, for market in globalization is based on the concept of 'buy now and pay later'. As against this Gandhiji considered economic decentralization as the fundamental principle and this is what we need today. Dr. Manmohan Singh also stood for decentralization when he said that "decentralization will be able to mobilize the grass roots knowledge and public awareness to prevent the misuse of public funds for private ends."[5] In India, democracy can succeed only when it is built up in a grass root manner. This can be done by following the Gandhian concept of *swadeshi*.

SWADESHI: AN ANALYSIS

Gandhi realized that much of the heart rending poverty of the masses is due to the ruinous departure from *swadeshi* in the economic life. His thesis was that India would not have been poor if the articles of consumption had not been brought from outside India. The broad meaning of *swadeshi* is the use of all home made things to the exclusion of foreign things. Gandhi believes that the economic good of all lies in strictly practicing the principles of *swadeshi.* It is a plea for protecting village industries which enjoys abundant manpower. We have to provide food, work and employment to our immediate neighbours. *Swadeshi*, is a doctrine employed for the protection of home industry. According to Manmohan Choudhary "the principle of *swadeshi* is a fundamental concept in Gandhian economic thought. It defines the relation of individual to his society and the larger world in terms of socially responsible economic behaviour."[6] Thus, the practice of *swadeshi* would result in innumerable self supporting and self contained units meeting their primary needs locally and exchange with other units such necessary commodities that are not locally producible.

Swadeshi spirit never allows exploitation of the raw materials of a country. It does not neglect the powerful manpower. Wasting time and money in producing goods which are unsuitable to the Indian, amounts to the negation of the *swadeshi* spirit. It is false *swadeshi.* At the same time, *swadeshi* does not mean boycotting foreign goods. Gandhi observes "any article is *swadeshi*, if it subserves the interest of the millions, even though the capital and talent are foreign but under effective Indian control".[7] *Swadeshi* is also one of the ways of non-violence and, therefore, a true believer of *swadeshi* will not harbour any ill-feeling towards foreign things. It is not a cult of hatred but a doctrine of selfless service that has its roots in *ahimsa*. Gandhi would be prepared to buy from any part of the world, things that are needed for the growth of his country, but he would insist on the use of *swadeshi* when such foreign things are sought to be imported that hamper the economic status of home industry. *Swadeshi*, thus is not an outright rejection of everything foreign. It is based on a feeling of concern for the economic and political stability of one's own country.

The concept of *swadeshi* comprises three propositions, the first being the reduction of wants by each individual consumer; the second, the reordering of preferences in such a way that it is made up mostly of goods produced in the neighbourhood; and the third is the cooperation of the consumer with his neighbour producer to make them both work effectively. This principle decries competition and stresses the need to promote cooperation between the consumer and producer, which in turn leads to a downward trend in cost function.

Swadeshi is one of the best ways of preventing manufacture of goods in abundance that creates unemployment and exploitation. If a person wishes to increase his business so as to supply also the needs of others than those who belong to that unit, he will find that no one else would be willing to buy his goods due to a moral responsibility towards his neighbours. Thus he would be prevented from developing into a large scale manufacturer. Even if the article produced elsewhere are more attractive than those produced locally, they will not be allowed to flood out the local products. At the same time, the local producer is encouraged to improve the quality of his products to come up to the standard of foreign goods. Thus the consumers will limit themselves to, and help to improve, the quality of local produce.

If the indigenous industries are not protected from foreign competition, our naive skill will be ruined and the villages which constitute the greater part of the country will not prosper. Therefore, *swadeshi* is specially meant for the basic unit of society, i.e., villages, where production is made for consumption, not for exchange. The basic principle of *swadeshi* is to produce for the fulfilment of the basic needs and not to produce for commerce, market and profiting. This requires the simplification of our economic structure. If the economy is restricted to small units, it can influence the people morally make them self dependent. That was why Gandhi was not only against the big industries of the foreign multinationals but also against the native multinationals which swallow the small scale industries, which make greater section of people unemployed. But he was not totally against industries and technology. In fact he wanted a balanced growth of both villages and cities, and small scale and big industries to form a harmonious peaceful and society. He wanted to free economy from greed. By his concept of *swadeshi* he wanted to construct an exploitation free society.

To conclude we can say that Gandhian concept of *swadeshi* from its economic view point is a belief in self reliant economy. It is a warning against the killing of native skills and putting the nation in the trap of others. It stands for the natural growth of people than to make some live in luxuries while others starving. It permits taking the help of other for building one's own economy but with great caution. If we enrich ourselves from others *swadeshi* welcomes it. But if we lose control over ourselves and fall between the endless wheels of exploitation, it is against the idea of *swadeshi.* "Gandhi's *swadeshi* principle exhorted people to remain contended with the local conditions and with the things that God provided for man's sustenance, instead of indulging in ruthless exploitation of other countries to obtain unnecessary luxuries".[8] Thus Gandhian concept of *swadeshi* from economic point of view stands for strong belief in self-reliance, balanced growth and human economics, i.e., the economics for larger and deeper life and not the economics for profit and market.

The New Economic Policy of India is a clear deviation from the ideals of *swadeshi*. This would result in foreign domination, downfall of indigenous industries and unemployment. The resultant economy would be a market economy, and is destined to create socio-economic disparities in society which in turn would generate conflicts. Hence, what is needed today is a cultural revolution to reduce wants and to adoption of *swadeshi.* This will, in turn, will promote cooperation among the people within the country and among the nations internationally.

NOTES

1. Romain Rolland (2008), *Mahatma Gandhi: The Leader of the Universal Peace and Liberty*, Delhi: Vijay Goel, p. 159.

2. Gandhi, M.K., *Young India*, 5.11.1925.
3. Jawaharlal Nehru (1982), *Discovery of India,* New Delhi: Jawaharlal Nehru Memorial Fund, p. 533.
4. Anthony. J. Parcl (2006), *Gandhi's Philosophy and the Quest for Harmony*, New Delhi: Cambridge University Press, p. 75.
5. Manmohan Singh, The Unfinished Business of Nation Building, *The Hindu*, Delhi, 15th August, 1997.
6. Choudhary, Manmohan (2000), *Exploring Gandhi*, New Delhi: Gandhi Peace Foundation 2000, p. 200.
7. Bhagvan, Vishnu (1976), *Indian Political Thinkers*, New Delhi: Atma Ram & Sons, p. 63.

15
Minimizing Ill-effects of Market Economy on Social Fabric: Gandhian Ethics as a Counter Force

Sheoraj Singh

INTRODUCTION

Someone has rightly uttered:

> *' Seene me zalan aankhon me tuphan sa kyun hai,*
> *Is shahar (read* Economy*) me har saksha pareshan sa kyun hai?'*

It is an opportune moment for all of us to ponder over the question raised in the above couplet as the world has turned a full circle in the vicious trap of its own making and finding no way out, is desperately looking towards Gandhian ethics for liberation from the trinity of perpetual want, conflict/tension, and the increasing mechanization of life

The world economy is passing through a phase of transition. The basic philosophy of wealth generation for the larger good of the masses has taken the back seat and the driving force behind the present economic order has become the principle of profit by any means, even by exploiting painfully the very people for whom it intends to exist. There seems no end to the exploitative machinery of global economy in near future and its impact is badly felt by one and all today. From the simple farmers in villages to the sophisticated economic players in the Wall Street, everyone is feeling the heat now. The economy seems to threaten its own very basis. A world in crisis is desperately looking towards better alternatives/Gandhian ethics for solving its recurring problems amidst its trial and error approach to create a generous market economy. What Gandhiji propounded way back in the early part of the twentieth century through his down-to-earth personal experiments and a programme for social reconstruction based on his idea of *Ram Rajya,* seems more relevant today. In fact, his concept of an ideal society is based the observance of ethical principles of living by every individual with an aim to overcome the so-called human limitations and reach a state of harmony in life so as to manifest the inherent divinity of the human race. Gandhian ethics are the eternal principles of righteous living, individually as well as collectively. And in this scheme of things, trusteeship is one of the guiding laws of life so far as economic activities are concerned.[1] In fact, when Gandhiji emphasizes that the earth has enough for the need of every human being but not enough for the greed of even a single human being, he is essentially pointing to the shared future of mankind.[2] His idea of economic independence and prosperity is not one of accumulating the resources for fulfilling our needs for a long period of time. On the contrary, it is for preparing us to enjoy the earthly life through increasing spirit of renunciation amidst prosperity in the true spirit of the *Upanishads—Ten Tyaktena Bhunjithah* (Enjoy thy wealth by renouncing it).[3]

Expanded in the words of Gandhiji, it means "Earn your crores by all means. But understand that your wealth is not yours; it belongs to the people. Take what you require for your legitimate needs and use the remainder for society."[4] Here, in the following pages, a humble attempt has been made to analyze larger social impact of market economy in a technologically globalized world-order. It establishes that the only panacea is an immediate reconstruction of the basic philosophy of wealth generation following Gandhian ethics. It has been logically pointed out that the greed for possessing more and more without realizing the personal-social evils arising out of this tendency has crippled the very fabric of our society. The solution tried so far by this economic order has not yielded the desired results because as Gandhiji pointed way back in 1930's that the exploitative economic machinery is bound to create class-war in one form or the other.

And wherever there is class war, whether in gross form or subtle, all our economic activities are bound to be exploitative. In an exploitative economy, every player wants to outsmart the other and a competitive mindset for commanding the means of production ensues and ultimately nobody gains in the long run. Everyone feels dissatisfied and life becomes mechanical. But there is a way out as pointed out by Gandhiji. This chapter, therefore, discusses how the market economy can reorient itself through the twin principles of trusteeship and non-violence to enhance the happiness-index of mankind and concludes that Gandhian ethics are more relevant today than ever before. As Gandhiji emphatically said, 'the owners of wealth should be trustees of their possessions and should use their talent to increase the wealth, not for their own sake, but for the sake of the nation/world and therefore, without exploitation.'[5] If this spirit of trusteeship gets imbibed in the right earnest in our economic activities, most of our problems will vanish automatically.

PRESENT GLOBAL ECONOMIC ORDER

Modern capitalist economy has given exclusive emphasis on wealth generation by exploiting natural and human resources. The result has been increasing mechanization and corporatization of life without due regards to basic human values. This economic order is heading from crisis to crisis with just fire fighting mechanisms to contain the damage to a tolerable level. But the fact is that if the system demands a basic change in its frame of reference, it cannot be brought about just by some superficial and cosmetic adjustments. What we need today is the rethinking about the very structural basis of our economy. Economics is not just a science of wealth generation but also a science of enhancing human welfare. But the market economy is based on creating artificial want for largely unwanted things in the larger sections of population in order to get the mass-scale produced goods consumed indiscriminately and then create a vicious cycle of flawed demand-supply network in which the humanity seems entangled. People are made to understand that earning a lot of money is the only purpose of their life. The whole life is geared to accumulation of wealth in order to fulfil the pseudo-needs of the individuals and societies. In the rat race of wealth-accumulation, we forget to adhere to the ethical principles of life and the consequent domination of brute forces in our daily life makes our life hellish. It is no wonder then that life loses its wonder and the charisma of creative living is out of our reach. The impact of market economy has not been very encouraging for Indian society. In fact, it has separated the concept of well-being from that of affluence. It has slowly started dehumanizing the individuals and society at the same time in pursuit of material affluence.

In words of Sri T.N. Chaturvedi; The inadequacy or near failure of various models of economics and political development in India (and the world) has been a cause of frustration and bewilderment to the intellectual class, most particularly, to those who have grown either in the traditions of nineteenth century liberalism, Fabian socialism or under the strong influence of Marxian thoughts and movements. Some of these intellectuals now feel the need for a more indigenous model which can simultaneously meet the challenges of the modern world and make use of the best aspects of Indian traditions through which alone people can genuinely be involved in and enthused for political and economic development.

MARKET ECONOMY AND ITS GUIDING PRINCIPLES

Market economy is based on the twin ideas of demand and supply. On one hand it tries to manufacture goods in bulk to reduce the unit cost of production but on the other it attempts to create bigger market for consumption of its products. It devises various strategies to enhance the production as well as the demand for goods and services in such a way that there seems to be always a balance between the two. It attempts to price the goods and services on the basis of market needs and the supply. But in case of essential commodities, balancing of prices on the basis of demand-supply balance fails and when prices go up, people feel the heat. And, this creates an opportunity for the market to exploit the common man by limiting the supply of such essential goods. Moreover, owing to the limitations of natural resources (and the means of production), the production of goods and services is also limited by various factors operating at a particular point of time. All these aspects contribute to soaring of the prices and the exploitative machinery of the market economy sets in. Now this exploitative tendency of market economy has far reaching impact on individuals and the society. In fact, the exclusive concern of economics has been economic growth indicated by a higher GDP and there is hardly any concern for simultaneous growth in human well-being. As Fullbrook (2004) points out that: the economists (read market economists) do not confuse economic growth with growth in the well-being and that if others confuse it that has nothing to do with them; the current measure of GDP is not designed for gauging the human well-being and that the economists and experts in national accounting devote 100 per cent of their efforts in measuring and using GDP and economic growth instead of directing only 50 per cent of their efforts in that direction and reserving the other 50 per cent for developing and designing alternative indicators that better reflect notions of well-being, human development, social development, sustainable development, etc.

Actually, the problem with market economy lies in its very foundation of exclusive concern for wealth generation disregarding the ultimate purpose of its effort. Human welfare hardly finds a place in its scheme of economic activities.

IMPACT OF MARKET ECONOMY ON INDIVIDUAL

Market economy seems initially advantageous for the individual as goods and services seem to be available on demand at competitive prices, but in the long run, the local economy is badly hit because of the principle of survival of the fittest operating in the play. Due to the disappearance of local self-sufficiency, the individual has to depend more and more on market for his very survival. And a time comes when all decisions of the individual are based on the trends of the market. This is really pitiable situation when the sovereignty of the individual gets mortgaged in the hands of the market. In fact, the individual apparently feels independent, but is not actually independent and very subtly gets caught in the cobweb of market-created pseudo needs. Survival becomes the basic and all-encompassing question for the person and he/she is hardly left with any time for leading a fulfilled life. The rat race for accumulation of wealth sets in very secretly and destroys the balance in life. Now, the individual is at the command of the market factors. The individual today is either caught in the dilemma of providing for the existential needs of the family or in the dream of getting rich overnight by any means whatsoever. The market mechanism is such that every new packaging and new gadget is made to seem essential for the survival of the individual. Thus one is hardly left with any time or energy or choice to decide for himself about his needs, aspirations, means and ends. Almost everything is being decided by the projections and trends of the market. The individuality of a person is getting lost in the crowd of madness for money-power. Insanity has taken the driving seat for journey of human life and the golden rule of contentment in human life has become outdated. Various kinds of pulls and pressures make the life full of tension and resultant depression. The joy of righteous living has become a thing of the past for most of us. Ethics, which used to be guiding force for human beings until recently, have become the things of forgotten past. Talking of ethics and ethical living is considered a sign of backwardness today. Trying to lead a contented life guided by ethics and values is a crime today. Self deception and so called smartness have become the laws of life. The increasing self-centredness of man is spoiling human relations and social life has become another name for crowd-mentality without the feeling of togetherness. Everyone seems to be in hurry to ensure a reasonable means of livelihood for the longest possible period of time but nobody bothers about the ways and means of life and living. Individual seems to be lost in wilderness of greed.

IMPACT OF MARKET ECONOMY ON THE SOCIETY AS A WHOLE

It has been found that if the individual is caught in the confusing economic scenario, no better is the lot of society. As the individual is the basic component of any society, social impact of market economy is not very encouraging. In the race of having greater control over the wealth, people find very little time to interact peacefully with one another. Everyone is in hurry for one reason or the other. The very fabric of affectionate relationship among the individuals seems strained and gets damaged in the process of fulfilling the market-driven needs. The society as such becomes just another mechanical entity, where material needs of man get fulfilled in a competitive way. Obviously, this results into the neglect of those who are not powerful contributors in the production or consumption of goods and services to satisfy market needs. Most of the people are sinking into misery, while a few are enjoying a life of luxury. Global inequalities, corruption, apathy, indifference to the human feelings and insensitiveness have become the hallmark of societies today all over the world.

Societies world over are witnessing the breaking of basic family structure, which is more apparent and devastating in Indian context. This has resulted into a disturbing chain reaction for the new generation, which segregates man from man. Patience, perseverance, fellow-feeling, sensitivity, considerations for others and, the most important of all, a sense of space and relaxation for oneself and the sacredness of life hardly find a place in the present scheme of life. And without these ingredients in place, it is next to impossible for human beings to enjoy the bounties of nature. Life today has become totally mechanical for most of us.

As has been witnessed world over, the social impact of market economy has put man against man. The social cohesion is missing because of over-indulgence of man in the process of production owing to the dictates of market-economy. There is increasing sense of alienation among the various constituents of society. The war is set in very subtle form and the society willingly forgets its own role to provide a conducive environment for *flowering of goodness* in man. The *response potential* of man is getting weakened and dulled with every passing day. People are physically living together but are hardly concerned for one another. Self-centredness is increasing and there is feeling of void among the individuals. Everybody feels the other to be a market factor, either guided by demand or supply. Humanity is slowly losing its humane touch and it is one of the most disturbing contributions of market economy that everybody seems busy but actually busy for nothing significant in life. Human values are getting neglected. Individuals hardly value eternal values of life for its own sake. Everything seems to be at the command of the market forces. If something is marketable, it has value otherwise not. The use and throw fashion has become the *mantra* of life. Humanity has got entangled in economic wilderness.

The social impact of market economy has really become disturbing. The growing alienation of man from himself, his surrounding nature, the immediate human concerns and the search for reality has created some of the following disastrous consequences:

1. Breaking of families and family ties;
2. Increasing sense of indifference among the individuals;
3. Lack of trust and trustworthiness;
4. General feeling of inadequacy/insufficiency and growing discontent in life;
5. Decreasing social cohesion;
6. Increasing mechanization of life;
7. Increasing instances of corruption in public life;
8. Degeneration of moral and spiritual values;
9. Growing tension and depression;

10. Disappearance of the traditional rural societies and economies;
11. Increasing corporate culture;
12. Disappearance of the innocence of childhood, carefree energy of the youths and godly detached compassion of the elders;
13. Increasing cleverness and decreasing simplicity of life;
14. Growing need for economic security as a primary source of happiness in life;
15. Exploitation of nature beyond the point of return; and
16. Despiritualization of life and so on.

Thus we find that the above mentioned disturbing social impact of market economy has troubled mankind a lot and there does not appear any viable alternative to mitigate the suffering of man in near future in the present economic philosophy of life.

DESPERATE SEARCH FOR A VIABLE ALTERNATIVE

As the world economy is passing through various phases of transition in quick succession, every individual feels the inadequacy of the market mechanism to provide for a satisfactory standard of living and fulfilment in life. No doubt, the market forces are also trying to have multiple permutations and combinations to suit the individual as well as collective needs of humanity, yet a desperate search is going on to have a solid foundation, a guiding principle and a viable alternative to the present chaotic economic activities and dissatisfactory way of life. The best products of the market are even not able to satisfy the human beings, not because of some defect in the product or the process but because of the flaw in the very perception of the feasibility of the market economy to ensure a want-free life for mankind.

A Gandhian Alternative

Mahatma Gandhi proposed a model for human development based on his experiences and experiments in life. In his scheme of life economics, ethics, religion, philosophy and spirituality were beautifully synthesized. The ultimate aim was realization of Truth and manifestation of non-violence in all aspects of human life. He said, "It is the fundamental law of Nature, without exception, that Nature produces enough for our wants from day-to-day, and if only everybody took enough for himself and nothing more, there would be no pauperism in this world, there would be no man dying of starvation in this world". Accumulation of wealth by any means was immoral and violent activity in his views. He emphasized on the purity of means as much as on the purity of ends. To him economics was not just a science of wealth creation but a moral science. In words of Prof. Sharma (2003), "the goal of Gandhian economics is not pure material benefits but advancement of humanity on its road to progress by strengthening the character and the development of personality of each individual engaged in such activity. Satisfaction of needs and moral elevation of individuals were not antithetical for Gandhiji".[18] He laid emphasis on self-sufficiency of villages and to him village economy was the centre of human growth. To him, urbanization, industrialization and mass production of goods as well as services were to be causes of human degeneration. At the centre of his economy was the ethico-spiritual man, who does not live by bread alone but is capable of producing his own bread and butter with the help of immediate environment in non-exploitative way and is strong enough to share his wealth for the welfare of all. The essence and culmination of his economy was in freeing man from wants and creating true brotherhood of man (*Vasudhaiva Kutumbakam*) as an essence of world peace and development of a globally inspiring model of human development.

Gandhian Ethics: What Is It and What It Means

Gandhian ethics are the principles of life based on the foundation of truth and non-violence. The ideals which Gandhiji advocated during his lifetime were not just ideas but were the powerful truths distilled out of his experiments with life in order to get nearer to the truth or God as he envisaged. Truth and non-violence were the two sides of the same coin for him and he very beautifully demonstrated the power of truth and non-violence in solving most of the then prevailing problems of life. As Sri Aurobindo points out—*'All the problems of existence are essentially problems of harmony'*, unless there is a harmony among the various dimensions of life of an individual, any plan for human happiness will have limited significance. What Gandhiji attempted was a life guided by ethics to reach the highest state of development, because ethics make a balance of material and spiritual aspects.

Truth and non-violence were the twin principles of Gandhian miracle and he regarded Truth as God. In his own words:

> Devotion to truth is the sole justification of our existence. All our activities should be centred in truth. Truth should be the very breath of our life. When once this stage in the pilgrim's progress is reached, all other rules of correct living will come without effort, and obedience to them will be instinctive. But without Truth, it is impossible to observe any principles or rules in life.

Gandhian ethics are essentially the code of conduct for making human life meaningful, contented, blissful and a highway to reach the God-State. The eleven observances he included as a way of life in his *ashram*—namely Truth, Non-Violence, *Brahmacharya*, Control of the palate, Non-stealing, Non-possession, Fearlessness, Removal of untouchability, Bread-labour, Tolerance, Humility were/are the foundationstone for spiritualizing and divinizing man in all dimensions.

Now the question arises—why do we need Gandhian ethics today? The answer is very simple. If we want fulfilment and joy in life, which have become a historical fact for a major portion of humanity, there is no other way. If we want the rampant corruption, wanton killing and widespread distrust and indifference (which have come as a package deal with exclusive material prosperity) to vanish from the individual and collective living, then there is no other way—*'Nanyo panthah Vidyate anayay'*. If we want our life to be inwardly and outwardly beautiful and harmonious, we have to resort to the true spirit of Gandhian ethics. In all our dealings we have to obey the spirit of trusteeship, and then only our economic prosperity will bring happiness in the true sense.

Relevance of Gandhian Ethics Today

As Gandhian ethics are the distilled wisdom of the ages to lead a life committed to truth and non-violence, they are more relevant today than ever before. The world is torn apart by violent activities of individuals and groups mostly in search for its ideal instrument of control over material wealth. Man is living under illusion of power of wealth and has lost touch with the inward beauty and strength, thereby creating a wide gulf between the reality and perception. Whatever external changes have come with science-technology and a plethora of techniques of wealth generation, there has been essentially no change in the human nature and needs for the last many centuries. There has not been an inch of addition in the height of man, so to speak. This is because no external wealth can add an inch to the stature of man unless man makes an effort to change himself from within, the kingdom of God is within and unless we turn our attention to inner strengthening of man, no amount of wealth can help us in solving our problems permanently.

The plethora of problems facing humanity today has basically arisen from our folly of distancing ourselves from the ethics/values in life. When wealth generation and satisfaction of wants became our sole preoccupation, the inner man got malnourished and this resulted into imbalance in life. This imbalance is the root cause of degradation in life. And in the modern age of jet-speed processes of production as well as consumption of goods and services, the inner starvation of man has become acute. Gandhian ethics are essentially the answer to the cry of humanity for saving it from this acute spiritual starvation and help mankind reach the godly state. In the words of Sri Aurobindo—

> "The force of man can be driven by God's force
> Then is he a miracle doing miracles
> For only so can he be Nature's king."

GANDHIAN ETHICS AND SUSTAINABLE GLOBAL ECONOMY

When one looks at the global economy, one finds unbalanced economic development of various parts of the world. Even in one particular country, the economic prosperity/development appear quite unbalanced. There are islands of the so-called prosperity amidst the sea of poverty and exploitation. Moreover, the revenue generation emphasizes on wrong means contrary to Gandhian thought and practice. A large portion of revenue is generated by the sale of liquor and associated addictive materials and the plea is given that this revenue will be used for social sectors affecting the lives of the so called underprivileged in a positive way. The ethical considerations are thrown to wind in the process. The vicious cycle continues and suffering grows in proportion. A poet has nicely described the situation in the following couplets:

> '*Kabhi nahi lag sakta yaron mayakhane me tala*
> *Ek-do-teen-char nahi, sara shahar hai pinewala*'
> (i.e., the liquor shop cannot be closed as not one, two, three people drink but the whole town is drunkard)

More and more people become addicted to alcohol and other bad habits and the problems continue to increase in quality and quantity. The saying proves correct—'*Jas jas suarasa badan badhava, tasu dun kapi roop dekhava'*.

Hence, it is the need of the hour to incorporate Gandhian ethics in our economic activities so as to bring lasting peace and prosperity for mankind. If we want to have a sustainable global economy, we have to nurture it on the principles of trusteeship for the welfare of all. As Kalam puts it beautifully, "perhaps there is so much conflict between peoples and nations because in our pursuit of prosperity and power, we have lost sight of ethical values." Gandhiji said, 'True economics stands for social justice, it promotes the good of all equally including the weakest and is indispensable for decent life...That economics is untrue, which ignores or disregards moral value. The extension of the law of non-violence in economics means nothing less than the introduction of moral values as a factor to be considered in regulating international commerce.'

In fact, the global conflict and struggle for supremacy is the direct result of absence of ethical considerations in commerce to a large extent. The exploitative economic regimes are the result of unethical practices in wealth generation. Hence, for a sustainable global economy ensuring peace and prosperity for mankind, Gandhian ethics is a must.

BLENDING OF GANDHIAN ETHICS AND MODERN ECONOMICS

If we want to make human life on this planet free from want, disease and destruction, we have to fundamentally change the way we regard our economic activities. We must learn to differentiate our needs from our desires, our illusions from the reality and simplify our life on the lines of Gandhian ethics. Unless we do so, our dream for a prosperous and peaceful world beyond any conflict will not be translated into reality. We have seen that the numerous permutations and combinations of models of economic development have failed miserably in solving the problems of man because of their basic limitation of confusing means for ends and not considering means as important as the ends. This dilemma is beautifully solved through Gandhian ethics and thus a prosperous economy based on Gandhian ethics paves the way of real enrichment and fulfilment in human life.

CONCLUSIONS

We can conclude by quoting from Marglin (2008):

> "Economists celebrate the market as a device for regulating human interaction without acknowledging that their enthusiasm depends on a set of half truths: that individuals are autonomous, self-interested, rational calculators with unlimited wants and that the only community that matters is the nation-state. However, market relationships erode other forms of community. In the past for example, people supported each other in adversity. A fire or illness was an occasion on which the community pitched in. Now if my house burns down, or I become disabled, I turn not to my neighbours but to my insurance company. Insurance may be a more efficient way to organize resources than a community engaging in mutual help, but the deep social and human ties that are constitutive of community are weakened by the shift from reciprocity to market relations."[23]

We can thus say that for modern man to live in harmony with the world outside and at peace within oneself, the best alternative seems to make our market economy geared to human welfare instead of its present pre-occupation with wealth manipulation. This can be best achieved through Gandhian ethics being incorporated as the guiding principles of our economic activities. As things stand today, we cannot revert to the model of *Gram Swarajya* of Gandhiji overnight, but it is within our hands to adopt, in spirit, the principles of individual as well as collective living rooted in Gandhian ethics for enrichment and fulfilment in life. In words of Sriman Narayan, this will ensure not just raising the *standard of our living* but also the *standard of life*.

NOTES

1. Gandhi, M.K. (1909), *Hind Swaraj*, Ahmedabad: Navjivan Publishing House, p. 33.
2. Gandhi, M.K. (1960): *Trusteeship*, Ahmedabad: Navjivan Publishing House, pp. 2-3.
3. Gandhi, M.K. (1959), *The Message of the Gita*, Ahmedabad: Navjivan Publishing House, p. 17.
4. Gandhi, M.K. (19), *India of My Dreams*, Ahmedabad: Navjivan Publishing House, pp. 14-16.
5. Hegde, B.M. (2010), Do We Have the Will to Make Poverty History; *Bhavan's Journal*, Vol. 57, No. 4; Sept. 30, 2010. Mumbai: Bharatiya Vidya Bhavan.
6. Kumar, Ravindra (2010): 'Love for Humanity: A Gandhian Perspective'; *Bhavan's Journal*, Vol. 57, No. 4; Sept. 30, 2010. Mumbai: Bharatiya Vidya Bhavan.
7. Manav Seva Sangha: *Dharma Vijnana in Sadhana Triveni*, Vrindaban, Mathura: Manav Seva Sangha, 2006, pp. 43-54.
8. Manav Seva Sangha: '*Vishva Shanti*' in *Sadhana Triveni*, Vrindaban, Mathura: Manav Seva Sangha, 2006, pp. 99-114.
9. Swami Ranganathananda (1966), *Eternal Values for a Changing Society*. Mumbai: Bharatiya Vidya Bhavan, pp. 114-15.
10. Gandhi, M.K. (2001), *Anasakti Yoga*, Ahmedabad: Navjivan Publishing House.
11. Kalam, A.P.J. Abdul (2002), *'Ignited Minds'*, New Delhi: Penguin Books India Pvt. Ltd.
12. Pratap, R. (2009), *Gandhian Management—The Paragon of Higher Order Management*, Mumbai: Jaico Publishing House.
13. Sri Aurobindo, (1996), *Essays on Gita*, Sri Aurobindo Ashram.
14. Sri Aurobindo (1996), *The Mother*, Pondicherry: Sri Aurobindo Ashram, Pondicherry, pp. 17-18.
15. Sri Aurobindo (1988), *Life Divine*, Pondicherry: Sri Aurobindo Ashram.
16. Vinoba Bhave (1996): *Thoughts on Education*, Varanasi: Sarva Seva Sangha.
17. Krishnamurti, J. (2002): *Beyond Violence*, Chennai: Krishnamurti Foundation India, pp. 3-4.
18. Sharma, J.N. (2003), *Alternative Economics: Economics of Mahatma Gandhi and Globalization*, New Delhi: Deep & Deep Publications.
19. Sriman Narayan (1970), *Relevance of Gandhian Economics*, Ahmedabad: Navjivan Trust & Publishing House.
20. Fullbrok, E. ed. (2004), *A Guide to What is Wrong with Economics*, London: Anthem Press.
21. Basham, A.L. and A. Bhattacharjee (1988), *The Father of the Nation*, New Delhi: Ashish Publishing House.
22. Ramachandran, G. and T.K. Mahadevan, (eds.) (1967), *Gandhi: His Relevance for Our Times*, New Delhi: Gandhi Peace Foundation.
23. Marglin, Stephen A. (2008), *The Dismal Science—How Thinking Like an Economist Undermines Community*, New Delhi: Oxford University Press.

16
Can *Swadeshi* Help Solve Contemporary Economic Problems?

D.M. Diwakar

All of a sudden in the year 2009 almost every forum with Gandhian overtone has started discussing the *Hind Swaraj*. Most of them including Government of India have little concern about the Gandhian alternative development paradigm. They are busy in celebrating centenary of the *Hind Swaraj*, as the funds are flowing to legitimize with the Gandhian legacy. Although Gandhi has often been used for convenience what he was not. A century ago Mahatma Gandhi reflected on encountering crises of civilization and brought a seminal document before the world in general and India in particular, i.e., the *Hind Swaraj* or Indian Home Rule. The *Hind Swaraj* is an interactive dialogue between Reader and Editor, which he visualized regarding his framework of *Swaraj*. For Mahatma, *Swaraj* is not merely transfer of power and governance from the British to the Indians[1] rather it is a blue print of an alternative vision and path of development, which focuses on social, economic, political and cultural emancipation with harmonious model of development based on cooperation. Gandhiji has been an ever evolving practitioner open to modifications in his strategies, which have been reflected in his writings but there is seldom change in the broader canvas of visions and goals. Explaining on the question as to when India can become free Gandhiji said: "If we become free, India is free ... It is *Swaraj* when we learn to rule ourselves... such *Swaraj* has to be experienced, by each one for himself."[2] In this whole treatise of the *Hind Swaraj* he emphasized on *inter alia* three important elements, i.e., "1. Real home-rule is self-rule or self-control. 2. The way to it is passive resistance: that is soul-force or love-force. 3. In order to exert this force, *swadeshi* in every sense is necessary."[3] These elements remained guiding force for Indian freedom struggle led by Gandhiji. However, the term passive resistance was replaced during the course of his practices when he evolved an original and more meaningful term *satyagraha*. Towards culmination of freedom struggle a day came when India was celebrating independence, but Gandhiji did not appreciate so much underlining his disagreement that so long there was communal strife in the country, people were unfed, half fed and ill-clad, joyous moment was not desirable. He believed that *satyagraha* and non-cooperation[4] remained sanctions of non-violent paradigm and *swadeshi* or *swaraj* which he called "poor man's *swaraj*", where 'no one is to be the first and none the last'[5], i.e., equality. For Gandhiji poor man's *swaraj* was the hallmark of *swaraj*. Unfortunately, vision of reconstruction of village worked out by Gandhiji, which runs through pages of Village *swaraj* was summarily rejected in his lifetime by his esteemed colleagues and the village could not attract desired focus of planned development. Needless to mention that during the days of freedom struggle against the British colonial rule in India, three most popular and basic agenda emerged from the people—land to the tillers, irrigation for every field, and work to every hand coming forward. Import substitution and self sufficiency was broader spirit and guideline for the development of the country when country was moving towards independence. However, the fact remained that ruling class succumbed to the priority of the Bombay Plan of industrialization, which dominated over other plans, i.e., Gandhian Plan prepared by Shrimannarayan and People's Plan prepared by trade unions. For the time being it appeared for many of us that national bourgeoisie took over the hegemonic role. However, this illusion could not continue for long when India succumbed to the pressure of United States to devaluate its currency and maintain humiliating silence during 1960s.

After transfer of power, from the British to Indian ruling class, many steps were initiated to counter the challenges of food self sufficiency through changing property relations (i.e., abolition of zamindari system), creating infrastructure and technological development. As a result, production and productivity has increased significantly. But access to food for poor always remained a big challenge till today, which is not only linked with production but also with sustainability of production and productivity and distribution. With the present regime of liberal policies and multilateral trade relations, meaning of self-reliance at the food front has been changed. Availability of foreign exchange ruled the scenario to secure food through trade and hence question of food security/insecurity emerged as one of the major concerns with new dimensions of challenges. Therefore, the question of food insecurity which has been closely linked with food diplomacy and food sovereignty even after the so-called green revolution, acquired strategic significance after obligatory import bindings of foodgrains under World Trade Organization Agreement on Agriculture. We are reminded of the messages of Gandhiji in the centenary year of the *Hind Swaraj* that *swaraj* could not be protected without *swadeshi* for long[6].

Generally questions are raised whether Gandhian concept of *swadeshi* is still relevant in the era of global market syndrome particularly when national rigidity is fading away and globalization is generally argued as anti thesis to *swadeshi*. In the present policy regime of globalization of market besides assurances of the elegant expectations and elusive deliverance, many concepts and definitions have also witnessed modifications and changes and so there is change in the concept of self-reliance also. It has been equated with purchasing power, (i.e., enabling payment of goods and services in the global market) assuming that everything will be at the disposal of foreign exchange. It is subjected to examination whether trade has ever been free from politics, specially, when it comes to sensitive items like food and energy. With the emergence of new regime of trade with World Trade Organization (WTO) impacts on millions of peasants also need to be examined. Policy makers have been talking of the issues of food insecurity but the more serious question is of implications on food sovereignty.

Objective assessment of the situation is an imperative need of the hour. This chapter is an attempt to examine the question of agrarian challenges and food sovereignty with a perspective of *swadeshi* as an alternative to globalizing market and industrialism. This exercise is divided in four parts besides introduction. Part one provides a brief account of the agrarian structure and status of food economy followed by contours of agrarian challenges in part two. Factual instances linked with the questions of food self sufficiency, security and sovereignty has been dealt in part three. Part four is intended to examine the framework of *swadeshi* to address the questions of marginalization along with food self sufficiency and sovereignty and finally part five is an endeavour to consolidate imperatives and options.

PART I
AGRARIAN STRUCTURE AND STATUS OF FOOD ECONOMY

Needless to say that agriculture continues to be the mainstay for majority of the population in India. Over 56.5 per cent of the workforce and 61.7 per cent of the rural workforce—35.9 per cent self employed and 25.8 per cent agricultural labours are still directly dependent on this sector for their livelihood[7]. Out of self-employed workforce majority of holdings are of marginal and small farmers. About 63 per cent holdings are of marginal farmers which have only 18.82 per cent operational holdings (Table 16.1). About 18.88 per cent small farmers have 20.17 per cent operational area. Semi-medium holdings were 11.66 per cent and operated 23.96 per cent of area and almost similar amount of area were operated by 5.44 per cent medium holdings and about 1 per cent of large holdings operated 13.21 per cent of area. This shows inequality in distribution of land.

Table 16.1: Per Cent Distribution of Holdings and Area Operated by all Social Groups in India

Sl. No.		1970-71	1980-81	1990-91	2000-01
1.	Marginal	50.98	56.39	59.44	63.00
2.	Small	18.92	18.08	18.84	18.88
3.	Semi-Medium	15.04	14.01	13.06	11.66
4.	Medium	11.17	9.08	7.11	5.44
5.	Large	3.90	2.44	1.55	1.02
6.	All Sizes	100.00	100.00	100.00	100.00
Percentage of Operated Area					
1.	Marginal	9.00	12.05	15.04	18.82
2.	Small	11.89	14.14	17.42	20.17
3.	Semi-Medium	18.50	21.15	23.19	23.96
4.	Medium	29.75	29.64	27.04	23.84
5.	Large	30.88	23.02	17.32	13.21
6.	All Sizes	100.00	100.00	100.00	100.00

Source: GoI, Agriculture Census 2000-01.

Table 16.2: Average Size of Operational Holdings in India (Excluding Jharkhand)

Size Group	1970-71	1980-81	1990-91	2000-01*
Marginal	0.40	0.39	0.39	0.40
Small	1.44	1.44	1.43	1.41
Semi-Medium	2.81	2.78	2.76	2.72
Medium	6.44	6.02	5.90	5.80
Large	18.10	17.41	17.33	17.18
All Sizes	2.28	1.84	1.55	1.32

Source: As cited in Table 16.1.

There is another point to note that number of small holdings remained almost constant in last 30 years with marginal variations. However, area under operation has increased. Moreover, number of holdings under medium and large categories of holdings has decreased over the years but area under their operation is disproportionately higher than other holdings. It is evident from the data that number of holdings has been increasing in different farm sizes consequent upon sub-division and fragmentation of land on account of natural attrition through population pressure.

Prevalence of inequality in distribution of land is also reflected in average size of holdings by size groups displayed in Table 16.2. Average size of marginal, small and semi-medium holdings remained almost stagnant with marginal variations. Average size of holdings for medium and large has also declined marginally. Taking all size together average size of holdings have been declining significantly. It is important to note here that Gandhiji was of the opinion that land belongs to God (Gopal) and he was against fragmentation of holdings.[8] Initially he advocated that zamindars should act as trustee of land but gradually he learnt in the process of freedom movement that the question of equity and access to land to the direct producer can help in eradication of poverty and, therefore, he changed his stands[9] and advocated that land should belong to the tillers: "No man should have more land than he needs for dignified sustenance. Who can dispute the fact that the grinding poverty of the masses is due to their having no land that they can call their own?"[10] Thus, he insisted on state initiatives for redistribution of land to the tillers for poverty eradication. However, land reforms remained a distant dream and unfinished agenda towards land to the tillers.

Despite the fact that agriculture has grown significantly, the contribution of agriculture has gradually been declining from 59.2 per cent of gross domestic product (GDP) in 1950-51 to 18.5 per cent in 2006-07[11]. Contribution of agriculture to GDP has been declining not only because the other sectors are growing fast but also because of continued neglect of this sector leading to decline in rural income. During pre green revolution (1951-52 to 1967-68) total economy grew by 3.7 per cent whereas agriculture grew by 2.5 per cent, crops and livestock by 2.7 per cent and non-agriculture grew relatively faster, i.e., 4.9 per cent as infrastructure building initiatives and community development programmes made a dent at the initial years of planning (Table 16.3). Interestingly average growth rate of total economy in post-green revolution period until 1980-81 was only 3.5 per cent and of agriculture and allied sectors was 2.4 per cent, and non-agriculture was 4.4 per cent which were slightly lower than earlier period. Growth rate of total economy in 1980s (1981-82 to 1990-91) known for wider dissemination of technology was 5.4 per cent.

Table 16.3: Average GDP Growth Rates of Agriculture and Other Sectors at 1999-2000 Prices (Per Cent)

	Period	*Total Economy*	*Agriculture & Allied Sectors*	*Crops & Live-Stock*	*Non-Agri-culture*
Pre-Green Revolution	1951-52 to 1967-68	3.7	2.5	2.7	4.9
Green Revolution	1968-69 to 1980-81	3.5	2.4	2.7	4.4
Wider Technology					
Dissemination	1981-82 to 1990-91	5.4	3.5	3.7	6.4
Early Reforms	1991-92 to 1996-97	5.7	3.7	3.7	6.6
Ninth and Tenth Plan	1997-98 to 2006-07	6.6	2.5	2.5	7.9

Source: GoI (2008): *Economic Survey 2007-2008*, p. 155.

Agriculture and allied sectors were also at their best at 3.5 per cent. Crops and livestock grew even higher at 3.7 per cent and non-agriculture by 6.6 per cent. This period was known best period of growth up to that period. During early reforms, i.e., between 1991-92 and 1996-97 total economy grew by higher rate of growth, i.e., 5.7 per cent. Agriculture and allied sectors and crops and livestock also grew by 3.7 per cent each. Non-agriculture also shown higher growth rate to the tune of 6.6 per cent. During Ninth and Tenth Plan total economy achieved highest rate of growth so far and non-agriculture was also high. However, agriculture and allied sectors and crops and livestock suffered deceleration later in last one decade (1997-98 to 2006-07) and grew only by 2.5 per cent. Crop-wise growth rates of area, production and yield suggest that overall growth rates of area, production and yield of all principal crops during 1949-50 to 2007-08 were 0.51, 2.57 and 1.64 per cent, for foodgrains 0.27, 2.35 and 1.77 per cent and for non-foodgrains 1.22, 2.92 and 1.40 per cent respectively (Table 16.4). It is claimed that agriculture has progressed significantly in terms of production and productivity and country has been relatively comfortable at food front also.

Table 16.4: Compound Growth Rates of Area, Production and Yield of Principal Crops since 1949-50 to 2006-07 (Base TE 1981-82=100)

Crop	*1949-50 to 2007-08*			*1949-50 to 1964-65*			*1967-68 to 2007-08*		
	A	*P*	*Y*	*A*	*P*	*Y*	*A*	*P*	*Y*
Cereals	0.32	2.69	2.02	1.25	3.21	1.77	–0.07	2.48	2.18
Pulses	0.08	0.56	0.50	1.72	1.41	–0.18	0.02	0.75	0.70
Foodgrains	0.27	2.35	1.77	1.35	2.82	1.36	–0.05	2.25	1.99
Non-Foodgrains	1.22	2.92	1.40	2.44	3.74	0.89	1.26	3.06	1.61
All	0.51	2.57	1.64	1.58	3.15	1.21	0.29	2.56	1.86

Source: *Agriculture Statistics at a Glance 2008*, Ministry of Agriculture, GoI. http://dacnet.nic.in/eands/At_Glance_2008/rates_new.html

Production of foodgrains increased from 50.8 million tonnes in 1950-51 to 216 million tonnes in 2006-07. In pre-Green Revolution period growth rates of all principal crops, in terms of their area production and yield were 1.58, 3.15, 1.21 per cent, foodgrains 1.35, 2.82, 1.36 per cent and non foodgrains 2.44, 3.74, 0.89 per cent respectively. Post Green Revolution data of growth rates suggest that area and production of all principal crops had lower rate of growth but yield registered higher rate of growth than that of pre green revolution period. So, far non-foodgrains are concerned, growth rates of area and production witnessed deceleration. However, productivity registered increasing trend from 0.89 per cent to 1.61 per cent. In case of foodgrains area declined, production registered lower rate of growth and yield rate increased.

Comparison of 1980s and 1990s suggests that in case of all principal crops area increased in 1990s but production and productivity registered deceleration. In case of foodgrains area declined, production and productivity encountered lower rate of growth than 1980s. So far non-foodgrains are concerned area, production and productivity indicated an increasing trend with deceleration, i.e., lower rate of growth than 1980s, as displayed in Table 16.5. However, during 2000-01 to 2007-08 there were overall sign of recovery reflected in growth rates of area, production and yield of cereals, pulses, total foodgrains, and taking all the principal crops together. We also know that on an average, this sector grew at the rate of 2.5 per cent during 1950-51 to 2007-08.

Table 16.5: Annual Compound Growth Rates of Principal Crops during 1980s and 1990s in India

Crop	1980-81 to 1989-90			1990-91 to 1999-2000			2000-01 to 2007-08		
	A	P	Y	A	P	Y	A	P	Y
1	2	3	4	5	6	7	8	9	10
Total Cereals	−0.26	3.03	2.90	0.04	−0.02	1.59	0.16	1.95	3.10
Total Pulses	−0.09	1.52	1.61	−0.60	0.59	0.93	1.91	3.42	1.65
Total Foodgrains	−0.23	2.85	2.74	−0.07	2.02	1.52	0.48	2.09	2.82
Non-Foodgrains	1.12	3.77	2.31	1.18	2.69	1.09	2.46	5.09	3.87
All Principal Crops	0.10	3.19	2.56	0.27	2.29	1.33	1.06	3.17	3.88

Source: Agriculture at a Glance 2008, GoI.

Per capita availability of cereals has gone up from 334.2 gram per day in 1950-51 to slightly higher level, i.e., 390.9 gram per day in 2005-06. However, per capita availability of pulses in reference period has gone down from 60.7 gram per day to 31.5 gram[12]. Caloric distribution has been indicating adverse movement. During 55th round of NSSO, i.e., in 1999-2000 about 74 per cent of rural households was below 2400 kcal[13] and after 61st round this figure went further down to the level of about 81.4 per cent[14]. If one looks at the production of foodgrains it is evident that with a few exceptions production has not declined significantly in recent years. Therefore, it is not simply the question of supply but of access and distributional aspects. But import of foodgrains has been made in the pretexts of food security generally at higher price than domestic. Import of cereals and cereal preparations are on rise in recent years. It has increased from 20 million dollars in 2000-01 to 26 million dollars in 2004-05 and further to 36 million dollars in 2005-06.[15] Moreover, obligatory binding of the import of foodgrains under WTO has become a rider on self sufficiency. We have been importing wheat from international market in the name of meeting requirements of foodgrains at much higher price than our farmers are paid.

PART II
CONTOURS OF AGRARIAN CHALLENGES

Indian agriculture irrespective of the size of holdings has been experiencing worst forms of crises culminated and manifested in starvation and tragic suicides of its producers, who have been feeding the nation. Besides unregistered starvation in backward regions in absence of employment at least at subsistence level, even diversified and prosperous agriculture of Punjab, petty cotton growers of Maharashtra, Andhra and Karnataka are also not spared from this trap. Expert Group on agrarian crisis underlines suicides as a disturbing symptom of deep-rooted crises that Indian agriculture has been confronting. Broadly two dimensions of agrarian crises—low growth with declining productivity and high dependence of population on lower farm income have been the root causes. Reflecting a little further stagnation, increasing risk in production and marketing, collapse of the extension system, growing institutional vacuum, and the lack of alternative livelihood opportunities, etc., are *inter alia* main factors behind agrarian crisis[16]. Challenges of the syndrome of fatigue at the front of technology, institution, policy and governance have been debated at length.[17]

Expansion of irrigation network, use of modern technology—HYV seeds, chemical fertilizer, pesticide combined, etc., changed cropping pattern remarkably. Cropping intensity also improved to the level of 134 per cent but percentage coverage of foodgrains did not change significantly until 1980-81. Coverage of total cereals hardly changed and remained at the level of about 75 per cent. During 1990-91 to 2000-01 it remained around 65 per cent. Coverage of oil seeds, fruits and vegetables almost doubled and area under HYV increased from 1.2 per cent of GCA to 41.17 per cent. Paddy coverage of HYV has increased from 0.56 per cent in 1966-67 to 17.34 per cent in 1998-99, wheat from 0.34 to 12.61 per cent, jowar from 0.12 to 4.89 per cent, bajra from 0.04 to 3.76 and maize 0.13 to 1.89 per cent of GCA.

Important factors *inter alia* for such poor performance was continued neglect of agriculture towards structural inequity, prevailing non-development syndrome in infrastructure, lack of adequate budgetary allocation of resources for investment. Agricultural investment to GDP witnessed declining trend over the years. During 1985-86 it was 2.3 per cent at 1993-94 prices, which declined to 1.6 per cent in 1989-90 and continued to decline further to 1.4 per cent in 1999-2000 and 1.3 per cent in 2003-04. Even at prices of 1999-2000 the level of investment in 2003-04 was 1.9 per cent and remained stagnated at 1.9 per cent only for three consecutive years, i.e., up to 2005-06.[18] This clearly indicated a decline in investment in real terms.

Realization at the level of the Planning Commission of the Government of India suggests that private investment cannot be sustained without sustained public investment. Thus, syndrome of non-development left this sector underperformed. Much hope is pinned on Bharat Nirman Yojana to expand irrigation network. But the provision made under this scheme in the budget of current financial year does not appear consistent with targets. With this speed the target of covering additional 10 million hectares under irrigation will take at least 17 years.

Cost of cultivation increased significantly with the increasing use of modern technology across the States. Difference in cost and price structure is another dimension for examination of the viability of the crops. For example, farm harvest price/cost of cultivating cotton ratio in 1997-98 in Haryana, was 0.8633 with respect to Desi and 0.9656 for American cotton and in Punjab 0.5515 and 0.6914 respectively. In Maharashtra price-cost ratio was 0.9452. Thus, farmers of these States were not in a position to recover even cost from the returns. In case of paddy Andhra Pradesh, however, was getting Rs. 445 price per quintal against cost of cultivation Rs. 436.77. Escalating cost of production with poor returns from agriculture amidst uncertainty of monsoon, risk of crop failures, absence of effective insurance cover, and almost non-existence of extension services pushed farmers into unprecedented hardships. Terms of trade remained against agriculture even after termination of industrial protection and devaluation of rupee in 1991.[19]

Data also suggest that about 40 per cent of the farmers did not like to continue with agriculture.[20] About 27 per cent were reluctant to continue in this occupation precisely because of non-viability. Inter-State variations were even higher than that of all-India figures. About 36 per cent of the farmers of Bihar, and West Bengal; 34 per cent of Orissa; 30 per cent of Haryana and Jharkhand; 29 per cent of Maharashtra; and even 28 per cent of the farmers of Punjab which is agriculturally one of the most developed regions; and Kerala, one of the most developed States in terms of social development indicators of the country; and Karnataka, and 30 per cent farmers of Haryana did not like agriculture occupation.

Encountering deceleration resulted into lower farm income and widening gap between agricultural and non-agricultural income. Therefore, major challenge is not simply to attain higher growth target in agriculture, which has been projected at 4 per cent in Eleventh

Five Year Plan, but to include agricultural labourers and marginal and small farmers participating in the growth process effectively. In order to make them to participate in the growth process institutional, infrastructure and technological constraints need to be addressed on priority basis. This sector by and large is dependent on vagaries of monsoon and unprotected from the risks of crop failures despite expansion of significant network of irrigation. Rising cost of cultivation, embedded with insufficient infrastructure support and slowing down of employment and income, left farmers trapped in the syndrome of indebtedness and despair.[21] NSSO survey report suggests that about 48.6 per cent of the farmers' households were indebted with an average outstanding loan amount of Rs. 12,585. Out of indebted farmers households, 31.3 per cent were from the category of landless and below marginal farmers; 29.8 per cent were from marginal farmers; and 18.8 per cent from small farmers category. Thus, altogether 80 per cent of the indebted households were from the poorest lot in terms of land in possession. Prevalent rate of indebtedness of landless labour households of rural area were 45.3 per cent, who owed on an average Rs. 6,121. With the increasing size of land in possession prevalent rate of indebtedness increased and so was the amount of loan. Considering per farmer loan amount by monthly per capita expenditure (MPCE), extent of indebtedness was higher in lower consumption bracket. With the increase in monthly per capita expenditure percentage of indebtedness decreased. However, amount of loan per farmer remained positive with the increasing monthly per capita expenditure. Indebtedness by social groups suggest that spread of indebtedness and loan amount was lowest in STs and second lowest in SCs. OBCs reported higher spread of indebtedness and amount of loan than SCs but lower spread and higher amount of loan than general category of social group. State-wise distribution of farmers' indebtedness suggests even more pathetic concerns than macro picture. Amount of loan taken was generally utilized for production and consumption purposes. Data suggest that 30.6 per cent of loan amount was spent for capital expenditure in farm business followed by current capital expenditure (27.8%). Non-farm business consumed 6.7 per cent. Thus, altogether 65 per cent loan amount was directly used for production purposes. Another 15 per cent was spent for social development and remaining 20 per cent was on marriage and other ceremonial occasions and on consumption expenditure. Medical treatment and other expenditure could meet significant proportion in some of the States.

Rural credit market has both formal and informal players. Formal players are government, cooperatives, commercial banks, whereas informal credit market is run by and large by moneylenders—often farmers, traders including dealers of inputs, other professionals, friends and relatives, and others operate as moneylenders. NSS data suggest that commercial banks remained major player in providing credit to farmers (35.6%) followed by cooperatives (19.6%) and government (2.5%). Altogether 57.7 per cent of credit taken by farmers was provided through institutional arrangements. Remaining 42.3 per cent credit market was controlled by informal players. These players may be categorized in one bracket of moneylenders with a few individual exceptions. It is evident from data in reference that credit extended by cooperatives and commercial banks emerged positively directed towards increasing size of holdings whereas credit extended by moneylenders had inverse direction. Landless households took 47.3 per cent loan from moneylenders alone. Adding extended informal usury network it came to 77 per cent. Near landless and marginal households took 56.7 per cent and 47.2 per cent of loan amount respectively from informal usury networks. State-wise variations suggest that non-institutional share of loan finance was higher in many States. Non-institutional finance controlled greater credit market to the tune of 68 per cent in Andhra Pradesh followed by Rajasthan, Assam, Bihar and Punjab. Although Maharashtra provided 83.8 per cent credit through institutional sources farmers were not free from distress and suicides. This suggests that provision of institutional credit is although important it alone cannot be sufficient to rescue the farmers from the syndrome of despair.

Performance of agriculture remained at lower profile with a few exceptions, thanks to unpredictable monsoon and indifference of the government towards this sector. As a result, employment in rural sector grew at declining rate.[22] Data from NSS rounds suggest that there was significant decline in employment in primary sector for both males and females.[23] Findings are supporting the apprehensions that National Rural Employment Guarantee Scheme with this speed cannot deliver the jobs to rural workforce, as implementation reports from different States is adding frustrations only. Another disturbing factor is decelerating real wage rates in agriculture and non-agriculture.[24] But the question is whether these were substantial to offset the decelerating impacts of primary sector on the income of rural economy. Decelerating growth rate suggests that this sector could not generate sufficient capital and investment even through private sector. Limited benefits of expansion of the post-green revolution technology could increase production and productivity but that also could not be sustained. Moreover, the gains could not be transferred significantly to rural poor in particular and farm sector at large in general. Rather due to lack of effective infrastructure and extension services, modern technology added confusions in absence of effective extension services, increased cost of production, and created environmental complications and imbalances added with greater intensity of exploitation of poor farmers through usury network of non-institutional credit market in absence of effective institutional credit support.

Market driven farms diversification has not necessarily designed differently but for the interests of corporate sectors, which exploited farms undermining ecological and fertility balance. Globalization and new trade regime has made framers condition vulnerable and exposed to uncertainty.[25] There is every possibility of worsening condition of poor farmers further with the emphasis on investment through corporate contract farming. Unless means of production is reoriented in favour of producers and meaningful employment and employability of poor cultivators are ensured through public sector initiatives for infrastructure development and input and output markets are regulated in the interest of producers it will be difficult to rescue farmers from the syndrome of distress and despair leading towards suicides.[26]

PART III
FOOD SELF-SUFFICIENCY, SECURITY AND SOVEREIGNTY

Achieving self-sufficiency at food front was the first and foremost task before the country identified during freedom struggle. After transfer of power, in order to unleash productive forces and to keep pace with rising demand of food and raw materials for development and providing employment to the masses of the country, abolition of zamindari system was initiated as one of the most radical steps for changing institutional arrangement. However, this tempo could not be sustained for achieving targets with a few exceptions. Tasks of land reforms and redistribution of land remained unfinished agenda and gradually it lost its steam and was relegated to background.

Although agriculture was accorded to top priority during First Five Year Plan, subsequently, from Second Five Year Plan onwards, it was pushed to the secondary position. Gradually, public investment in agriculture lost its priority and thereby self-reliant development path suffered a major setback. Gradually, it has reached as low as 1.9 per cent of the GDP. It is worth mentioning here that agriculture never got proportionate share of investment corresponding to its contribution of GDP. For example, if one takes year 2005-06 for reference, agriculture contributed 18.5 per cent of GDP, which is the lowest so far. Out of 34 per cent of total investment agriculture should have received about 6.29 per cent of GDP as proportionate share in natural course and without any favour. If one calculates due share of agriculture it becomes obvious that this sector has suffered continuous discrimination and neglect since Second Five Year Plan. As a result, private investment could also not be sustained in absence of support system and back up.

Many of us have very high appreciation of green revolution on its face value of increasing production. Appreciating their innocence and ignorance of the fact, they may not be clubbed with commitment to promote the interest of multinational agribusiness. But fact suggests that United States' "Food Aid" and "Food for Peace" which were aimed at promoting US agribusiness market for surplus, were offered as new instruments of neo-colonial rider over policy of aid receiving country. This was very much evident from the annual report of the US President in 1966 on PL-480.[27] This was followed by green revolution technology sponsored by the Rockefeller Foundation and later teamed up by the Ford Foundation to secure the interest of multinational agribusiness but in the pretext of growing demands of foodgrains and raw materials and to rescue farm sectors from low income syndrome. Green revolution technology consisted of High Yielding Variety (HYV) of seeds, plenty of water, chemiçal fertilizer, pesticides, fungicides and herbicides. HYV seeds have been less resistance of disease than traditional variety. Green revolution in India was introduced with imported liquid ammonia based energy instead of indigenously available abundance of naphtha. Supply of these new inputs-seeds, chemical fertilizer and machinery were tied with USAID loan to developing nations including India. United States (US) and the World Bank put heavy pressure on India to promote multinational agribusiness joint ventures to provide enough space to import inputs and machinery from US, even India could have supplied many of them. US fertilizer plants were based on liquid ammonia when plenty of indigenous naphtha was available.[28] We have lost many indigenous seeds in this process of HYV seed replacement and indirect transfer of seed control. Thus, self reliant guidelines and spirit of development gradually lost its space.

Many of us, who count achievement of green revolution at food front can well be appreciated, should be ready to recognize irreparable loss of indestructible power of the soil risking sustainability of agriculture. We all know that most parts of the country still lack nutritional mapping of the soil. Only a few States have recently started. Therefore, we are yet to acquire comprehensive knowledge about the nutritional deficiency of the soil of our country. Collapse of our extension services have been acknowledged by the highest office of the country. Disproportionate ratio of Nitrogen (N), Phosphorus (P) and Potash (K) has been critically disturbing the nutritional map of soil in absence of proper extension services and awareness, which has created environmental chaos. Recently, Indian Agriculture Research Institute (IARI) came out with findings that pathogens and insect population are strongly dependent upon temperature and humidity. ncrease in temperature and humidity would change their population dynamics, resulting in crop production loss. It was found that contribution of agriculture to green house gas emission, particularly of methane from paddy fields, enteric fermentation in ruminant animals and nitrous oxide due to application of chemical fertilizer. Global warming in short run is likely to favour agricultural production in Europe and North America and negatively impact crop production in South Asia, Africa and Latin America which will in turn affect international food supply, prices and trade. Impact of the global climate change on Indian agriculture indicates the possibility of loss of four to five million tonnes in wheat production with every rise of one degree Celsius temperature throughout the growing period even after considering carbon fertilization. Irrigation potential is likely to be decreased in near future in the Indo-Gangetic plains. The gross emission from Indian agriculture is likely to increase significantly in the future, if attempts are made to boost food production by excessive use of chemical fertilizer. Coverage of green revolution remained skewed and confined to a few pockets in absence of proper infrastructure, i.e., irrigation, extension services, support system and technological access. Dynamics of rising cost uncovered through inefficient administered prices, uncritical diversification, non-responsive support system, unfavourable terms of trade of agriculture, etc., compounded the challenges of food self-sufficiency.

In the Uruguay Round 1986, USA argued to end the regime of food self sufficiency. With the onset of reforms and liberalization concept of self sufficiency was replaced by food security through trade. Self reliance was given a new meaning which was defined by purchasing power underlying assumption of free trade. World Trade Organization was established to ensure level/playing field and the rule of the game was set to follow the logic of comparative advantage maximization and disadvantage minimization on the line of Ricardo and improvement thereafter through reciprocal demands by J.S. Mill and offer curves by Alfred Marshall, and also at par with the purchasing power by Gustav Cassel, which I have dealt at length elsewhere.[29] Thus, food security by way of trade assumes free access to commodity at market price where non-economic factors will not influence irrespective of the economic status of a country. But this level playing field is a myth between land and capital starved poor nations and land and capital surplus rich nations. Moreover, the trade has seldom been away from diplomatic complications and free in real sense in the history. Creation of different subjective boxes, particularly green and blue and sanitary and pheno-sanitary proviso are the testimony under which developed nations have manipulated their subsidies and trade restrictions. Moreover WTO could not be effective to impose pressure on rich countries to reduce their domestic subsidies which have been distorting trades. Rich countries have manoeuvered access through provision of obligatory imports of foodgrains to the poor nations. Access to rich market of the world has not been ensured freely. Free access of labour from poor country to rich country is another area. Therefore free trade is nothing but freedom of capital to flow in the poor countries for profit.[30]

Food sovereignty is the responsibility and autonomy of any country to meet the demand of respective country in normal and exceptional situation. We have seen the aid linked loan and technology imposed by the US and the World Bank. India could face many such situations in the past. India had to devalue her currency despite her unwillingness to get foodgrains under PL-480 in 1960s. India had to maintain humiliating silence in favour of US even if she was important leader of the non-alignment movement during US Vietnam war forced by two consecutive droughts. Pakistan and many other countries were forced to join military alliance led by US, as they were facing droughts. Undoubtedly green revolution brought some relief for many of the countries including India. Therefore, India could take independent position at the time Bangladesh war in 1971. However, during 1975 US took a cruel decision to identify only a large number of smaller countries to save from starvation for diplomatic game of numbers and India was kept in negative list. In the early 1990s, US turned down India's request for wheat on the pretext that India permitted supply of one boatload rice to Cuba which was arch enemy of the United States.[31] It will be quite refreshing to our memory when India introduced green revolution technology, Mexico extended its substantial support for HYV seeds of wheat and now following uncritical diversification for horticulture Mexico herself has become dependent on US for food. Being a small country in size perhaps she can afford to import food and survive. But a country like India, China and Russia cannot ignore their huge requirement of foodgrains. Nor it is possible for any country to supply sufficient foodgrains to these nations without vested interest when they face natural calamities. Thus, we can see that food has never been free from diplomatic relations and bilateral preoccupations. Privatization and unaccountable participation of multinational in agriculture through diversification and seed control brought the farm sector in disarray and irreparable loss and agrarian crises rocked farmers.

When one discusses supply side of agriculture one should not oversight that agriculture in India is not merely a production industry like developed nations, it is a major source of livelihood for the majority of the masses for generations beyond the commercial mechanism of market, profit and trade and is a mark of sovereignty. Moreover wheat surplus nations are rich nations—US, Canada, Western Europe, Australia, and Argentina and they are in need of market for their surplus foodgrains. Rice surplus nations are smaller. Thailand and Vietnam are notable among them but Regional Trade Agreement has also been brought under the bindings of WTO. We know that last year India has paid much higher prices to wheat imports. Even this year our Agriculture Minister is facing problems to procure wheat despite paying higher prices. Thus, food insecurity crisis is knocking our doors and sovereignty is at risk. What are the alternatives?

PART IV
DOES *SWADESHI* PROVIDE AN ANSWER?

Self-sufficiency in food, which has been the matter of basic concerns, has always been linked with the question of freedom and sovereignty. Question of self sufficiency and self reliance came up at higher plane and with better articulation on the board of political agenda when *swadeshi* movement was launched as an instrument of protest to boycott foreign goods on August 7, 1905 against British conspired partition of Bengal.[32] *Swadeshi* movement was later supported and adopted in Calcutta Congress under the leadership of Dadabhai Naoroji in 1906. It is for the first time when "*Swaraj*, Boycott, *swadeshi* and National Education became the four cardinal points of the Congress programme"[33] on the national agenda. Since then, with the progress of Indian freedom struggle, *swadeshi* added wider canvass as a tool for struggle and a vision for reconstruction of an alternative society. Gandhiji reiterated the importance of *swadeshi* and self-sufficiency in food and clothes repeatedly to acquire and protect *swaraj* of a country.[34]

Discourse of *swadeshi* as an anti thesis of globalization has often been misquoted and misappropriated with Gandhian context of 'global village' by policy makers and mainstream official academics to defend globalization of market. While mixing these two diagonally opposite concepts, (i.e., global village and globalization of market), one should not lose the sight that unlike global market based on competition, profit and exploitation, Gandhian context of the 'oceanic circle' of villages, is a manifestation of 'innumerable villages' with composite picture of a complete republic, self reliant, independent yet interdependent, equipped with sufficient highly skilled talents of workforce to command markets outside for their quality products, perfect sanitation, free from avoidable dusts, industrial education as central factors in schools integrated with art, craft, and health, based on local endowments, cooperatives and non-violence, along with space for non-cooperation and *satyagraha* as sanction to *gram swaraj*.[35] Thus, global village is an 'ever widening and never ascending oceanic circle' of 'innumerable villages'[36] full of cultural lives having complementary symbiotic and harmonious relations with *swadeshi* from local to global sphere.

Swadeshi in words of Gandhiji running through pages of his collected works has many dimensions. A few of them are placed here for conceptual clarity. "*Swadeshi* is an eternal principle whose neglect has brought untold grief to mankind. It means production and distribution of articles manufactured in one's own country."[37] It is not a temporary but permanent boycott of foreign goods to the extent of redundancy.[38] It is a "part of the non-cooperation programme"[39] and "solid action".[40] It provides employment and saves foreign exchange against imports and economic drain which has been the cause of poverty.[41] It has much larger meaning than a boycott. "It is a constructive programme."[42] Gandhiji was convinced about the efficacy of *swadeshi* and said: "It is through *swadeshi* that we shall get *swaraj*"[43] provided it is followed uncompromisingly.[44] In his view "*swadeshi* means fiscal autonomy" and "*swadeshi* may be called *swaraj* also".[45] He used '*swadeshi* or *swaraj*' interchangeably[46] and he considered *swadeshi* as a golden key to *swaraj*.[47]

Swadeshi is one of the important dimensions of this alternative paradigm of development, which should be examined in an integrated framework and not in isolation. *Swadeshi* for Mahatma Gandhi has deeper meaning and wider domain of religious, political and economic life[48] than in notional and symbolic sense of attire and consumption, observance of which has a 'subtle moral bearing'.[49] "*Swadeshi* is intended not so much to bring pressure upon the Government as to demonstrate the capacity for sacrifice on the part of the men and women of India".[50] Use of force is also not acceptable to propagate and popularize the idea of *swadeshi*. "It must be a mark of freedom and respectability".[51] He was of the view that "He who serves his neighbour serves the world".[52] Observance of *swadeshi* is to identify with neighbours and surroundings on priority basis even if one has to forgo many considered essentials.[53] Mahatma Gandhi delivering his speech on *swadeshi* at Missionary Conference in Madras on February 14, 1919 said:

> "*Swadeshi* is that spirit in us which restricts us to the use and service of our immediate surroundings to the exclusion of the more remote.... In the domain of politics, I should make use of the indigenous institutions and serve them by curing of their proved defects. In that of economics, I should use only things that are produced by my immediate neighbour and serve those industries by making them efficient and complete where they might be finding wanting. It is suggested that such *swadeshi*, if reduced to practice, will lead to

> millennium. And as we do not abandon our pursuit after the millennium because we do not expect quite to reach it within our time, so may we not abandon *swadeshi* even though it may not be fully attained for generations to come."[54]

Analysing further with an alternative world view he rooted his historical insights and deducted inferences about the mass poverty which according to him is the result of the 'ruinous departure from *swadeshi*'.[55] *Swadeshi* begins from household economy and gets expansion throughout the world but basic spirit of the expansion of activities remains consistent with neighbourhood and utilitarian framework away from competitive market. "An individual's service to his country and humanity consisted in serving his neighbour. ... it was their duty to support their farmers, their artisans, such as weavers, carpenters, etc."[56] In other words *swadeshi* advocates facilitics for lives with mutual cooperation and interdependence and not for exploitation and faceless profits as globalization does. In pursuance of *swadeshi* every village will be self supporting and self contended. However, one has to find his/her neighbour for exchange of commodities that is not possible to produce locally.[57] This in no case is the situation of going back to barter mode but of occupation based on cooperation, quality training and improvement. If we are able to solve the problems at household level and in the neighbourhood, through them we will be serving the whole nation and humanity. But "To use foreign articles because we do not like indigenous one is to be a foreigner".[58] Therefore, *swadeshi* demands sacrifice of the liking for foreign goods.[59] Gandhiji was of the view that if the economy of which the people could not well order their own needs of food and clothing was not at all fitted to enjoy *swaraj*. Without food and clothes there is hardly any country on the earth where people could retain their *swaraj*. If they could manage their *swaraj* it could be 'devilish *swaraj*' and the people of that country must either deceive or exploit other countries by their act and their diplomacy and obtain their food and clothing or they must do so by force. History suggests that those nations that failed to maintain their economic independence for want of policy of *swadeshi* has fallen. Therefore, fiscal autonomy in real terms makes *swadeshi* meaningful.[60] "Real reforms that India needs, is *swadeshi* in its true sense."[61] But it is "more than reforms"[62]. "India's freedom was always bound up with the adoption of *swadeshi*".[63] Thus, *swadeshi* is patriotic and exclusive and also inclusive.[64] It is a mission to create an alternative order and, therefore, "*swadeshi* is *satyagraha*".[65]

It is not merely rhetoric, attire and native pride but a solution of misery, unemployment and poverty also. Therefore, simply producing things in a geographical domain may not serve the objectives of *swadeshi* if the initiatives do not cater employment and livelihood to masses to get rid of deprivation of basic necessities. Edifice of *swadeshi* although started with the concept of production to defeat the colonial interest but extended to employment generation and removal of poverty.[66] If one browses through the writings of Gandhiji, dependence on women for the success of *swadeshi* movement in India has been articulated several times in his speeches and communication as *swadeshi* is aimed to earn a modest livelihood.[67] He was emphatic in his view while joining home rule league in 1920 and said: "India's economic emancipation and moral regeneration can only be achieved through *swadeshi*. I would, therefore, exact a promise from every candidate for election to the Legislative Assembly that he would not be afraid to levy a tariff on foreign goods to any extent necessary for protecting Indian industry".[68] Ironically today our government has been busy in removing tariffs in favour of multinational and transnational companies even at the cost of closing down 'petty producers' initiatives even in the retail sectors. Clarifying aims of *swadeshi* in 1922 Gandhi said: "The aim of *swadeshi* or *swaraj* can be and is simply this that, the starving people of India may be fed, famine may be banished from the country, the chastity of Indian women may be safeguarded and Indian children in the country may get a little milk."[69] Explaining purest form of *swadeshi* with an example of cloth Gandhi emphasized on "the use of hand-woven clothes made out of hand-spun yarns"[70] because he was concerned for clothing needs next to food, and value of import as economic drain from the country to acquire those amount of clothes at that time. Of course employment generation remained basic issues linked with *swadeshi* initiatives.

Therefore, *swadeshi* could be an answer to provide opportunity of livelihood for masses, whose marginalization has become speedier in the process of globalization. Thus, basic essence of *swadeshi* is to use local resources, technology and manpower to utilize them for the benefit of the local first on the priority basis with friendly environment. This also ensures natural propriety of the son of the soil. Nothing is acceptable from the outside of the locality at the cost of local livelihood. It is essential to say no to the outside product so long local resources have not been utilized and exhausted fully. This can give employment, eradicate poverty and provide facilities to local first, instead of becoming market for profit seeking riches. Thus, *swadeshi* is a strong hypothesis which has not been operative for validity test. This hypothesis suggests that the agrarian crises that we have discussed above might not have occurred in India, if we would have followed *swadeshi* model of development. If this concept of *swadeshi* is to be extended to the global context, issues of deprivation in absence of basic wellbeing of the poor starving billions of masses of the globe can be addressed. Therefore, in the micro framework of a national boundary *swadeshi* can be an instrument for redress of deprivation and discrimination at local level and in macro-global context as well. Therefore, *swadeshi* can be an effective paradigm for the redress of unemployment, poverty, starvation, and discriminations being encountered by poor and poor nations anywhere in the world. However, this needs an alternative process of development away from the present dominant approach. Obviously, this will not be approved by the beneficiary of this development model. Gandhiji was aware of this fact and, therefore, he suggested strategies as well anticipating insensitiveness of rich community addicted for profit through market competition. "But who is to stop her great millionaires from entering into the world competition? Certainly, not legislation; the force of public opinion, proper education, however, can do a great deal in the desired direction".[71]

PART V
IMPERATIVES AND OPTIONS

Above analysis suggests that livelihood concerns of the majority of the people in India dependent on agriculture have been aggravating with faster pace of globalization of market. Green revolution technology initially appeared a relief to maintain food self sufficiency but in the long run it could not be sustained. Environmental complications have emerged with many dimensions. Thus, it created a market for rich nations depending on their technology and production. Now with changing policy regime from food self sufficiency to food security through trade has made the situation worse without providing any viable alternative. Historical accounts suggest that food has never been free from politics. Therefore, expecting free access in the food market on the strength of foreign exchange is a dangerous proposition. Ineffectiveness of WTO to regulate rich nations is a testimony to this proposition. Moreover, alienation of poor peasants from land as their livelihood through commercialization in the interest of big business in the name of production and productivity has danger of accentuating unemployment, poverty and social tensions. Farmers are forced to commit suicides in the coils of diversification and value added unprotected agriculture. Therefore, it does not seem prudent to repeat the mistakes of the green revolution experience to complicate the situation further without critical scrutiny of implications in the name of second green revolution. Scientific researches are the evidences which suggest that uncritical use of chemical fertilizer may result in further loss of production and productivity of the soil. Unless an alternative strategy is worked out to provide meaningful livelihood and employment to the masses society may not live in peace and harmony. Therefore, reinventing *swadeshi* with composite research and development inputs in favour of poor of the nations is the need of the hour. With the present pace of structural transformation there is little scope for unskilled workforce dependent on agriculture to enter in the emerging market. In the syndrome of global melt down job losses have been rampant and threatened livelihood even in organized sector for skilled labour. Any attempt to undermine the livelihood of toiling billions will inevitably lead to further deterioration in the social harmony and peace.

Now if we reflect on the present situation of the world right from industrial revolution and colonial expansion to globalization of capital and global melt down with their agencies like IMF, IBRD and WTO, and results, particularly in the contexts of the marginalized sections and nations, it becomes necessary to recall Gandhi and his discourse in the *Hind Swaraj*, which is a blue print of an alternative vision and path for development. The *Hind Swaraj* needs to be unfolded and reinvented with reinforced role of self control, *satyagraha* and *swadeshi*[72] to mobilise and educate people to build their own society towards addressing basic questions of structural violence rooted in the present development paradigm.[73] Categorical conviction of Gandhiji in concluding chapter of the *Hind Swaraj* is guiding light towards the path of action: "We shall get nothing by asking; we shall have to take what we want, and we need the requisite strength for the effort and that strength will be available to him only who will act."[74]

NOTES

1. Gandhi, M.K. (1938), *Hind Swaraj or Indian Home Rule*, Ahmedabad: Navjivan Publishing House, pp. 26-28.
2. *Ibid.*, Ch. XIV.
3. *Ibid.*, Ch. XX.
4. *CWMG* (The Collected Works of Mahatma Gandhi), New Delhi: Publications Division, Ministry of Information and Broadcasting, Government of India, Vol. 18, p. 185.
5. Gandhi, M.K. (1959), *India of My Dreams,* Ahmedabad: Navajivan Publishing House, pp. 9, 73, 76, 100.
6. *CWMG*, Vol. 16, p. 495.
7. National Sample Survey Organisation (NSSO), 61st Round, 2006, Report No. 516, p. 23.
8. Gandhi, M.K. (1962), *Village Swaraj* (Compiled by H.M. Vyas), Ahmedabad: Navajivan Publishing House, p. 65.
9. Diwakar, D.M. (2009), "Gandhi on Equity and Land Relations in Independent India", *Gandhi Marg*, January-March, Vol. 30, No. 4.
10. Gandhi, M. K., *Village Swaraj, op. cit.*, p. 98.
11. Government of India, *Economic Survey*, Ministry of Finance, New Delhi, 2007, p. 1.
12. *Ibid.*
13. NSS *Report No. 471.*
14. *Ibid.*, No. 513.
15. Government of India, *Economic Survey, op. cit.*
16. Radhakrishna, R. (2007), *Expert Group Report on Agrarian Crisis in India*, New Delhi: Government of India.
17. Narayanamoorthy, A., "Deceleration in Agricultural Growth: Technology Fatigue or Policy Fatigue?" *Economic and Political Weekly*, Vol. 42, No. 25, June 23, 2007; See also B. Behera and P. Mishra, "Acceleration of Agricultural Growth in India: Suggestive Policy Framework", *Economic and Political Weekly*, Vol. 42, No. 42. October 20-26, 2007.
18. Government of India, *Economic Survey, op. cit.*
19. Bhalla, G. S., The State of the Indian Farmers, G. Parthasarathi Memorial Lecture in 88th Annual Conference of the Indian Economic Association, December 28, 2005.
20. NSSO, Indebtedness of Farmer Households in India, Report No. 498, 59th Round (January-December 2003), 2005.
21. Diwakar, D.M., "Inclusive Growth in India: A Case of Structural and Agrarian Challenges", *India Economic Review*, Vol. 4, 31 December, 2007.
22. Bhalla, G. S., *op.cit.*
23. NSSO, 60th Round, *Report No. 506.*
24. Sharma, H. R., Recent Trends in Wage Earnings of Agricultural Labourers: State Level Analysis for Different Social Groups, *Arth Vijnana*, Vol. XLVII, Nos. 3-4, September-December, 2005, pp. 329-344.

25. Vidyasagar, R. and K. Sunianchandra (2003), *Study on Farmers' Suicides in Andhra Pradesh and Karnataka*, CSD, NIRD, 2003.
26. Sainath, P., "Farming: It's What They Do", *The Hindu*, May 24, 2007, p.11; see also "Suicides are About the Living, Not Dead", *The Hindu*, May 21, 2007, p.13; Vidarbha, "Packaging an Anniversary", *The Hindu*, August 31, 2007; "It's Official: Distress up, Suicides Appalling", *India Together*, 22 November 2006, courtesy *The Hindu*, p.11; "When farmers Die", *India Together*, http://www.indiatogether.org/2004/june/psa-farmdie.htm; B.B. Mohanty, "We are Like the Living Dead: Farmer Suicides in Maharashtra, Western India", *Journal of Peasant Studies*, Vol. 32, No. 2, April, pp. 243-276, 2005; see also Srijit Mishra, "Farmers' Suicide in Maharashtra", *Economic and Political Weekly*, Vol. 41, No. 16, April 22-28, pp. 1538-45, 2006, see also, "Suicide Mortality Rates Across States of India", in the same issue p. 1567, 2006.
27. Rao, G.J.R. (1984), "Development of Capitalism in Indian Agriculture: Role of Multinationals and Multilaterals", in Kishna Rao, Y.V., *et al.*, (eds.), *Peasant Farming and Growth of Capitalism in Indian Agriculture,* Vijayawada: Vishalandhra Publishing House, pp. 219-20.
28. *Ibid.*, pp. 220-21.
29. Diwakar, D. M., "Implications of New International Trade Regime on Indian Agriculture: Perspectives of Food Sovereignty", *The Indian Economic Journal*, 88th Annual Conference 2005, Volume Part-I, Indian Economic Association, pp. 248-260. See also D.M. Diwakar, *Agriculture and Industry: Dynamics of Imbalances*, New Delhi: Manak Publications.
30. *Ibid.*
31. Dasgupta, Biplab (2001), "Food Security and Globalisation", in Asthana, M.D., and Medrano, Pedro (eds.): *Towards Hunger Free India: Agenda and Imperatives*, New Delhi: Manohar, World Food Programme.
32. Gandhi, M.K., *Hind Swaraj or Indian Home Rule*, *op. cit.*, Ch. II.
33. Dutt, R.P. (1940), *India Today*, Calcutta: Manisha Granthalay, Second Indian Edition, 1970 (reprint 1983), p. 330; see also Suniti Kumar Ghosh, "The Tragic Partition of Bengal", *Indian Academy of Social Sciences*, 2002, pp. 167-68.
34. *CWMG*, Vol. 16, p. 495.
35. *Harijan,* 26-07-1942; 10-11-1946.
36. *CWMG*, Vol. 85, pp. 32-34.
37. *Ibid.*, Vol. 16, p. 480.
38. *Ibid.*, Vol. 18, p. 248.
39. *Ibid.*, Vol. 20, p.16.
40. *Ibid.*, Vol. 17, p. 331.
41. *Ibid.*, Vol. 16, p. 30.
42. *Ibid.*, p. 481.
43. *Ibid.*, p. 18.
44. *Ibid.*, Vol. 18, p. 416.

45. *CWMG.*, Vol. 16, p. 124; Vol. 18, p. 416.
46. *Ibid.*, Vol. 23, p. 11.
47. *Ibid.*, Vol. 14, pp. 7, 59-60; Vol. 15, p. 197.
48. *Ibid.*, Vol. 13, p. 261.
49. *Ibid.*, p. 104.
50. *Ibid.*, Vol. 18, pp. 180, 196.
51. *Ibid.*, Vol. 20, p. 491.
52. *Ibid.*, Vol. 16, p. 80.
53. *Ibid.*, Vol. 13, p. 231.
54. *Ibid.*, p. 219.
55. *Ibid.*, p. 222.
56. *Ibid.*, Vol. 16, p. 30.
57. *Ibid.*, Vol. 13, pp. 222-223.
58. *Ibid.*, Vol. 15, p. 305.
59. *Ibid.*, Vol. 18, p. 97.
60. *Ibid.*, Vol. 15, pp. 487-89.
61. *Ibid.*, Vol. 16, p. 335.
62. *Ibid.*, Vol. 18, p. 21.
63. *Ibid.*, Vol. 16, p. 495.
64. *Ibid.*, Vol. 13, p. 224.
65. *Ibid.*, Vol. 16, p. 260.
66. *Ibid.*, Vol. 23, pp.10-11.
67. *Ibid.*, Vol. 15, pp. 291, 307; Vol.18, p. 275.
68. *Ibid.*, Vol. 17, p. 370.
69. *Ibid.*, Vol. 23, p. 11.
70. *Ibid.*, Vol. 15, p. 306.
71. *Ibid.*, Vol. 13, p. 222.
72. Gandhi, M.K., *Hind Swaraj* or *Indian Home Rule*, *op. cit.*, Ch. XX.
73. Diwakar, D.M., "Exploring *Satyagraha* against Contemporary Global Structural Violence", *Gandhi Marg*, April-June 2007, pp. 71-92.
74. Gandhi, M.K., *Hind Swaraj or Indian Home Rule.*

17

Journey of *Khadi* and Village Industries: From 'Livery of Freedom' to 'Fabric of Livelihood'

Raunak Ahmed

India is primarily an agrarian economy. A large section of its population earns its livelihood by farming. Apart from agriculture, KVI plays an important role in the rural economy. It fulfils the local needs of the people and at the same time generates employment as it is labour intensive in nature. From centuries it was an integral part of village life; from prehistoric age to medieval period spinning and weaving were in practice. In the ruins of the great civilization of Mohenjodaro, the tools used for spinning were found. The evidences provide it with more legitimacy that KVI were always a part of the Indian life. The handicrafts, cotton and silk fabrics earned lot of revenue for India. During the seventeenth and eighteenth century the Indian exports succeeded in placing it among the affluent nations of the world. It was during the pre-British rule that the KVI witnessed boom and the Indian economy as a whole. As far as the village economy was concerned, it was equally self-sufficient and operated on the principle of self-reliance. Though the division of labour was caste-based, each individual contributed to village community in their own unique way. The village industries chiefly drew their raw materials from agriculture within the village and also used to supply the finished products within the village. The need of the village was simple; hence it was met by village industries which utilized the local manpower, used locally available raw materials and created its local market. People exercised full freedom and control on their produce and raw materials and market and similarly profit. The handicraft sector which is the part of village industries enjoyed a better position in comparison to other village industries. It produced articles that had great demand in urban areas and abroad. Some of the articles appealed to the elite class and thus these handicrafts had assured market all over the world. The skills and specialization to produce these aesthetic articles was possessed by people of different communities and regions. Each region is specialized in a particular kind of product which is skilled-based and labour-intensive. Even in contemporary times, they have a distinct place in the market. The handicrafts industry has a great potential to generate employment and preserve the age old crafts and skills of the country. The KVI had an advantageous position during the seventeenth and eighteenth century.

Then came the era of Industrial Revolution. It was a crucial phase and a turning point in the history of KVI. Greed, in the form of profit maximization accompanied Industrial Revolution. It changed the entire gamut of international trade and similarly, the fate of Indian KVI. As a result of colonization, Great Britain found a potential market and provider of raw materials in India. During the nineteenth century, particularly in the mid of nineteenth century, it became difficult for KVI to compete with the machine-made goods as the latter was cheaper and the former was expensive due to its labour intensive character. Hence, the age old source of livelihood of people became endangered. During the beginning of twentieth century a large percentage of them were forced to become agricultural labourers or migrated to urban areas in search of livelihood. The Industrial Revolution marked a paradigm shift as the place of home-made products was replaced by factories and men were replaced by machines. The production by the masses was converted into mass production and the trend is still continuing. It was the decaying phase of the KVI. Different exploitative strategies were adopted by the rulers to destroy production and market of KVI. High tax rate for purchase of cotton is one such example. Similarly, the scenario changed for those involved in hand weaving and spinning. *Khadi* too had a long journey and a history of struggle for existence.

The rays of hope emerged out of this political injustice in the hands of merciless power when Mahatma Gandhi united the nation to raise their voice against the exploitative and devastative British Government. The leading Congress leaders like Bal Gangadhar Tilak had the single opinion that the reason of Indian poverty and backwardness is destruction of KVI. It was the period of 1919 to

1921 when a great transformation took place in the history of *Khadi* when Gandhi launched *Khadi* Programme in 1919 and further by the establishment of *Khadi* production centre in 1921 at Kathiawar (Gujarat). Soon it became a symbol of liberation and identity of freedom struggle. It gained national identity when the All India Spinners Association was established in 1925 for the implementation of programme throughout the country in a decentralized manner. Rahul Ramagundam well explained it when he said, "If *Khadi* was to spread it could only be through decentralized channel. The All India Spinners Association founded in 1925 was an effort towards the creation of decentralized network. Gandhi called it a purely philanthropic initiative."[1] Gandhi found KVI as the prime occupation for the self-reliant villages and India of his dream. It found place in Gandhi's constructive programme in 1935 and the whole set of strategies was formulated for the revival of KVI with special emphasis on *Khadi*. Anthony Parel explained *Khadi* as Gandhian tool which had multi-dimensional reach and influence. It is clear when he said, "*Khadi*, together with spinning and the spinning wheel, was probably the most important Gandhian political symbol. It aided the realization of four types of values which had immediate political relevance: First, economic self-sufficiency; secondly, mastery over machinery; thirdly, social and political harmony between the rich and the poor; and finally, the value of *swaraj* or national independence."[2] Nehru called *Khadi* a Livery of freedom movement. The support of Gandhi for the regeneration of KVI is clear as evident in his letter to C. Vijayaraghavachariar, he mentioned, "I am now living with the staff of All India Village Industries Association. We are trying to reproduce, so far as it is at all possible for us, the village life, and we content ourselves with what village can produce."[3] Gandhi's associates like J.C. Kumarappa worked for the promotion and rejuvenation of *Khadi*. A major shift took place after 1947 when in the Independent India, the slogan '*Khadi* the livery of freedom' lost its voice and the Planning Commission laid more emphasis on heavy industries. The large-scale industries were neither proved to be successful for employment generation nor for welfare of majority. The planning model in the post-independence era failed to acknowledge rural poverty as the central objective of development. In Jagdanand Jha's words, "The Mahalanobis model of economic growth adopted in our successive plans has belied our expectation particularly in relation to employment generation and poverty reduction."[4]

IMPORTANCE AND RELEVANCE OF KVI IN THE INDIAN ECONOMY

We can say that KVI is an integral part of the Indian economy. Since its beginning, it has been playing an important role in the growth and development of the national economy, though in recent decades, not much has been done to support its expansion or contribution to GDP (Gross Domestic Product). But GDP alone cannot decide the human development which is an important component of a balanced growth trend. As T. Krishnamurthy said, "Growth in GDP alone cannot bring justice and establish a peaceful society."[5] With the very nature of the Indian economy, which is characterized by large percentage of rural India in its fold, the KVI has all the potential to prove as a major developmental engine for the progress and development of rural masses. It can provide employment opportunities with much less capital investment. As Kulwant Singh Pathania stresses, "total production of *Khadi* caters to less than two per cent of the actual needs of the country. Yet *Khadi* has employed over two million people and provided them with a considerable level of living wages."[6] Hence, it is clear that the KVI holds an important place in labour surplus country like India. It provides a way out to rural masses at the time of leisure months of farming and act as an additional source of income too. Since it ensures them an income in the villages itself, it also reduces migration to urban areas. KVI promotes self-reliance, cooperation and entrepreneurial abilities which are essential prerequisites to fight back rural poverty. It has a unique quality to project the culture, heritage and mastery of rural Indians. It overcomes the limitation of large-scale industries and can be established in the most difficult and remote areas. KVI is sustainable as it is eco-friendly in nature and thus sustainable. This aspect of KVI makes it unique and an important area of research and development in this globalised world. According to World Commission on Environment and Development, "In general industries and industrial operation should be encouraged, that are more efficient in terms of resource use, that generate less pollution and are based on the use of renewable rather than non-renewable resource, and that minimize irreversible adverse impact on human health and the environment."[7] It makes use of the limited available resources and materials which are considered to be waste at times. The masses are directly involved in the production, management as well as distribution; hence it promotes leadership skills in the workers. Its importance further increased due to the percentage of the women involved at all the levels of production. It thus contributes indirectly to women empowerment through economic independence. A contemporary example is Shri Mahila Griha Udyog Lijjat Papad. In September 1966, KVIC formally recognized the institution. It is symbolic of women empowerment and entrepreneurial ability guided by Gandhian thoughts. Malathi Ramanathani said, "The institution aimed at promoting self-employment, dignity of labour and earning capacity of women working from home. With time, this was to be consciously developed as a discourse and an ideology, based on Mahatma Gandhi's concept of trusteeship."[8] It also covers the risk of market fluctuation as the KVI products are consumer goods; hence it ensures a continuous demands of goods. If we analyze the long term goals, we would find that KVI ensures a balanced regional industrial development. A country like India which has huge population, poverty, unemployment and limited capital, the only alternative that suits the economic and social condition is KVI. At the time of environmental degradation, when the world is concerned about global warming, the recycling features of village industries are unique. The example given by Yogesh Chandra Sharma explains the recycle features of KVI very well: "Last but not the least, cotton *Khadi* tailor cutting and old rags as well as the ravings and yarn wastes are used as the raw materials for producing the high quality handmade papers in the process, valuable forests of soft wood and bamboos, which form the raw materials for paper mills industries, are saved to maintain the equilibrium in the eco system."[9] In order to overcome the regional disparity in income and growth, decentralization is a major prerequisite which was envisioned by Gandhi. KVI is a step towards this goal. It empowers the artisans and rural people to have direct control over their produce. It thus encourages just social order. The KVI reduces the pressure on urban areas to provide the migrated rural population with employment opportunities and civic amenities to support their life. In today's scenario, the villages are increasingly becoming dependent on urban areas for their needs; in the absence of village industries, the goods are supplied from urban areas to rural areas which exhaust manpower and include overhead charges. KVI reduces this unnecessary expenditure as the locally produced goods will be marketed and consumed locally. KVI is a life supporting factor which improves the standard of living of rural masses; hence rural industrialization through KVI is the need of the hour. If we look into the production of *Khadi* it has a series of interlinked activities or processes like spinning, weaving, etc. Each of the process is simple and requires minimum skills. The KVI industries are struggling for survival in this age of globalization, industrialization and liberalization. It is crucial to realise the place that KVI holds in our economy. There is need to bring balance in regional disparity due to industrial development through the progress and expansion of KVI. It is rightly cited by Avadhesh Kumar, "It is time to recall that with the intervention of *Khadi* and Village Industries programmes much ice can be broken. But for this a closer analytical look on the present state of affairs of KVI is a must."[10]

PRESENT STATUS OF *Khadi* AND VILLAGE INDUSTRIES

Gandhi envisaged the liberation of country not only from the exploitative foreign rule but also from poverty, untouchability, unemployment, etc. To bring holistic development in India and to make the development sustainable, he always advocated reliance on indigenous resources and human skills. KVI is a way to make the change long lasting. Even after increase in the pace of industrialization and urbanization, we cannot ignore the importance of KVI. The urban areas are still dependent on rural areas to ensure their food security. In order to attain this security it is the fundamental obligation of city dwellers to retain rural population in rural areas which could only be achieved through year long employment guarantee to them. KVI, with all its uniqueness, is in accordance with our village economy, which only can ensure the above mentioned objective. It is crucial to realise the dream of Mahatma Gandhi so that the effect of development would cut across and percolate to the so-called deprived sections of society. Before bringing the desired change in the state of affairs of KVI, it is important to understand as to where we stand today. To decide the future direction of development of village in India, there should be an analytical view regarding the present status of KVI.

KVI is considered to be the part of small industries. It covers a wide range of activities and industries such as handicrafts, handloom, sericulture, manufacture of *ghani* oil, pottery, soap and paper, etc. Some of the industries such as handicrafts are particularly urban-based. Few of them such as handloom come under the periphery of both. According to *Khadi* and Village Industries Commission, "Village industry means any industry located in a rural area, population of which does not exceed ten thousand or such other figure which produces any goods or renders any service with or without the use of power and in which the fixed capital investment (in plant and machinery and land and building) per head of an artisan or a worker does not exceed fifteen thousand rupees."[11] These industries are highly diverse in nature and have their own institutional set-up and working mechanisms. The problems and challenges faced are also diverse in nature. The pattern of development, status and future prospect also varies in kind. To be precise, while analyzing the status of KVI, here it would be focussed on the *Khadi* and Village Industries Commission (KVIC) which is the prime institution of development of KVI. It was established in 1957 under the Village Industries Commission Act 1956. It has a wide range of responsibilities, from the execution of development programme to financial power as well as research assistance for development of KVI. The irony is that KVIC is regulated by the Central Government but it is not able to achieve its objectives and the numbers of achievements are much lesser than the numbers of failures. In spite of the Government policies, programmes and promises to ensure that the benefit would reach the target group, the organization is far behind in achieving its goal. One of the major reasons is government finance; in L.C. Jain's words, "KVIC on its own cannot adopt such a strategy since the method of financing of KVIC itself by the government compels tedious procedures."[12] Thus, the goals and objectives of KVIC are not well formulated and often face negligence at the implementation level. The very two-tier delivery mechanism of the Commission is at bay. Also the figures presented and the limitation explained by M.R. Rajagopalan give an unheard account in this free market economy. "At present, *Khadi* production is only 0.4 per cent of the total textile production. It gives employment to some 12 lakh persons. To increase it to even one per cent requires tremendous organizational steps."[13] The budgetary support to KVIC is clear from Table 17.1.

Table 17.1: Budgetary Support to KVIC *(Rs. crore)*

Year	*Allocation (RE)*		*Funds Released*	
	Plan	*Non-Plan*	*Plan**	*Non-Plan*
2007-08	650.40	84.82	622.99	82.80
2008-09	1104.95	107.63	1104.94	107.62
2009-10	919.20	192.41	836.00	192.38
2010-11*	1524.41	155.60	1013.21@	132.58@

Source: Ministry of Micro, Small and Medium Enterprises (MSME) Annual Report 2010-11.

But we should not blame this dependence on KVIC; it is equally important to find the root of the problem and the possible alternative. With all subsidies and rebate in the name of promotion, the textile sector which has *Khadi* and handloom sector in its fold has not witnessed much progress. "The cloth production during 2007-08 was 56,025 million sq. m. The compound annual growth rate during the last five years works out to 5.34 per cent. The total production of cloth by all sectors, i.e., mill, powerloom, handloom, hosiery and *Khadi*, wool and silk is anticipated to be 54,966 million sq. metres, during 2008-09 (Prov.) due to slowdown in economy."[14] Minoo R. Masani rightly said, "The KVIC, which was recently castigated by the Prime Minister for leaning more and more on government resources and subsidies, does not seem capable of carrying out this enormous task, and there is no alternative agency in existence which can undertake it with competence and vigour."[15] The very value of self-reliance on the foundation, of which *Khadi* once stood, is eroding gradually. In order to bring back the true spirit of KVI and improve its present status it is required to view their objectives and feasibility of its achievement in the backdrop of market challenges and formulate the future course of action.

KVI IN THE GLOBALISED WORLD

Globalisation is a process that has become well accepted and practiced phenomena. There is hardly any part of the globe which is untouched with the ever expanding reach of globalization. It has its influence on global politics, economy and as well as social life of a common man. From the cloth to food and even the water we consume is part of globalised world. The KVI is also not an exception; it has witnessed the impact of globalization that has become threat for its survival. The world is shrinking under the umbrella of globalization and claim to avail better opportunities. If we analyze the process of globalization, it will not be difficult to conclude that industrialization and development in the name of globalization viewed rural areas as the hub to cater to their needs of raw materials. The MNCs had never come near to the noble intention of rural development or an attempt to mainstream of the rural masses in the process of development. With profit maximization in mind they have tapped the minds of urban mass with much emphasis on middle income group consumption pattern, thereby creating fake sense of lack through mass media. Like the man cannot live in isolation so a country cannot live in isolation with globalization; hence, it becomes important to understand and develop strategies to remain part of the process of globalization yet protect the integral and indigenous knowledge of livelihood. KVI is one form of it. The task is indeed difficult but not impossible. A wise economic planning, keeping in mind the lowest of the low individual of the democratic India, can lead to economics of all or I would rather put it globalization for all. Without equipping the KVI sector to compete in the globalised market we have opened the doors of our economy. As Jaya Jaitly said, "The present economic policy will allow the import of all consumer items from anywhere in the world, giving a final blow to our village products in the market place."[16] In this world of competitive market economy the KVI has number of reasons to fallback. Except for some upgradation of the spinning wheel, there are not much technological developments. Difficulties in raw material access and less market development for the KVI are some of the drawbacks. The KVI products are confined to the KVIC outlets supported by subsidies and rebates. One can find rare international brand perfumes in multi-branded stores but rarely find KVI products. The problem is also identified in the Eleventh Five Year Plan document where it states, "The sale of *Khadi* production is only through the departmental outlets of either the institutions or those of the KVIC or State KVI boards. The focus is on charity and appealing to the goodness of people's hearts not on the value of the product itself."[17] Though the problem has been acknowledged, the corrective measures are witnessing the reverse in financial allocations "The outlay for industry and minerals is Rs. 46,922 crores. Out of this Rs. 6,334 crores is the total outlay for the entire village and small industries sector or a mere 7.4 per cent."[18]

It is time to redirect our attention to contemporary industrial development policies which are neglecting indigenous goods and industries such as KVI. Due to welcoming of almost all the multinational corporations the allocation of our resources are diverted towards their benefits such as agricultural land and raw material. The increase in consumerism has increased the production but not employment opportunities. Eminent economist E.F. Schumacher said, "One of the most fateful errors of our age is the belief that the problem of production has been solved. The advantage of big machine is held out as yielding large production with few workers and increase in leisure."[19]

The product promotion strategies of global and national brands have advance marketing and advertising techniques which are successful in capturing and turning the heads of the buyers. Whereas the KVI's weak brand building methods confined to a few fashion shows, as the only promotional tool is facing tough market competitions. Few fashion shows and association of top designers' names would not make much difference unless the products are made and marketed to appeal to the hearts of the common man. In the words of Geetanjali Parikh, "Marketing of *Khadi* would not have been a problem if the changes in consumption pattern and preferences were not so fast and the globalization had not influenced the product mix of the markets so significantly."[20] KVIC should appeal to the government to meet their advertising expenses on different media sources with special emphasis on TV as the cost for the 30 seconds commercial advertisement on TV is approximately Rs. 2 lakh, which the poor KVI could not meet. The support thus provided will be more sustainable than the subsidies provided. Though the KVIC is under the nurturing of central government but still there is no national level body or organization to look after the marketing needs of KVI products. The KVIC is burdened with multi-tasking in limited resources. It is rightly pointed by S.N. Singh, "There is no organization at the national level to take exclusive care of the marketing of the products of rural industry. In the stricter sense most of the rural industries function without a proper understanding of the market behaviour and market structure."[21]

As far as export is concerned, free market is the slogan of global trade. The plight is that the export efforts for the KVI products are still exploring possibilities and often undertaken on experimental basis with few exceptions. The KVI products have immense potential to grab international market specially handicrafts products, fashionable *Khadi* garments, bamboo products, herbal products, etc. But it has failed to avail the opportunity. Given below is Table 17.2 which explains the performance of KVI.

The data available presents a pessimistic story but there are optimistic examples such as effort of Uttar Pradesh KVIB for export of KVI products is an example for all and worth acknowledging. With the combined effort of Trade Fair Authority of India the team under the guidance of Vice Chairman of the Board had visited to Mauritius and succeeded in promoting Indian KVI export. Similar initiative was taken by an American in Indian setting that took the

Table 17.2: Performance of *Khadi* and Village Industries Sector

Year	Value of production (Rs Crore)		Value of Sales (Rs Crore)		Cumulative Employment (Lakh Persons)	
	Khadi	V.I.	Khadi	V.I.	Khadi	V.I.
1	2	3	4	5	6	7
2007-08	543.39	16134.32	724.39	20819.09	9.16	90.11
2008-09	585.25	16753.62	799.60	21948.59	9.50	94.41
2009-10	628.98	17508.00	867.01	23254.53	9.81	98.72
2010-11*	510.91	12317.13	784.63	15868.70	10.01	101.18

Source: Ministry of Micro, Small and Medium Enterprises (MSME) Annual Report 2010-11.

**Upto December 2010.*

shape of the most loved and recognized brand of national and international market called Fabindia. John Bissell revived the handloom in India and written an entire new story and fate of the Indian handloom industry. From 1960, the year of its establishment till today, Fabindia climbed the ladder of success with devotion, innovation and exploration. During 1960s even under export restrictions and restricted trade possibilities which were further worsened under limited mode of communication John Bissell never gave up the idea of export. His effort for revival of Indian handloom is clear in the words of Radhika Singh when she said, "The date was 16th August, 1958, and the boss, Lakshmi Jain, was to be proved wrong. John Bissell stayed on. In fact, he never left. Two years later he started a company called Fabindia which slowly became synonymous with the revival of handloom in India."[22] Similar efforts could be made by other organizations and State KVIBs. Gandhi's humble spinning popularized *charkha* that was used as a non-violent weapon of political and social change in colonial India. But the time has changed, so as the symbol of change, that is *charkha*. It is time to realize the need to separate this act of spinning from Gandhian socio-political weapon and revise the theme of KVI holistically as a means of livelihood and an alternative to fight back rural unemployment. It is the need of hour to establish the association between KVI and globalization rather than perceiving it as a threat to its survival.

Challenges Faced

The simple fabric called *Khadi* is no more 'Livery of Freedom' or 'Fabric of Freedom' but it is still a 'Fabric of Livelihood' for millions of poor weavers. They are dependent on this humble thread to get two square meals a day. In T.Krishnamurthy's words, the employment viability of *Khadi* is apparent as follows: "*Khadi* sector employs 20 spinners, mostly women to produce the same quality of yarn which is produced by a single power operated spindle."[23] In spite of the long list of merits that KVI holds, it is facing a serious downfall. It is on the verge of losing its importance that it once had in the Gandhian era. KVI is a way to accomplish the objectives that have not been achieved till now. There are a number of reasons which are responsible for the hibernation of KVI. Some of them are as follows:

1. The prime reason is shift in the realization of the needs of the rural masses. The government has failed to acknowledge the contribution of KVI and ignored its developmental needs to make it profitable for village population. The rural India is still far behind in its contribution to India's GDP. The very nature of KVI that is labour-intensive makes it expensive and difficult to compete with the machine-made products. To correct this limitation, the government has to provide KVI with rebate. This results in yet another limitation, as the *Khadi* outlets wait for long time to get the reimbursement by the government. Though the immediate benefit goes to the account of buyers, the motive to benefit the KVI by increasing the sale takes longer to reach them. Due to this gestation period, this profit cannot be considered a true benefit for KVI.
2. Most of the sale is expected during the rebate season which is for a limited period in a year. The rest of the days are days of less sales for KVI which result in the unsold stocks thereby worsening the situation. This pressure keeps on mounting with the increase of the unsold stock every year. As M.R. Rajagopalan puts it, "At the moment, the *Khadi* institutions appear to be surviving on the oxygen in the form of rebate they get from the *Khadi* Commission and the State *Khadi* Board."[24]
3. The employment that KVI sector generates makes it

important that government should provide KVI with assistance and support, free from conditions such as tax. However, the scenario is reverse as the government is charging 4.5 per cent from *Khadi* whereas earlier it was interest free. T.Krishnamurthy pointed out, "The extent of support that *Khadi* sector gets from the government is a pittance compared to what other government enterprises and MNCs get in the normal course. Take for instance Maruti Udyog."[25]

4. Another gigantic problem is the very hierarchy of the institutional structure. The complexities of the delivery system in the KVIC structure. Y.A. Panditrao too identified the need to strengthen the institutional structure of KVI; "To impart strength to the unorganized artisans of cottage and village industries, there is immediate need to recognize them under the institutional fold or to bring them under umbrella organisation."[26]
5. KVI is facing serious challenges and only a radical and revolutionary shift in machinery, infrastructural improvement, improvements in institutional finance and similar efforts could bring desired change and bring KVI into focus again. Gandhi advocated spinning and favoured *Khadi*. He was not against machinery but the mode of production that deprives the masses from employment was unacceptable for him. He encouraged scientific improvement in the simple tool of spinning and weaving. Today KVI is standing at crossroads. The problem is low level of production. It is a vicious cycle, low quality of products lead to lesser sales which result in low profits to workers. If we look into the affairs of other village industries such as oil pressing, even in twentyfirst century the village oil pressure have not seen any improvement in the technique of production and still work with the bullock driven age old oil *ghani*. Lack of training and research innovation and absence of technological upgradation in KVI is dissatisfactory.
6. Another hindrance is the inadequate quantity and good quality of raw material. The increase in the demand of raw materials by big industries and manufacturing units is leading to increase in their dependency on villages. This, in turn,

has been creating problem for KVI to get raw materials at reasonable prices.

7. Another issue of concern is marketing and finance. Over the period of time, the consumer's needs are changing with higher level of awareness regarding fashion. In case of KVI, the efforts to understand the market and requirements of consumer are completely absent. In the absence of proper market research, the hope for betterment is dismal. In this developed market economy of banking and finance, the workers/artisans engaged in KVI are dependent on money lenders for credit at exorbitant rates of interest. The co-operative banks do not provide credit support to artisans as they have nothing to offer as security. Even after the launch of Integrated Rural Development Programme, the services for financial assistance remain inadequate. As T.Krishnamurthy says, "To carry on *Khadi* programme as at present, that is, on a commercial basis which means production for sale, government's support, we should at the same time try to develop *Khadi* on individual self-sufficiency basis that is '*Swavalambi Khadi*'."[27]
8. To understand the trend of development of KVI, it is necessary to look into the development trends through the lenses of planning and programmes. As Vadilal Dagli stated, "The work of KVIC will have to be reviewed in the backdrop of the policies laid down in the plans."[28] It is a matter of serious concern that the production of KVI has declined considerably over the last few decades. To provide solutions to these problems, there is a need to study in depth all these issues mentioned above. Integrated efforts of KVI along with the government and non-government organizations is a must. There is a need for innovative ideas and research that can bring incredible changes. Some of the suggestions are listed as below.

SUGGESTIONS

The labour-intensive character of KVI automatically includes it in the priority list of development. It has already been discussed that it is major sector of employment for the rural Indians and unemployed youth. There are numerous promises that have been time and again discussed in our Plans by the Planning Commission but most of them either remain under the dust of the files or do not get implemented. Some of the suggestions and possible alternative in this chapter are:

1. There is a need for improvement in the implementation of the programmes to ensure that the benefit should reach those, for whom it is meant. The monitoring agencies should be decentralized and should be outsourced to voluntary organizations. Avadhesh Kumar explains that the "central initiatives on development are dependent on the State's ability to ensure that the schemes are able to reach target audiences."[29]
2. The KVI should be equally nurtured as we are nurturing the culture of MNCs in our nation. To overcome the structural institutional problems in KVIC, there is a need to establish coordination through collective endeavour and cooperation in the identification of common goal. The change is needed in the area of financial support for KVI which could not be achieved only by dependence on banks but the fund raising activity. The KVIC itself can be revamped as fund raising agency.
3. The role of Panchayat cannot be overlooked as it is the grass root level organization that understands the needs and difficulties of rural masses. It should be empowered to take up the responsibility of KVI, "The self-sufficient village economy is an alternative solution and in this context the role of institutions in the rural sector like the village Panchayat and rural multi-purpose co-operatives can play a vital role."[30]
4. The KVI products were once a way of life. But to make it sustainable there is a need to revive the *swadeshi* spirit and familiarize it with the masses. Most of the plans are formulated by the urban intellectuals who do not understand the rural settings. It is thus important to make them understand the KVI in the backdrop of rural masses and their needs.
5. To bring self-reliance in the KVI sector, it could be linked with self-help groups. The self-generated SHG funds could be utilized for production. To ensure the sale of production, more and more voluntary organizations should come forward. They should work for product betterment and should work

to create market opportunities. The sincere effort could make the dream of prosperous India come true.

6. The State accountability and proactive role for KVI development should be increased and should be coordinated by the centre as KVI is the only viable option to generate employment and reduce migration to urban areas. The number of *Khadi* outlets should be increased at the same time and it should adopt new marketing techniques.
7. The national and regional channels could be used to advertise KVI products. The cost of publicity could be covered by the government. However, today mass media's responsibility of generating awareness and voicing the concern on behalf of deprived sections of society is negligible. M.R. Rajagopalan remarks "The media in our country are dancing to the tunes of globalization and contemptuous of *swadeshi*."
8. The need of the time is to adopt a balanced approach and make the effort to institutionalize the art of spinning. It should be linked with modern educational system. It could be a part of curriculum and could be introduced in extracurricular activities. This effort would help each child to understand its importance and worth. They should be made to recognize it as part of the Indian culture and understand the role that it had once played for country's freedom.
9. Another effort that can save KVI from downfall is networking. Strong networking skills are required in order to establish the web of agencies, so that there are collective efforts for the progress and development of KVI. Also *Khadi* outlets can collaborate with other village industries such as goods made from cane and bamboo which has demand in the urban market. This will give a unique identity to both. Also it would bring back the spirit of self-reliance in KVI sector. The model of Andhra Pradesh Government could be adopted and facilities of small *haats* could be provided to the producers. This will limit the role of the middle man and the producers will have total right on the profit of the sale. In order to have the desired change, planning should be based on the real grass roots development. Therefore, before taking action well designed research is a prerequisite for proper planning and execution.

CONCLUSION

KVI play a vital role in the progress and development of country's economy at large and rural economy in particular. India is a country with large population and majority of them are rural based. The utilization of human capital can bring radical changes in the graph of prosperity. One way to achieve this target is KVI. The features of KVI are in consonance with the social, economic and physical features of India. But the irony is that we still have this popular notion that the root to success travel through big industries and fast urbanization. In this race we have left behind the eco-friendly and sustainable KVI. The need is to identify the available possibilities and also adopt new strategies and action. The recent example is National Rural Employment Guarantee Scheme. It is an example of new strategy adopted by the government. It has neither utilized the potential of the people nor given direction to it. The very nature of the programme is making the rural masses labourers, while many of them have hidden skills which have not been identified. There is a need to recognize the age old skills and work which still can be revived to suit the need of villagers such as KVI. There are a number of ways towards improvements but a sincere effort is needed to bring positive change. The KVI can rise through such integrated effort. There is a need to revisit and revive the Gandhian spirit and possible way to establish positive and progressive relation between KVI and globalization.

NOTES

1. Ramagundam, Rahul, '*Khadi* and Its Agency: Organising Structure of Philanthropic Commerce', *Social Scientist*, Vol. 32, No. 5/6, 2004, p. 63.
2. Parel, Anthony, 'Symbolism in Gandhian Politics', *Canadian Journal of Political Science*, Vol. 2, No. 4, 1969, p. 517.
3. *Collected Works of Mahatma Gandhi*, Vol. 60, p. 203.
4. Jagdanand, Jha. (1999), *Khadi and Village Industries in Economic Development*, New Delhi: Deep & Deep Publications, p. 17.
5. Krishnamurthy, T., '*Khadi* and Village Industries: The only Solution', *Sarvodaya*, Vol. 3, No. 4, 2005, p. 37.
6. Pathania, Kulwant Singh and Surender Singh Mehta (2011), *Khadi and Village Industries: Status, Problems and Challenges*, New Delhi: Regal Publications, p. 75.
7. Report of the World Commission on Environment and Development: *Our Common Future*, 2010, p. 213.

8. *Lijjat Patrika*, Issue.7, September 1984, pp. 4-5, cited in Malathi Ramanathani, "Women and Empowerment: Shri Mahila Griha Udyog Lijjat Papad", *Economic and Political Weekly*, Vol. 36, No.17, 2004, p. 1690.
9. Sharma, Yogesh Chandra (1999), *Cotton Khadi in Indian Economy*, Ahmedabad: Navjivan Publishing House, p. 48.
10. Avadhesh, Kumar, "Gandhian Vision of Poverty Alleviation: Reform or Wind Up KVIC-Need of The Hour", *Gandhi Marg*, Vol. 26, No. 4, 2005, p. 469.
11. Cited in N.Kannan Nair, "Cottage and Village Industries—Need for Technological Development", *Gandhi Appropriate Technology and Rural Development,* New Delhi: Gandhi Smriti and Darshan Samiti, 1995, p. 290.
12. Jain, L. C., "Village Industry: In Search of Plan Parentage", *Economic and Political Weekly*, Vol. 23, No. 1/2, pp. 29-30, 1988.
13. M.R., Rajagopalan., "Globalisation and Employment of KVIC with Special Emphasis on Values", *Sarvodaya,* Vol. 1, No. 2, 2003, p. 13.
14. For details see Outcome Budget 2010-2011, Ministry of Textile, Government of India, p. 7.
15. Masani, Minoo R., "India: Problem with the Sixth Five-Year Plan", *Asian Affairs,* Vol. 6, No. 2, 1978, p. 99.
16. Jaitly, Jaya, 'Village Industry: Struggling to Survive', *Economic and Political Weekly*, 1994, Vol. 24, No. 15, p. 845.
17. Eleventh Five Year Plan, Vol. 3, Planning Commission, Government of India, p. 120.
18. Jaitly, Jaya, *op. cit.*
19. Schumacher, E.F. (1973), *Small is Beautiful: A Study of Economics as if People Mattered*, London: Blond and Briggs Ltd., p. 1.
20. Parikh, Geetanjali (2011), *History of Khadi*, New Delhi: National Book Trust, p. 80.
21. Singh, S.N., and Kamal Taori (1991), "Marketing Rural Industry Products: Experiments and Experience in Uttar Pradesh", *Economic and Political Weekly*, Vol. 26, No. 8, p. M-21.
22. Singh, Radhika (2010), *The Fabric of Our Life: The Story of Fabindia*, New Delhi: Penguin Books India Pvt. Ltd., p. 4.
23. T. Krishnamurthy, "*Khadi* and Village Industries: The Only Solution", *Sarvodaya*, Vol. 3, No. 4, 2005, pp. 35-36.
24. M.R., Rajagopalan, "Globalisation and Employment by KVIC With Special Emphasis on Values", *Sarvodaya*, Vol. 2, No. 2, 2003, p. 13.
25. T., Krishnamurthy, *op. cit*, p. 36.
26. Y.A. Panditrao, 2003, p. 31.
27. T. Krishnamurthy, *op.cit.*, p. 36.
28. Dagli, Vadilal, "*Khadi* and Village Industries", *The Indian Economy*, Bombay: Commerce Publications Division, 1976, p. 5.
29. Avadhesh, Kumar, *op. cit.*, p. 469.

30. Bhumali, Anil, "Relevance of M.K Gandhi's Ideal of Self Sufficient Village Economy in twentyfirst Century", *Sarvodaya*, Vol. 2, No. 1, 2004, p. 34.
31. M.R. Rajagopalan, *op. cit.*, p. 13.

REPORTS CONSULTED

1. Eleventh Five Year Plan, Vol. 3, Planning Commission, Government of India.
2. Outcome Budget 2010-2011, Ministry of Textile, Government of India.
3. The World Commission on Environment and Development: Our Common Future, 2010.
4. Evaluation Report Study on *Khadi* and Village Industries Programme, Planning Commission, Government of India, March 2001.
5. *Khadi* and Village Industries Commission, Annual Report, 2007-2008.
6. Ministry of Agro and Rural Industries, Annual Report, 2006-2007.
7. Ministry of Micro, Small and Medium Enterprises (MSME) Annual Report, 2010-11.

18

Relevance of the Concept of Village Republic in a Globalised Economy

Vandana Sinha

India is a land of villages. It is true that there has been a significant growth and expansion of cities after Independence and migration from rural areas to urban centres is on the increase, the fact that majority of Indians still live in rural areas. There are more than 6 lakh villages in India and about 65 per cent of the population lives in villages. No development in India, thus, can be considered to be realistic unless it caters to life and living of the rural population.

Unfortunately, the importance that village India deserves is not getting in the development policies of India today. No government-whether Central or State seems to be truly concerned with the integrated development of villages. These short-sighted development policies have resulted in confining the village economy to crop farming and unplanned growth of cities where half of the population lives in slums.

The gulf between cities and villages, the rich and the poor therein is widening day by day while our government and media talk about 'Shining India' and 'Vibrant India'. The number of millionaires and billionaires is increasing at a faster pace while millions of our people are starving and dying. Farmers are commiting suicide and corrupt officials and businessmen are looting the people and converting cities into slums, and villages into homesteads where only the aged and children live. Government of India has now chosen 100 towns and cities of the country to be developed as Smart Cities. How can they develop smart cities without developing smart villages?

We are accustomed to look to the statistics of national and per capita GDP as measure of development and the government machinery backs it by putting the rosy picture of increase in per capita income as an indicator of development. Both the print and electronic media are full of these raw data and people are carried away by this media hype. We want India to get the tag of 'Developed Nation' by 2025 unless and until the Physical Quality of Life (PQL) of each and every family improves to such an extent that each citizen of India is able to fulfil at least his/her basic needs and has an access to the basic amenities of life.

Can this be achieved in the next one decade? The answer is 'Yes' if and only if we follow the Gandhian philosophy of *Swaraj, swadeshi* and development from below with modifications necessitated by new developments which took place in recent years.

THE HURDLES ON THE PATH OF DEVELOPMENT

Globalization armed with GATT treaty and other policies of the government, viz., SEZ in favour of the capitalists and big industrialists are a great threat to the villages of India. Thousands hectares of fertile lands are taken away from the farmers in the name of public interest and given to the industrialists both Indian and foreign, at a rate lower than the market rate. Industrial Corridors, Coastal Corridor, Ganga Express Way, Yamuna Express Way, etc., displace millions of farmers each year in the name of development without provisions for their rehabilitation. Interestingly, the acquisition of farm land in favour of Corporates and MNCs is being done under provisions of a British law passed in 1894.

Though the procurement prices of foodgrains have increased almost annually, the farmers rarely get their dues. They have to go through the middlemen who fleece them. The situation takes a grimmer turn when we look at our import and export policy which is heavily tilted in favour of the traders and industrialists. It imports foodgrains from other countries at a price much higher than what it pays to its own farmers.

Globalisation, Liberalisation, and Privatisation (GLP) have allowed foreign Multi-national Companies (MNCs) to enter into our market in a big way. They are taking control over our economy at a very fast rate. They have entered the industrial, mining, forest, water and now the farm sector. They are gradually taking control over retail market by launching huge retail Mals and the farming sector by contract farming.The process of acquiring farm land is on and if the

MNCs get full control over agriculture and its allied activities, *viz.*, sowing, pre- and post-harvesting activities including marketing of foodgrains, then it is almost certain that the limited economic capacity of farmers and small local businessmen would not be able to match them and slowly they will be in full control of the MNCs. This is going to kill the very base of Gandhi's village republics.

Indian Economy: Historical Background

It is true that much of India still lives in villages and depends for its livelihood on farming but it is a misconception that Indian economy before the Industrial Revolution was only agrarian. Indian farmers have never been engaged in agriculture-related work for more than six months in a year. For rest of the time they were engaged in dairying and other village based industries.

Even in the era of Indus Civilization, India's trade with far off countries was a flourishing business. Trade and industry based cities like Mohenjo-Daro, Harappa, Kalibungam and Lothal existed even at that time. The British, to promote their own industrial products, destroyed Indian industrial base.

India was so prosperous that even in medieval times it was a centre of attraction for the whole world. The Muslims invaded and occupied India but made it their home. Every nation sent its emissaries to India. Ancient and even latter Medieval India was full of foreign students and traders who came here to seek knowledge and wealth. The arrival of Europeans changed the scenario. They treated India as a colony and source of economic and political power. Columbus set for India but landed in Central America; Vasco-da-Gamma was luckier; he sailed along the West African coast and circled the Cape of Good Hope to reach India. The writings of British of the time reveal how India's wealth was drained to U.K. They brought the Railways and other means of transport and communication to furher strengthen their hold on India.

Gandhi, the great freedom fighter consistently fought for the freedom of India and advocated self-reliant villages based on agriculture and small-scale cottage industries. Spinning wheel became a symbol of the self-reliant village based development. Following excerpt from a letter written by Romain Rolland, a close associate of Gandhi to Stefan Zweig in 1930 points to Gandhi's mission. "Since English domination has undermined the village crafts which added to the insufficient profits they drew from the land, millions of men have been reduced to poverty and malnutrition. The most urgent problem is to bring back craftsmanship, of which the simplest form, accessible to all and bringing in sure returns, is the spinning wheel."[1]

Upholding Principles and Moral Values

Self Reliance of Mahatma Gandhi is built on certain moral principles. His way of living clearly puts emphasis on the importance of love, peace, and freedom. His boycotts and religious beliefs make him an excellent figure for self reliance. At a time of British rule, he convinced thousands of Indians to peacefully protest the captivity of India. Essentially, Mahatma is the role model for all persons practicing self reliance. Emerson wrote "Who so would be a man, must be a nonconformist." Gandhi, either with intent or not, became consumed with these non-conformities. During the age of technology and intelligence, Gandhi was all about returning to the basic principles of living. He believed self-sufficiency was an important stepping stone in achieving personal sovereignty. When the whole world lathered itself in the benefits of technology, Gandhi stuck out like a red dress at a funeral. He would not give in to the pandemonium that was consuming the most powerful nations. Instead, Gandhi spun his own cloths, and was able to provide nourishment for himself with a small farm he owned in India.

At the time of his life, Britain was a humongous political power. They had control over many nations, including India. To end the colonial rule of this powerful country was the goal of Mahatma. When Parliament passed a law forbidding Indians to make salt, he was outraged. But through his practices, no amount of outrage would ever make this pacifist take arms. May be the most powerful revolt, civil disobedience, was used to repeal this restraining law. Never before had civil disobedience seen such a large mass of people. More than 60,000 of his loyal followers travelled to the sea to make salt with him until the law was repealed. Britain was shamed by this unresisting force and gave in to the power of disobedience. This was essentially a living example of the principle of 'Self Sufficiency'.

His rejection of 'modern' or Western civilization was all encompassing. He described it as the 'Kingdom of Satan' polluting everyone it touched. Modernization in the form of industrialization, machinery, parliamentary government, the growth of the British

Empire and all the things that most people regarded as progress, Gandhi rejected. In opposition to modern civilization he counterposed ancient Indian civilization with its perceived emphasis on village communities that were self-sufficient and self-governing. He was concerned with the stranglehold that Western civilization had over India. The materialistic values that the British Raj imposed on India had to be countered by the spirituality of Ancient India. Time and time again throughout his life he would return to this theme of the need to revert to what he called their 'own glorious civilization' which was far superior to anything modern society could offer.

Education: Gandhian Way

Given Gandhi's values and his vision of what constituted a truly civilized and free India, it was not surprising that he developed firm views on education. Education not only moulds the new generation, but reflects a society's fundamental assumptions about itself and the individuals which compose it.

Though Gandhi himself went to England to study law, he soon realized the futility of western education for Indian people. Later in his life he was to declare that 'real freedom will come only when we free ourselves of the domination of Western education, Western culture and Western way of living which have been ingrained in us. Emancipation from this culture would mean real freedom for us'.

As we have seen, Gandhi had not only rejected colonial education but also put forward a radical alternative. So, what was this alternative? What was so radical about it?

Within this context of the need for a machineless society, Gandhi developed his ideas on education. The core of his proposal was the introduction of productive handicrafts in the school curriculum. The idea was not simply to introduce handicrafts as a compulsory school subject, but to make the learning of a craft the centrepiece of the entire teaching programme. It implied a radical restructuring of the sociology of school knowledge in India, where productive handicrafts had been associated with the lowest groups in the hierarchy of the caste system. Knowledge of the production processes involved in crafts, such as spinning, weaving, leather-work, pottery, metal-work, basket-making and bookbinding had been the monopoly of specific caste groups in the lowest stratum of the traditional social hierarchy. Many of them belonged to the category of 'untouchables'. India's own tradition of education as well as the colonial education system had emphasized skills such as literacy and acquisition of knowledge of which the upper castes had a monopoly.[2]

Gandhi's proposal intended to stand the education system on its head. The social philosophy and the curriculum of what he called 'basic education' or *Buniyadi Talim* thus favoured the child belonging to the lowest stratum of society. In such a way it implied a programme of social transformation. It sought to alter the symbolic meaning of 'education' and to change the established structure of opportunities for education.

Why Gandhi proposed the introduction of productive handicrafts into the school system was not really as outrageous as may appear. What he really wanted was for the schools to be self-supporting, as far as possible. There were two reasons for this. Firstly, a poor society such as India simply could not afford to provide education for all children unless the schools could generate resources from within. Secondly, the more financially independent the schools were, the more politically independent they could be. What Gandhi wanted to avoid was dependence on the State which he felt would mean interference from the centre. Above all else, Gandhi valued self-sufficiency and autonomy. These were vital for his vision of an independent India made up of autonomous village communities to survive. It was the combination of *swaraj* and *swadeshi* related to the education system. A state system of education within an independent India would have been a complete contradiction as far as Gandhi was concerned.

He was also of the opinion that manual work should not be seen as something inferior to mental work. He felt that the work of the craftsman or labourer should be the ideal model for the 'good life'. Schools which were based around productive work where that work was for the benefit of all were, therefore, carrying out education of the whole person—mind, body and spirit.

The right to autonomy that Gandhi's educational plan assigns to the teacher in the context of the school's daily curriculum is consistent with the libertarian principles that he shared with Tolstoy. Gandhi wanted to free the Indian teacher from interference from outside, particularly government or State bureaucracy. Under colonial rule, the teacher had a prescribed job to do that was based on what the authorities wanted the children to learn. Textbooks were mandatory so that Gandhi found that 'the living word of the teacher has very little value. A teacher who teaches from textbooks does not impart originality to his pupils'. Gandhi's plan, on the other hand, implied the end of the teacher's subservience to the prescribed textbook and the curriculum. It presented a concept of learning that simply could not be fully implemented with the help of textbooks. Of equal, if not more importance, was the freedom it gave the teacher in matters of curriculum. It denied the state the power to decide what teachers taught and what they did in the classroom. It gave autonomy to the teacher but it was, above all, a libertarian approach to schooling that transferred power from the State to the village.

Gandhi's basic education was, therefore, an embodiment of his perception of an ideal society consisting of small, self-reliant communities with his ideal citizen being an industrious, self-respecting and generous individual living in a small cooperative community.

For informal educators, we can draw out a number of useful pointers. First, Gandhi's insistence on autonomy and self-regulation is reflected in the ethos of informal education. Gandhi's conception of basic education was concerned with learning that was generated within everyday life which is the basis on which informal educators work. It was also an education focused on the individual but reliant on co-operation between individuals. There is also a familiar picture of the relationships between educators and students/learners:

A teacher who establishes rapport with the taught, becomes one with them, learns more from them than he teaches them. He who learns nothing from his disciples is, in my opinion, worthless. Whenever I talk with someone I learn from him. I take from him more than I give him. In this way, a true teacher regards himself as a student of his students. If you will teach your pupils with this attitude, you will benefit much from them.[3]

Lastly, it was an education that aimed at educating the whole person, rather than concentrating on one aspect. It was a highly moral activity.

Swadeshi and *Swaraj* for a Sustainable Economy

The two terms *swaraj* and *swadeshi* taken together represent the type of society that Gandhi was looking for *swaraj*, very badly translates as independence/autonomy/home rule/self-rule. *Swadeshi* can be translated as self-sufficiency or self-reliance.

Gandhi advocated everything of our requirement to be produced in the country itself and for this he used the term *swadeshi.* Though the term was used for a movement to boycott the British goods even if they were convenient and superior to our goods it was used in a wider context. Gandhi defined the term as "that spirit in us which restricts us to the use and service of our immediate surroundings to the exclusion of the more remote."[4] He wrote "Much of the deep poverty of the masses is due to the ruinous departure from *swadeshi* in the economic and industrial life. If not one article of commerce had been brought from outside India, she would be today a land flowing with milk and honey. But that was not to be. We were greedy and so was England…"[5] "I think *swadeshi* not as a boycott movement undertaken by way of revenge….India cannot live for…any other country before she is able to live for herself; and she can live herself only if she produces everything for her requirements within her own borders…."[6] On Economic localization within India he said, "If we follow the *swadeshi* doctrine it would be your duty and mine to find our neighbours who can supply our wants, and to teach them to supply them where they do not know how to proceed…"[7]

Swaraj literary means self-governance or "home-rule" (*swa*—"self", *raj*—"rule") but the word usually refers to Mahatma Gandhi's concept for Indian independence from foreign domination. *Swaraj* lays stress on governance not by a hierarchical government, but self governance through individuals and community building. The focus is on political decentralization. Since this is against the political and social systems followed by Britain, Gandhi's concept of *swaraj* laid stress on India discarding British political, economic, bureaucratic, legal, military, and educational institutions.

Gandhi gave to *swaraj* the content of an integral revolution that encompasses all spheres of life. "At the individual level *swaraj* is vitally connected with the capacity for dispassionate self-assessment, ceaseless self-purification and growing self-reliance", Politically *swaraj* is self-government and not good government (for Gandhi, good government is no substitute for self-government) and it means a continuous effort to be independent of government control, whether it is foreign government or whether it is national. In other words, it is sovereignty of the people based on pure moral authority. Economically, *swaraj* means full economic freedom for the toiling millions. And in its fullest sense, *swaraj* is much more than freedom from all restraints, it is self-rule, self-restraint and could be equated with *moksha* Adopting *swaraj* means implementing a system whereby the state machinery is virtually nil, and the real power directly resides in the hands of people. Gandhi said, "Power resides in the people, they can use it at any time."[9] This philosophy rests inside an individual who has to learn to be master of his own self and spreads upwards to the level of his community which must be dependent only on itself. Gandhi said, "In such a state (where *swaraj* is achieved) everyone is his own ruler. He rules himself in such a manner that he is never a hindrance to his neighbour"; and also "It is *swaraj* when we learn to rule ourselves."[10]

Swaraj for Gandhi was not simply a question of ousting the British from India and declaring independence. What it implied was a wholly different type of society. He did not want the British to be replaced by Indians doing exactly the same. If that was all they achieved, they would not have achieved true freedom but merely the same type of government run by a different set of men. He wanted the value system and life style of the British Raj to be done away with and totally replaced by a simpler, more spiritual, communal life. This new type of society, reflecting the old values of pre-colonial days, was to be based on the village.

Gandhi's vision for a new India entailed that 'every religion has its full and equal place'. (He was totally opposed to the partition of India on religious lines). Equally, 'there would be no room for machines that would displace human labour and that would concentrate power in a few hands'.[11]

In his *Collected Works* there is a passage, written in 1942, that amplifies his ideas on the role of the village. He states that 'my idea of village *swaraj* is that it is a complete republic, independent of its neighbours for its own vital wants, and yet interdependent for many others in which dependence is a necessity'. He continues:

> Thus, the first concern of every village will be to grow its own food crops and cotton for its cloth. It should have a reserve for its cattle, recreation and playground for adults and children. Then, if there is more land available, it will grow *useful* cash crops, thus excluding *ganja*, tobacco, opium and the like. The village will maintain a village theatre, school and public hall. It will have its own waterworks, ensuring clean water supply. This can be done through controlled wells or tanks. Education will be compulsory up to the final basic

> course. As far as possible every activity will be conducted on the co-operative basis. There will be no castes such as we have today with their graded untouchability. Non-violence with its technique of…non-cooperation will be the sanction of the village community. There will bc a compulsory service of village guards who will be selected by rotation from the register maintained by the village. The government of the village will be conducted by a council of five persons annually elected by the adult villagers, male and female, possessing minimum prescribed qualifications. These will have all the authority and jurisdiction required. Since there will be no system of punishments in the accepted sense, this [council] will be the legislature, judiciary and executive combined to operate for its year of office.[12]

Gandhi was quite certain that any village could become such a republic straight away without much interference even from the colonial government because he believed that their sole effective connection with the villages was the collection of village taxes. All that was needed was the will to do it. He referred to his ideal state as one of 'enlightened anarchy in which each person will become his own ruler'. It is interesting to see that throughout his writings on the autonomous self-sufficient village communities we see echoes of the anarchist lifestyles proposed by such writers as Tolstoy or Thoreau in the nineteenth century.

Gandhi explained his Vision in 1946

"Independence begins at the bottom.. Thus, every village will be a republic…having full powers. A society must be built in which every village has to be self-sustained and capable of managing its own affairs… It will be trained and prepared to perish in the attempt to defend itself against any onslaught from without.. Thus, ultimately, it is the individual who is the unit. This does not exclude dependence on and willing help from neighbours or from the world. It will be a free and voluntary play of mutual forces… In this structure composed of innumerable villages, there will be ever widening, never ascending circles. Growth will not be a pyramid with the apex sustained by the bottom. But it will be an oceanic circle whose centre will be the individual. Therefore, the outermost circumference will not wield power to crush the inner circle but will give strength to all within and derive its own strength from it."[13]

Gandhi was undaunted by the task of implementing such a utopian vision in India. He believed that by transforming enough individuals and communities society at large would change. He said, "It may be taunted with the retort that this is all Utopian and, therefore not worth a single thought... Let India live for the true picture, though never realizable in its completeness. We must have a proper picture of what we want before we can have something approaching it."[14]

Self-reliance: Gandhian Way in the Present Context

Gandhi was a great thinker and a great reformer too. He foresaw the threats of the market economy to our villages and propounded the theory of *sarvodaya*, *swaraj* and *swadeshi*. He put forward *charkha*, which was a symbol of cloth sufficiency at that time. It might have lost its glory these days but the morale behind this is still relevant. Gandhi talked about "production by masses" in place of "mass production". He did not condemn machinery or industrial techniques, insofar as they bring help and relief to humanity; his quarrel is merely with their murderous excesses and the morbid myth of economic overproduction.

Gandhiji talked about self sufficiency of the villages based on local resources. To him local means 5 miles or 8 km. In the present era this could be a circle having a radius of 10-15 km or cyclable distance. Self sufficiency does not mean that each and every item that is in need will have to be produced in a village or a cluster of villages for that matter. Gandhi often evoked the ideals of self-reliance and self-help in regard to individual, the village, the working class and the nation, yet he sought not to overdo it. In his own words, "Let us not....forget....man's social nature....If it is his privilege to be independent, it is equally his duty to be interdependent...It will be possible to reconstruct our villages so that the villages collectively and not individually, will become self-contained, so far as their clothing requirements are concerned."[15]

Four-tier Cluster based Approach

We could go for four-tier cluster based development where we start at the household activities and end up at heavy industries that manufacture goods and machines which need high precision and cannot be produced at local level for various reasons.

This approach hinges on the theory that most of our just needs can be fulfilled locally and a cluster of villages exchange its excess goods with another cluster. It is not necessary that each and every cluster produces or manufactures same things but primary processing for at least 80 per cent of the resources found within the boundary of a cluster would be a must.

The 4-tier approach is as follows:

1. **Household Activities:** These activities will be taken at the family level or group level, e.g., SHG level. This takes care of 80 per cent needs of the family. Most of the primary processing would be done at this level.
2. **Common Facility Centre at Cluster Level:** There would be a multipurpose centre at the cluster level consisting of 4-6 villages where plants and machinery for secondary processing of household level will be available and primary processing of such things which could not be taken at the family level would be done here. These centres would also serve the purpose of Primary Centres for Vocational Training.
3. **Advance Facility Centre at Block Level:** District is too big a unit for development at least in bigger States like U.P., M.P. and Bihar, etc. Thus, Block is a natural choice for setting up an Advanced Facility Centre. Blocks within the same district or even nearby districts can sit together to decide the industry and means of sustainable livelihood best suited for them and could go for the same. Interdependencies of Blocks would be taken care of. These centres would also serve the purpose of Advance Centre for Vocational Training.
4. **Higher Centres of Heavy Industry:** These would be located as per the suitability anywhere but not at the cost of fertile land. Everywhere there is wasteland and there should be a policy decision to locate the factories on this type of land. These industries would manufacture machines and goods necessary for the centres down in the hierarchy. Research Centres would also be clubbed in this level.

It is very necessary that we see this four-tier approach not in isolation for fulfilling our economic needs only. This has to be amalgamated with Gandhiji's idea of *Nai* or *Buniadi Talim* along with his views on the need of practicing moral values.

CONCLUSION

Since achieving *swaraj* could not be possible without the elimination of all forms of domination, Gandhi decided to undertake a number of constructive activities aimed at reducing the dependence of Indians from the British and simultaneously also making them self-reliant. Therefore, he founded many voluntary organisations throughout his life to carry out such social welfare programmes. The All India Spinners Association, the All India Village Industries Association, the Harijan Sewak Sangh and the Leprosy Foundation were some of the organizations he formed. The thrust of all these activities was social and not political. Gandhi also decided to popularise the spinning wheel in India to make hand-spun cloth out of *khadi*. The intention was to reduce India's dependence on foreign made cloth. This movement called *Khadi Movement* later gained fame by the term *swadeshi* Gandhi himself spun and weaved cloth from spinning wheels and handlooms in his *ashram*. The spinning wheel or the *charkha* became a symbol of the Indian freedom struggle, and was incorporated into many flags.

Although Gandhi's aim of totally implementing the concepts of *swaraj* in India was not achieved, the voluntary work organizations which he founded for this purpose did serve as precursors and role models for people movements, voluntary organizations and some of the non-governmental organizations that were subsequently launched in various parts of India. The Bhoodan movement which presaged land reform legislation activity throughout India, ultimately leading to India discarding the *zamindari* system, was also inspired by the ideas of *swaraj*.

It is high time we pay heed to the teachings and practices of Gandhiji towards Self Reliant Villages which he aptly thought to be the only way towards a prosperous India. It is a hard fact to swallow that a nation which owes its independence to a person whom it calls Bapu never followed his path. The Gandhian idea of *swaraj* outlined in his book *Hind Swaraj* was not acceptable to many Congress leaders. Jawaharlal Nehru later dismissed it as "completely unreal" and declared that neither he nor the Congress had ever considered the picture presented in it. The Congress treated *swaraj* more as a politically inclined goal demanding complete political independence from the British.

There is an old proverb "Better late than never". Working for Bapu's dream of *sarvodaya, swaraj and swadeshi* into reality will be the true homage to the *Rashtrapita* in place of the customary gathering on the occasion of his birthday and the martyrdom day.

We should remember what Gandhi often termed as a golden key to development "Whatever we do should be judged by the fact as to whether its impact reaches the last man or not".

NOTES

1. Mark Lindley (2007), *J.C. Kumarappa: Mahatma Gandhi's Economist,* Mumbai: Popular Prakashan (quotes from Romain Rolland letter to Stefen Zweig, 1930).
2. Programme of Action of the *National Policy on Education* of 1986, which emphasis promotion of culture and creativity in school children, SUPW curriculum may also include, Pottery, Clay Modelling, Paper Mache, Mask Making, Tie & Dye, Rangoli, Wall decoration, Cane work, Bamboo work, Book binding, Paper toys.
3. M.K. Gandhi, "Talk to Khadi Vidyalaya Students", Sevagram: *Sevak,* 15 February 1942; *CWMG,* p. 269.
4. M.K. Gandhi, *Young India,* 17-6-1926, p. 218.
5. *Ibid.*
6. *Ibid.*
7. M.K. Gandhi, *Young India:* April 4, 1929.
8. M.K. Gandhi, *Young India,* December 8, 1920, p. 886. See also *Young India,* August 6, 1925, p. 276 and *Harijan,* March 25, 1939, p. 64.
9. M.K. Gandhi, *Young India,* June 28, 1928, p. 772. *Ibid.*, December 8, 1920, p.886 (See also *Young India,* August 6, 1925, p. 276 and *Harijan,* March 25, 1939, p. 64.
10. M.K Gandhi, *Hind Swaraj or Indian Home Rule,* Gandhi, 1909 and 1938 editions.
11. M.K. Gandhi, *Harijan,* July 28, 1946.
12. M.K. Gandhi, *Harijan,* 26 July, 1942, p. 238.
13. Anthony J. Parel, 1997. *Hind Swaraj and Other Writing.*
14. M.K. Gandhi, *Harijan,* 28 July 1946. *CWMG,* Vol. 85, pp. 32-34.
15. Mark Lindley, *op. cit.*

19
On the Concept of Village Republic: Gandhi, Nehru and Ambedkar

Pradeep Kumar Jha

Village has for long been viewed as a convenient entry point for understanding the "traditional" Indian society. It signifies the authentic native life, a social and cultural unit uncorrupted by outside influence. It is an invaluable observation centre where one could see the "real" India, its social organization and cultural life. By observing a village one could generalize about the social processes and problems to be found occurring in great parts of India. It is a representative unit and an important ideological category of the modern Indian imagination. It is not a place where people live it had a design, which reflects the basic values of Indian civilization. In case of India village acquires the status of primary unit representing social formation of the entire civilization. The "caste system" and the "village communities" are the two most important categories through which Indian society can be understood. It was during the British colonial rule and through the writings of the colonial administrators that India was constructed as a land of "village republic". Sir Charles Metcalfe the provisional Governor-General of India (1835-36) had called the Indian village communities "the little republic".

> "The British colonial rulers obviously had their own political reasons for representing India as they did and imputing qualities such as autonomy, stagnation and continuity to the village life in the subcontinent. It helped them justify their rule over the subcontinent to their people back home in Britain. Since the villages had been autonomous republics, the rulers of India were anyway always outsiders".[1]

Leaders of the nationalist movement despite disagreements and differences in their ideological orientations or political agenda, the village remained a core category through which most of them conceptualized or thought of "traditional" Indian social life. For most of the nationalist movement leaders, village represented "the real" India, the nation that needed to be recovered, liberated and transformed. The nationalist freedom movement was also a moment when the futures of India were being visualized. Their notions of India's pasts or its traditional social order invariably reflected their future visions or the alternative agenda they had for free India. Village remained a core category in their scheme of things. There was a virtual agreement on the fact that village represented the core of the traditional social order of India. However, the attitudes of these leaders towards the village varied considerably. They disagreed, both on the merits of traditional Indian village and also on the place it should have in the future India of their visions. Gandhi, Nehru and Ambedkar are the three most important leaders of modern India because they played a critical role in India's struggle for freedom from colonial rule and are the symbols of India's independent nationhood. Their legacy is also imbibed in the perspectives they articulated on India, its past and its possible future.

In quest for independence Gandhi needed a different set of ideas that would de-legitimize the British rule over India. Such an ideology required construction of a difference that would establish the sovereign identity of India and restore its cultural confidence. The idea of village came in very handy in this endeavour. He emphatically recognizes the centrality of village as he says, "For me, India begins and ends in the villages".[2]

Gandhi conceived a normative structure of the village community. The community is based on the guiding principles of harmony, love, we-feeling, consensus and intimacy. Village community is not a mere population within legally established limits rather the village-community is a social system with integrated functional sub-systems in the spheres economic, educational and political. Gandhi visualized various functions of ideal-type village community, although he was aware of the term "community disorganization". Gandhi adopted non-violent method for the smooth functioning of the village community because violent methods for conflict-resolution lead to "community disorganization" as one of the operational principles of the village community. His opinion was that, "as far as possible every activity will be conducted on the cooperative basis".[3]

If the conflict is inevitable, Gandhi showed no hesitation in launching *Satyagraha* to resolve the issue. His view is clear in the following words, "Non-violence with technique of *Satyagraha* and non-cooperation will be the sanction of the village community".[4]

Gandhi institutionalized non-violence with its technique *Satyagraha* and non-cooperation to resolve conflicts in society. Institutionalized non-violent methods for resolving conflicts in society protect the community from disorganization. In addition to *Satyagraha* and non-cooperation, Gandhi emphasized on three basic norms for the smooth functioning of the village community:

1. "There will be no caste as we have today with their graded untouchability".[5] It is clear that Gandhi was against the existing social stratification that hampered the growth of a socially and economically healthy village community.
2. *Swaraj* is the ultimate goal of Gandhi's ideal type village. He pleaded for economic equality, and levelling down of the rich in order to achieve the poor man *Swaraj*. This makes his point clear in the following words, "economic equality is the master key to non-violent independence. Working for economic equality means abolishing the eternal conflict between capitalists and labour; it means the levelling down of few rich in whose hands is concentrated the bulk of the nation's wealth on the one hand, and levelling up of the semi-starved naked millions on the other. A non-violent system of government is clearly impossible so long as the wide gulf between the rich and the hungry millions persists".[6]
3. The third norm for ideal type village community is the duty of a man to serve his neighbour. To Gandhi serving one's neighbour means serving the world. A village cannot be called community unless good neighbourhood relation is developed. The village has to be self-governing and it would be self-sufficient in the matter of basic needs food, clothing and shelter. Gandhi's village is not agricultural community rather it would be an "agro-industrial" community. The village government functions in such a way that ensures the growth of agro-industrial community. In Gandhi's words, the structure of *Panchayat* in a village is as follows: "the

> government of the village will be conducted by the *Panchayat* of five persons annually elected by the adult villagers male and female possessing minimum prescribed qualifications. These will have all the authority and jurisdiction required. Since, there will be no system of punishments in the accepted sense, this *Panchayat* will be the legislature, judiciary and executive combined to operate for its year of office".[7]

Gandhi was a lover of face-to-face village community and so he wrote, "My imaginary village consists of 1,000 souls. Such a unit can give a good account of itself, if it is well organized on a basis of self-sufficiency".[8]

There are two major criteria for considering the size of the village. The first is economic and a self-sufficient village ensures that the basic necessities of life are met. The second is political and the small size of village ensures that the villagers actively participate in the process of decision-making. Law making power is assigned to the *Panchayat* and all the adult of the village must be in a position to participate in political activity. The village elects five persons for a fixed time of office. The general body of adult persons will supervise the executive and judicial functions of the *Panchayat*. In Gandhi's scheme people's participation in decision-making of the village community is the pre-requisite for political decentralization. *Swaraj* can be achieved only when people have a direct say in the management of village polity.

The jurisdiction of village government is not only confined to administrative work but also the *Panchayat* has been entrusted with economic functions, which in turn reconstructs the village into self-sufficient village community. Self-sufficiency of a village is seen in terms of food, cloth and other basic necessities. If a village cannot produce in its own area it will get it from other village. Gandhi spelled out in clear words, "only an arrogant man claim to be independent of everybody else and the self-contained".[9]

Interdependence of village means that reconstruction of rural life is practical only when one or more neighbouring village forming a cluster will be grouped for achieving the target of self-sufficiency in certain productive items. The supreme consideration is the grouping of village is economic viability. The governing organization of the village is responsible for the socio-economic affairs of the locality in order to achieve self-sufficiency as the ultimate goal. A *Panchayat* has to monitor the process of exchange of materials with the other villages. The surplus produce of a village will be supplied to other village to obtain in exchange what it cannot produce.

After Gandhi, Nehru was perhaps the second most important and influential leader of India's Freedom Movement. He was an important ideologue of Indian National Congress and he also became the first Prime Minister of India. Though, Nehru worked under leadership of Gandhi and gave him a good deal of respect, his ideas with respect to India's past and his vision of a new future of India was different from that of Gandhi. The idea of the Indian village community is quite central to Nehru's notion of traditional India. He came across the 'realities' of rural masses during his encounters with the then rural India, which was very different from what Gandhi saw and felt. His importance lies in the fact that he was the first Prime Minister of India and played a vital role in shaping development policies and programmes of the country. His comments on how rural India should be developed reflect his notion of Indian village. In *Discovery of India* he has given his ideas on the traditional Indian society. He apparently looked at the "old" social structure of Indian society from an evolutionary perspective and his approach to the understanding of Indian past was historical. He identified "the autonomous village community, caste and the joint family" as the three basic concepts of the old Indian social structure and it had something in common with the traditional societies in general all over the world as the organizing principles were the same everywhere.

> "In all these three it is the group that counts, the individual has a secondary place. There is nothing very unique about all this separately, and it is easy to find something equivalent to any of these three in other countries, especially in medieval times".[10]

He further elaborated his "organic" notion of an integrated traditional village society in the following text:

> "...The functions of each group or caste were related to functions of other castes, and the idea was that if each group functioned successfully within its own framework, then society as a whole worked harmoniously. Over and above this, a strong and fairly successful attempt was made to create

a common national bond which would hold all these groups together—the sense of a common culture, common traditions, common heroes and saints and common land to the four corners of which people went on pilgrimage. This national bond was of course very different from present day nationalism, it was weak politically, but socially and culturally it was strong".[11]

Unlike Gandhi, Nehru did not celebrate the old "village republics" of India despite having the same sources of their understanding of India's past.

He said the same what Metcalfe and later Marx said about the Indian village communities.

> "Foreign conquests brought war and destruction, revolts and their ruthless suppression, and new ruling classes relying chiefly on armed force... The self-governing community, however, continued. Its breakup began only under the British rule".[12]

Regarding the village *Panchayats* and political spirit of the traditional India, he reinforced the prevailing notion about the village society as having been economically stagnant and community-oriented but democratically organized. The traditional social structure emphasized the duties of the individual and group and not their rights.

> "The aim was social security: stability and continuance of the group; that is of society. Progress was not the aim, and progress therefore had to suffer. Within each group, whether it was the village community, the particular caste, or the large joint family, there was a communal life shared together, a sense of equality, and democratic methods".[13]

He emphasized the village republics had long degenerated into a society that was marked by various ills. There was a crystal clear shift in his discussion on village life as he moved closer to contemporary times. He becomes more and more critical of the past structures, particularly of caste-based hierarchies, which should have no place in modern society. Contrary to Gandhi, Nehru saw no virtues in reviving the traditional social order. He can be best located in his modernist outlook. His disposition is best illustrated in the following passage from *Discovery of India*:

> "...the ultimate weakness and failing of the caste system and the Indian social structure were that day degraded a mass of human beings and gave them no opportunities to get out of that condition—educationally, culturally or economically ....In the context of society today, the caste system and much that goes with it are wholly incompatible, reactionary, restrictive and barriers to progress. There can be no equality in status and opportunity within its framework nor can there be political democracy and much less, economic democracy".[14]

Compared to both Gandhi and Nehru, Ambedkar considers village as a site of exclusion and discrimination. Ambedkar was the one who had a firsthand experience of village-life and that too of looking at it from below. The experiences of a childhood and humiliations of being a dalit had shaped his political outlook and also his perspective on the village. Ambedkar's writing could be called a dalitist and subaltern view on the village. He, unlike Gandhi does not celebrate village without any qualification. He is diametrically opposed to celebrated ideals of village pronounced by Gandhi.

Ambedkar tried to understand the Indian society and village life in civilization terms. Despite recognizing the obvious cultural diversities, the social structure of the Indian village was the same everywhere. He saw the Indian civilization as being a Hindu civilization. More importantly, he did not see dalits as a part of this Hindu society. The structure of village settlements too reflected this basic principal. Quite like the Hindu civilization, village too was divided:

> "The Hindu society insists on segregation of the Untouchables. The Hindu will not live in the quarters of the Untouchables and will not allow the Untouchables to live inside Hindu quarters....It is not a case of social separation, a mere stoppage of social intercourse for a temporary period. It is a case of territorial segregation and of a *cordon sanitaire* putting the impure people inside the barbed wire into a sort of cage. Every Hindu village has a ghetto. The Hindus live in the village and the Untouchables live in the ghetto".[15]

For Ambedkar, village presented a model of the Hindu social organization. It was the working plant of the Hindu social order, where one could see the Hindu social order in operation in full swing. Though he frequently used the expression of the Indian village but the village did not include the untouchables, who lived outside, in the "ghetto".

> "The Indian village was not a single unit. It was divided into two sets of populations: 'touchable' and 'untouchable'. The touchables formed what he called, the major community and the untouchables a minor community. The touchables lived inside the village and the untouchables lived outside the village in separate quarters. The touchables were economically the dominant community and commanded power; the untouchables were a dependent community and a subject race of hereditary bondsmen. The untouchables lived according to the codes laid down for them by the dominant 'touchable' major community. These codes laid guidelines regarding their habitations; the distance they ought to maintain from the 'Hindus', the dress they should wear; the houses they should live in; the language they should speak; the names they should keep. They could not build house having tiled roofs; they could not wear silver or gold jewellery".[16]

Though Ambedkar was educated in the West, he was sceptical of Western and colonial writing on the Indian society. Ambedkar saw "village community" more in historical terms as it has been derived from the Western/colonial imagination of India, especially from the writings of Sir Charles Metcalfe such a notion of village community came to be accepted by the upper/dominant caste Hindus and the leaders of the independence movement projected it in a positive light. "The average Hindu was always in ecstasy whenever he spoke of the Indian village. He regarded it as an ideal form of social organization to which he believed there was no parallel anywhere in the world".[17]

According to Ambedkar, the governing normative structure of the village was no way close to democracy. Exclusion, exploitation and untouchability were the hallmark of village life. Not only did the upper/dominant castes force the untouchables live outside the village in the ghetto, the untouchable were also excluded from most of village festivals.

> "When the whole village community was engaged in celebrating a general festivity such as *Holi* or *Dashara*, the untouchables must perform all menial acts which were preliminary to the main observance. The duties had to be performed without remuneration".[18]

He concluded his views on village republic:

> "This is the Village Republic of which the Hindus are so proud. What is the position of the Untouchables in this republic? They are not merely the last but are also the least....in this Republic there is no place for democracy. There is no room for equality. There is no room for liberty and there is no room for fraternity. The Indian village is a very negation of a Republic. The republic is an Empire of the Hindus over the Untouchables. It is a kind of colonialism of the Hindus designed to exploit the Untouchables. The Untouchables have no right... They have no rights because they are outside the village republic and because they are outside the so-called village republic, they are outside the Hindu fold".[19]

CONCLUSIONS

The above exposition clearly shows that there is no uniformity of approach in treating village as a homogenous, inclusive, and undifferentiated category. Gandhi had a reformist vision and thought that India could recover its lost self and true freedom only through the reconstruction of her villages. Nehru did not want to revive the old community but to develop the village through new technology and abolition of outdated structures. From Ambedkar's point of view those who were made to live outside the village and were treated as untouchables, the so-called virtues of traditional living turn into oppressive structures. The hope for the untouchables did not lie in its revival and reconstruction, or even in its development.

NOTES

1. Surindra Singh Jodhka, "Nation and the Village: Images of Rural India

in Gandhi, Nehru, and Ambedkar" Gopal Guru, (ed.) (2005), *Atrophy in Dalit Politics,* Mumbai: Vikas Adhyayan Kendra, p. 104.

2. Gandhi, M.K. in a letter to Nehru written on August 23, 1944.
3. Gandhi, M.K. (1963), *Village Swaraj*, Compiled by H.M. Vyas, Ahmedabad: Navjivan Publishing House, p. 31.
4. *Ibid.*
5. *Ibid.*
6. *Ibid.*, p. 37.
7. *Ibid.*, pp. 31-32.
8. Gandhi, M.K. (1949), *India of My Dreams.* Ahmedabad: Navjivan Publishing House, p. 98.
9. Gandhi, M.K., *Village Swaraj*, *op. cit.*, p.65.
10. Jawaharlal, Nehru, (1964), *The Discovery of India*, New York: The John Day Company, p. 244
11. *Ibid.*, p. 248.
12. *Ibid.*, p. 246.
13. *Ibid.*, p. 252.
14. *Ibid.*, p. 254.
15. Ambedkar, B.R. (1948), *The Untouchables: Who Were They and Why They Became Untouchables*? New Delhi: Amrit Book Company, pp. 21-22.
16. Moone, V. (1979), *Dr. Babasaheb Ambedkar's Writings and Speeches,* Vol. V, Bombay: Government of Maharashtra, pp. 18-19.
17. *Ibid.*, p. 19.
18. *Ibid.*, p. 22.
19. *Ibid.*, pp. 25-26.

20

Kibubutzim and Moshavim: Israel's Village Republics

R.P. Misra

Mahatma Gandhi wanted Indian villages to be restored to their original status as self-reliant republics. The modernists of India who were wedded to Marxist or capitalist philosophy considered this concept retrogressive. Urbanization and absorption of 700,000 villages in the ever growing cities and towns of India was and still is considered to be a progressive step that India should pursue. This chapter takes the reader to Israel where Gandhi's village republics continue to prosper, the challenges of globalization faced by them notwithstanding. India can learn a lot from the Kibubutzim and moshavim of Israel and reshape and restructure its rural development policies, it has followed ever since it emerged as an independent nation in 1947.

KIBUBUTZIM: THE COMMUNITY-CENTRIC VILLAGE REPUBLICS OF ISRAEL

Israel has two types of rural settlements of relevance to India. They are kibbutz and moshav. In Hebrew, the plural of these terms is kibubutzim and moshavim. The former are communal settlements while the latter are cooperative settlements. The author had an opportunity to visit a few of these settlements and was impressed by their management and governance. Given below are details of their origin, goals and objectives, governance and management.

Kibbutz is a unique rural community dedicated to mutual aid and social justice. Its socio-economic system is based on the principles of joint ownership of property including land, equality in income, production, consumption and education. "From each according to his ability, to each according to his needs" is the goal of the community. It is a voluntary homestead and only those who choose to be a part of it, can live in it.

Most of the kibubutzim are laid out following a similar plan. The residential area include homes and gardens of members, playgrounds for every age group, and communal facilities such as a dining hall, auditorium, library, swimming pool, tennis court, medical clinic, laundry, grocery and the like. Close to the living quarters are sheds for chickens, dairy cattle, and one or more industrial plants. A few metres away from the centre are the agricultural fields, orchards and fish ponds. People either walk or use bicycles to get from place to place within the kibbutz. Electric carts are available for the disabled and elderly.

Kibbutz is a democratic institution; it has a general assembly consisting of all adult members. It serves not only as a decision-making body but also as a forum where members may express their opinions and views. It formulates policy, elects its officers, authorizes the budget and approves entry of new members. The day-to-day affairs like housing, finance, production planning, health, and culture are handled by elected committees. Each kibbutz has three full-time officers: a secretary, who is the top officer of the community, treasurer, and work-coordinator. The chairpersons of some of the committees, together with the secretary form the kibbutz executive. A member of a kibbutz is called a *kibbutznik* (in Hebrew).

Historical Background

Kibubutzim came into being before the State of Israel was established in1948. The first kibbutz was established in 1909 at Degania, located south of Lake Kinneret by a group of Jewish pioneers on land acquired by the Jewish National Fund. These founding fathers were young men and women who came mainly from Eastern Europe. They came not only to reclaim the soil of their ancient homeland, but also to forge a new way of life. Their task was not easy: a hostile environment and desolate land neglected for centuries, scarcity of water, lack of agricultural know-how and inexperience, and shortage of funds were among the many hurdles they faced. They could overcome these obstacles because they were committed to the ideal they had before them, i.e., to create a new world following their religious beliefs.

They succeeded in developing thriving communities which played a dominant role in the establishment and building of the state of Israel.

In 2010, there were 270 kibubutzim in Israel with memberships ranging from 40 to more than 1,000. Most of them have 300 to 400 adult members, and a population of 500 to 600. In all, approximately 130,000 people (about 2.5 per cent of the country's population) live in kibubutzim (Table 20.1). Most kibubutzim can trace their origin to one of three national kibbutz movements, each identified with a particular ideology.

Economic Base

The founders of kibubutzim considered tilling of the soil of their ancient homeland and transforming city dwellers into farmers an ideal, not just a way to earn a livelihood. Over the years, the land that was barren once bloomed with field crops, orchards, poultry, dairy and fish farming. More recently, organic agriculture has become the mainstay of their economy. What made the kibbutz bloom was hard work and advanced farming methods. They now account for a large percentage of Israel's agricultural output.

To begin with, production activities of the kibubutzim were limited to agriculture, horticulture, fish-farming and related activities. Today virtually all kibubutzim have expanded into the manufacturing of a wide range of products, from fashion clothing to irrigation systems. The majority of kibbutz industry is concentrated in three main branches: metal work, plastics and processed foods.

Table 20.1: Number of kibbutzin and their Population

Year	*Number of kibubutzim*	*Kibbutz Population*
1910	1	—
1920	12	805
1930	29	3,900
1940	82	26,550
1950	214	67,550
1960	229	77,950
1970	229	85,100
1980	255	111,200
1980	270	125,100
2000	268	117,300
2010	270	—

Most industries are small, employing less than 100 workers. Many kibubutzim have pooled their resources and established regional enterprises such as cotton gins and poultry-packing plants, as well as providing a gamut of services ranging from computer data compilation to joint purchasing and marketing. The kibubutzim contribute 33 per cent of farm produce and 6.3 per cent of manufactured goods while they contain just 2.5 per cent of national population. Tourism is another source of income. Many kibubutzim have recreational facilities like guest houses, swimming pools, horseback riding, tennis courts, museums, exotic animal farms and water parks for both national and foreign tourists.

As the population of the country increased and urban centres expanded laterally, some kibubutzim became suburbs of cities. Such kibubutzim now offer such services as commercial laundries, catering, factory outlet stores and child care, including summer camps.

People living in kibubutzim value labour (Gandhi's bread labour). Concept of dignity of labour elevating the most menial job, with no special status, material or otherwise attached to any task is one of the eternal values of the people.

Table 20.2: Employment of the Members of Kibubutzim in Various Activities

Sl. No.	*Branch of Economic Activity*	*Per cent*
1.	Agriculture & Fisheries	24
2.	Industry & Quarries	24
3.	Tourism, Commerce & Finance	11
4.	Transportation & Communication	5
5.	Building & Utilities	1
6.	Public & Community Service	18
7.	Personal Services	17

Each member is assigned a task for a given length of time. The routine functions such as cooking and management of dining hall are carried out on a rotation basis. Each branch of economic activity is headed by an elected coordinator. He is responsible for organizing the work of the different branches and for implementing production and investment plans. Although management positions are increasingly professionalized, the kibubutzim have adopted various methods of administration and organization to adapt their economic structure to the needs of the times without losing a sense of mutual responsibility and equality of work.

Women are equal participants in the labour force, with jobs in all parts of the kibbutz open to them. However, in contrast to kibbutz women two generations ago who sought to prove their worth by doing "men's work", today a majority of them prefer jobs in education, health and other services. Older members receive suitable work assignments according to their health and stamina.

Most of the members work in their kibbutz. Some are employed in regional kibbutz enterprises and a few are sent out by the kibbutz to perform educational and political functions under the aegis of its national movement. A few pursue their own special talent or profession outside the kibbutz framework. The income of these outside workers is turned over to the kibbutz.

The occasional lack of personnel for factories, agricultural tasks, tourism services and other jobs necessitates hiring paid workers, although this practice is contrary to the kibbutz principle of self-reliance in labour. Many kibubutzim host young volunteers from Israel and abroad for periods of one month or longer in exchange for work, thus partially solving the dilemma of obtaining outside labour.

Table 20.3: Number of Workers both Internal and Hired (1990-2000)

Year	*Number of Workers*	*% of Hired Workers*
1990	18,791	29.9
1992	20,223	40.7
1994	22,958	48.6
1996	25,673	56.4
1998	26,843	62.0
2000	29,290	66.7

Source: Kibbutz Industry Association.

SOCIO-ECONOMIC ROLE OF KIBBUTZ

Kibbutz, being a communal society, assumes responsibility to meet the basic needs of its members throughout their lives. It allows individuals to develop to their fullest potential, while demanding responsibility and commitment from each person to contribute to the welfare of all members of the community. The feelings of security and satisfaction engendered by belonging to a small, closed community make the life of kibbutz members satisfying.

In the early stages of its evolution, the kibbutz society took precedence over the family unit. In time, the community became increasingly family-centred. Today, in the context of a normal society of grandparents, mothers and fathers, aunts and uncles, sons and daughters, the kibbutz still offers a level of cooperation which provides a social framework and personal economic security. But compared to the past, kibubutzim today offer their members a much wider range of individual choices. Members have more latitude in all aspects of their lives, from the selection of clothing and home furnishings to where and how to spend their vacations. More opportunities are available to participate in higher education, and the special needs of artists and writers are recognized, with time given them to pursue their own projects. Although no money actually changes hands, members allot themselves a predetermined amount of credit each year to spend as they wish.

The kibbutz is not only a form of settlement and a lifestyle; it is also an integral part of Israeli society. Before the establishment of the state of Israel and in the first decade of the statehood, the kibbutz looked after such central functions in the community as immigration, defence and agricultural development. Once the state took control of these functions, the interaction between the kibbutz and the society at large decreased, but did not stop. Apart from the active involvement in the country's political life, the kibubutzim have carried out various national tasks over the years.

A good number of kibubutzim run five-month study courses for new immigrants, which combine intensive Hebrew language instruction, in-depth tours of the country and lectures on various aspects of Israeli life, and work on the kibbutz. Those participants who decide to stay in the kibbutz may apply for membership. Some kibubutzim adopt youth from disadvantaged families them up to high school. Some of these young people continue to live on the kibbutz and become its members. Their factories and farms account for 9 per cent of Israel's industrial output, worth US$8 billion, and 40 per cent of its agricultural output, worth over $1.7 billion.[1] Some Kibubutzim had also developed substantial high-tech and military industries. For example, in 2010, Kibbutz Salsa, containing some 200 members, generated $850 million in annual revenue from its military-plastics industry.[2]

Cultural Activities

Cultural activities abound in kibubutzim with films and professional performances presented frequently in community auditoriums. Further, closed circuit television offers programmers geared to the interests and tastes of the members for several hours daily. The kibbutz movements sponsor a number of professional groups, including a symphony orchestra, chamber ensembles, modern and folk dance troupes, choirs and a theatre company, which perform regularly in Israel and abroad. Some kibubutzim have museums which specialize in subjects such as archaeology, nature, art, Jewish history and the development of the land of Israel; they attract the community members as well as visitors in large numbers.

Education of Children

Unlike former times when children lived in children's houses each kibbutz maintained, children in most of the kibubutzim today sleep at their parents' home until they reach high school age. But much of their day-time is still spent with their peers in facilities adapted specifically for each age group. Parents are getting increasingly involved in their children's activities. Thus, the family unit is gaining more importance in the structure of the kibbutz community. The women who 75 years ago insisted on being released from domestic chores are now insisting on more parental involvement in the upbringing of young children and for allocating women more time at home with their families.

Children thus grow up knowing the value and importance of work that everyone must do. The educational system from the nursery school to the university emphasizes cooperation in daily life. Youngsters are assigned duties and take decisions with regard to their peer group. Young children perform regular age-appropriate tasks, older children assume certain jobs in the kibbutz and, at high school level, they devote one full day each week to work in a branch of the kibbutz economy.

Each kibbutz has an elementary school; the older children attend a regional kibbutz high school serving several area of kibubutzim. This helps children experience a broader range of academic subjects and social contacts. At all age levels, accommodations are available for youngsters with special talents or needs. Nearly 40 per cent of all kibbutz children come back to the kibbutz they were born after army service. Thus, a majority of kibbutz members today grew up in the kibbutz and decided to build their life there.

FUTURE OF KIBUBUTZIM

With time, the sense of identification that the members had with their kibbutz has decreased. This process originated both from personal frustrations among them resulting from internal processes and from the growing stratification and inequality due to the growth of capitalistic practices.[3] Over the years, some kibbutz members established professional careers outside the kibbutz, accumulating power, privileges and prestige.[4] The balance between individual values and values of the kibbutz began to tip, and work motivation was affected. An emphasis was placed on social compensation to encourage productivity. These processes occurred in parallel with a severe economic crisis.

The privatization processes led to the decline of cooperative beliefs all over the world including the Israeli society, affected the moral and structural support of kibubutzim, and captured the imagination of the new generations of the kibubutzim. The kibubutzim were built to create a permanent and institutionalized social framework and a pattern of conduct that would successfully handle the implementation of shared values. The attempt to place such a regular pattern required creativity in the adoption of kibbutz practices to its growth and changing kibbutz system and encompassing society, but kibbutz leadership suppressed innovators and critical thinkers, causing either failures to deal with changes or adoption of capitalist solutions that negated kibbutz basic principles.[5]

The kibubutzim had a rural pattern of human settlements, while over the years the Israeli society began adopting urban patterns of settlements. The lack of match between the patterns of the kibbutz society and the majority of the Israeli society, appealed the strong linkage between the kibubutzim with the entire Israeli society, a principle that did not allow the continuation of the collaborative model (because of the internal weakening and the loss of the all-Israeli legitimacy).

The kibubutzim were established during the pioneer period and were the fulfilment of the Zionist vision, during that period of time every member was required to give the maximum from himself for the good of the collective: the kibbutz and the state. In addition, as a group it was easier to deal with the common problems of the individuals—which allowed the recruitment of a large number of people for maintaining the safety of the community at that time and, therefore, this way of life was suited for the Zionist goals more than other forms of life at that time.

The original concept of the kibubutzim was based to a large extent on self-sacrifice of its members for the sake of abstract foundations and not on the cancellation of work and, therefore, after the pioneer period the linkage between the kibbutz members decreased, due to the decline in the pioneering spirit and the decline in the importance of the self-sacrifice values.

When the kibbutz was perceived as an initiator for values and national objectives, it was very much appreciated in the Israeli society and it was easier for the members to identify themselves with the kibbutz, its function and its significance. With the decrease of its appreciation and the minimizing of the social significances in the Israeli society, the kibbutz identity weakened.

The kibubutzim were not capable of dealing with the increase in the standard of living in order to keep the communal values relevant, which eventually led to the changes in patterns of life of many members, undermining the relevancy of the communal framework, which was not adapted to this.

The globalization processes and the kibbutz failure to block them exposed the kibbutz society to a different type of culture. For example, after kibbutz members were allowed to have television sets in their own homes, they were exposed to 'the good life' in which people were compensated for their work and could buy themselves different luxurious items. The kibubutzim were not able to deal with these processes.[6]

The collapse of the Communist bloc resulted in the weakening of Socialist beliefs around the world, including in the kibbutz society. During the 1980s, following the peak of the kibubutzim crisis, many peoples started leaving their kibubutzim, and there was considerable tension due to the economic situation. In order to cope with the situation, some kibubutzim began to change in various ways.

The changes that occurred could be divided into three main types:

1. Extensive privatization of the kibbutz services: in fact, such privatization had been introduced over the past two decades in many kibubutzim. Most of these privatization processes, however, were made in matters that were considered relatively minor. Currently, many kibubutzim that have privatized (some of them with subsidies) have also privatized

the education and health systems, which were once considered untouchable.

2. *Differential Wage*: One famous characteristic of the kibubutzim was that each kibbutz member received an equal budget according to his or her needs, regardless of what job they held. In many kibubutzim, members are now paid differentially based on the work they do.
3. *Association of Properties*: It refers to the transfer of some of the properties belonging to the kibbutz, in its capacity as a cooperative commonality, to the ownership of individual kibbutz members. This is actually true privatization (unlike the services privatization). These assets include the homes where the members live and a sort of a 'stock' in the manufacturing component of the kibbutz. This change allows kibbutz members to sell and bequeath both types of properties, within certain limitations.

Since, the mid-1990s, the number of kibubutzim making significant changes in their lifestyle continued to grow, while the resistance to these changes gradually decreased, with only a few dozen kibubutzim still functioning under more traditional models. It is important to note, however, that each kibbutz has undergone different processes of change. There are many people, outside and inside the kibubutzim, who claim these changes bring the end of the kibbutz concept. Among the communities that had recently officially ceased being kibubutzim are Megiddo in the Jezreel Valley, Hag Goshrim in the Upper Galilee, Beyt Nir in the Negev, etc.

These processes have created the "renewing kibbutz" a kibbutz settlement pattern not fully based on the original values of the kibbutz. Kibubutzim continuing under the original kibbutz values are associated with the 'collaborative model'.

New Models

By the second decade of the twenty-first century, three distinct models of kibbutz had emerged:

1. Traditional collective *kibbutz* known as *kibbutz shitufi*, in which each member is compensated equally regardless of what work he does;

2. Mixed model *kibbutz* known as *kibbutz-meshulav*, wherein each member gets a small percentage of his salary along with a basic component given equally to all members; and
3. Renewing *kibbutz/kibbutz mithadesh* in which a member's income consists solely of his income from his work and sometimes includes income from other kibbutz sources.[7]

According to a survey conducted by the University of Haifa, 188 of all kibubutzim (72%) are now converted to the 'renewing kibbutz' model, which could be described as more individualistic kibbutz. Dr. Shlomo Getz, head of the Institute for the Research on the Kibbutz and Cooperative Idea believes that by the end of 2012, there will be more kibubutzim switching to an alternative model. Robinstein has concluded that after years of declining membership and productivity, the kibubutzim have started making a comeback. In 1997, kibbutz production was valued at NIS (New Israeli Shekel) 20 billion. In 2006, the figure grew to NIS 27 billion. During the same period, the kibubutzim erased a collective debt of NIS 700 million and turned a NIS 1.2 billion profit. "Differential pay was introduced into the kibbutz structure; management has become increasingly professionalized; and the community and business structures have been separated, ... The community has retained its ideology of equality as much as possible, whereas the business enterprise has operated according to market-driven parameters. Today's kibubutzim still manage their funds in such a way that the weak, elderly and those members unable to earn high wages are cared for."[8]

Today's kibbutz is the accomplishment of three generations. The founders, motivated by strong convictions and a distinct ideology, forged a society with a unique communal way of life. Their children, born into the kibbutz framework, worked hard to consolidate its economic, social and administrative structures. The present generation, which grew up in an established and prosperous society, is applying its energies and talents to meet the challenges of modern life in the technological age.[9]

Some fear that by adjusting to changing circumstances, the kibbutz is abandoning many of its original principles; others believe that this ability to adapt and compromise is the key to its survival. Whatever lies ahead, as long as the kibbutz maintains its democratic nature, and the spirit of voluntarism, commitment and idealism, continues to motivate its members, it will have creative and compelling resources with which to meet the demands of the future.

MOSHAVIM: THE COOPERATIVE VILLAGE REPUBLICS OF ISRAEL

Moshav is a type of Israeli human settlement of individual farmers getting together to constitute a cooperative agricultural community. It was pioneered by the Labour Zionists during the second wave of aliyah. A member of a moshav is called a 'moshavnik'. The moshav is similar to kibbutz with emphasis on community labour. It was designed as part of the Zionist state-building programme following the green revolution in the British Mandate of Palestine during the early twentieth century. Unlike the collective kibbutz, farms in a moshav are individually owned but are of fixed and equal size. Workers produced agricultural products on their lands using individual and/or pooled labour and resources and distribute the products to meet their needs.

Moshavim are governed by an elected Council which levies a special tax to meet the cost of community projects and facilities. The tax is the same for all households of the community. Thus, good farmers were better off than bad ones. In communal kibubutzim all members enjoyed the same living standard. Number of moshavim has declined but a good number of them have managed to survive. In all there are 448 moshavim in Israel.

There are several variants of moshavim. The following two are the most common among them:

1. *Moshav Ovdim* (*workers' moshav*). It is the most common type and relies on cooperative purchasing of supplies and marketing of produce; the family or household is, however, the basic unit of production and consumption. Land is allotted to households or individuals. At present there are 253 such settlements.
2. *Moshav Shitufii* (*collective moshav*). It is a collective smallholder's settlement that combines the economic features of a kibbutz and social features of a moshav. Farming is done collectively and profits are shared equally. It is closer to the collectivity of the kibbutz. Although consumption is family or household-based, production and marketing are collective.

Unlike the moshav ovdim, land is not allotted to households or individuals, but is collectively worked. At present there are 195 such settlements in Israel. Today, there are 187 moshavim shitufiim in Israel.

The members moshavim have access to a range of mutual help instruments maintained by the national Moshavim Movement. These include a mutual insurance company, a mutual help fund, a mortgage bank for moshavim, and a pension and retirement fund for individual moshav members. In the past, the Moshavim Movement created a system of regional service cooperatives for supply of farm inputs and for marketing and processing of farm products for its members. These regional cooperatives were similar to those established by the Kibbutz Movement for kibubutzim and included fruit packing and canning facilities, livestock feed mixing, poultry and meat processing plants, egg sorting and packing, and refrigerated storage facilities.

The Moshavim Movement, like all settlement movements in Israel, is a cooperative federation formed by primary village-level agricultural cooperatives (moshavim and moshavim shitufiim). Israel has eight such federations. Close to eighty per cent of the agricultural output of Israel is produced on cooperative farms. As mentioned earlier, the first moshav, Nahalal, was established in the Jezreel Valley (also known as the Valley of Esdraelon) on September 11, 1921. By 1986 about 156,700 Israelis lived and worked on 448 moshavim.

Because the moshavim retained the family as the centre of social life, it was far more attractive to traditional Mizrahi (immigrants Muslim countries) who came to Israel in 1950s and 1960s. They were averse to bold experiments, like communal child-rearing, equality of the sexes, practiced in more radical communal kibbutz. These immigrants moshav (*moshav olim*) were able to absorb and integrate oriental immigrants. It allowed them a much steadier ascent into the middle class than did life in some newly developing towns. For this reason, the moshav became largely a Mizrahi institution, whereas the kibbutz movement remained basically an Ashkenazi institution.

Since, the 1967 war, both the moshavim and kibubutzim have relied increasingly on outside, particularly Arab labour. Financial instabilities in the early 1980s hit many moshavim hard. High birth rate made it difficult to absorb all the young people wishing to remain in the community. By the late 1980s, an increasing number of moshav members came to be employed in non-agricultural jobs outside the community. So, some moshavim began to resemble suburban or exurban villages whose residents commuted to work. In general, moshavim never enjoyed the elite status enjoyed by the kibubutzim and their prestige declined during 1970s and 1980s.

Moshav Shitufi

A moshav shitufi is a type of cooperative village which in matters of organizational principles stand between the kibbutz and the moshav. A classical moshav (formally known as *moshav ovdim*, or *workers' moshav* is a village-level service cooperative that takes care of farm services (such as marketing, supply, and credit for its members, while all production and consumption activities are handled at the level of families and households. A classical kibbutz is a village-level production cooperative, with all production, consumption, and service decisions handled collectively. Moshav shitufi is an intermediate form, in which production and services are handled collectively, while consumption decisions remain the responsibility of the households. Moshav shitufi members are engaged in agriculture and industry in the village and also work in various professions outside the community, contributing their salary to the collective.

The first moshav shitufi was established in 1936 in Kffar Hittim in Lower Galilee. Moshav shitufi has never been as widespread as moshav ovadim or kibbutz. Thus, at the end of 2006, there were 40 such cooperative villages in Israel, compared with 400 moshavim and nearly 300 kibubutzim. The population in moshavim shitufim was around 18,000, compared with 350,000 in moshavim and kibubutzim combined. There have been numerous instances in the history of cooperative agriculture in Israel when a kibbutz or a moshav reorganized as moshav shitufi, and *vice versa*. Moledet, the second moshav shitufi created in Israel in 1937 was a kibbutz and then reorganized in 1944 as moshav shitufi and reverted to the original name *Moledet* in 1957.

SIMILARITIES BETWEEN VILLAGE REPUBLICS OF GANDHI AND KIBUBUTZIM AND MOSHAVIM

The transformation of Indian villages into republics of Gandhi's dream is far more problematic than establishment of kibubutzim and moshavim in Israel. The Jews who migrated to Israel from different parts of the world had an ideological mission to create a new world. Judaism was considered by these migrants an expression of the covenantal relationship that God established with the Children of Israel. The immigrants wanted to convert Israel into that covenantal paradise. Once they settled down, new realities of life and living came to the fore. They had to make changes in the internal structure and external relations of the kibubutzim and moshavim. These changes at times went against the very ideology on which these settlements were founded. But the fact that many of these institutions have survived to this day, points to something that was lasting.

Indian villages had undergone tremendous changes in response to changing political, social and economic contexts. By the time Gandhi came into picture, they were no longer self-governing human settlements they were once upon a time. His mission was to reinvent them as village republics. In 1934, he resigned from the Indian National Congress over his differences with other leaders on the purity of ends and means. He established the All India Village Industries Association at Wardha and devoted most of his time towards reorganization of Indian villages. Gandhiji started experiments in the elements of rural life-style such as revival of village crafts and agro-processing industries, village cleanliness, diet reforms, etc., so that villages could be developed as ideal human settlements to live in. One of his major thrusts was removal of untouchability.

Before moving to Sevagram village in April 1936, Gandhi had started experiments to revitalize various small-scale industries at Wardha. He trained many workers in rural reconstruction work such as making *neera* from palm trees, jaggery, etc., and in dairy, leather work, pottery, oil pressing, bee-keeping, etc. He shifted the headquarters of All India Spinners' Association to Sevagram.

In Sevagram Ashram, *neera* was served to all inmates in the morning. Hand spinning and weaving (*khadi* cloth) was the hub around which all the village industries were built. Gandhi's mission was not limited to economic diversification; he thought he could rebuild and preserve the Indian village culture and made the villages the centres of cultural transformation. There was no place of ignorance, uncleanliness, laziness and jealousy in Gandhi's village republics in making.

Since, 1936 till his last, Gandhiji stayed in Sevagram Ashram and carried out various experiments. The man, who fought the mightiest empire of the world, also developed and demonstrated a new way to create a non-exploitative and non-violent social order. He launched three nationwide *satyagraha* movements: the Civil Disobedience in 1921-22 which had to be suspended later because of breakdown of the moral discipline and eruption of violence against the British; the Salt March in 1930; and the Quit India Movement of 1942.

"My Idea of village *swaraj* is that it is a complete republic, independent of its neighbours for its own vital needs and yet interdependent for many others in which dependence is necessary. Thus every village's first concern will be to grow its own food crops, and cotton for its cloth. It should have reserve for its cattle, recreation and playground for adults and children. Then if there is more land available, it will grow useful money crops, thus excluding *ganja*, tobacco, opium and the like.

The village will maintain a village theatre, school and hall for meetings and marriages and various social and cultural activities. It will have its own waterworks ensuring clean water supply. This could be done through controlled wells and tanks. Education will be compulsory up to the final basic course. As far as possible every activity will be conducted on the co-operative basis. The caste distinctions and untouchability will stand abolished.

Non-violence with its technique of *satyagraha* and non-co-operation will be the cornerstone of village community. The security of the village will be the responsibility of the village guards who will be selected by rotation from the register maintained by the village. The government of the village will be conducted by a Gram Panchayat of five persons annually elected by the adult villagers, male and female, possessing minimum prescribed qualifications. These will have all the authority and jurisdiction required to efficiently manage the village affairs. Since there will be no system of punishments in the accepted sense, this Panchayat will be the legislature, judiciary and executive combined to operate for its year of office.

I have not examined here the question of the relations with the neighbouring villages and the Centre if any. My purpose is to present an outline of village government. Here is perfect democracy based upon individual freedom. The individual is the architect of his own Government. He and his village are able to defy the might of the world. For the law governing every villager is that he will suffer death in the defence of his and his village's honour.

To model such a village may be the work of life-time. Any lover of democracy and village life can take up a village, treat it as his world and sole work, and he will find good results. He begins by being the village scavenger, spinner, watchman, medicine-man and school master all at once. If nobody comes near him he will be satisfied with scavenging and spinning."[10]

"The villagers should develop such a high degree of skill that articles prepared by them should command a ready market outside. When our villages are fully developed there will be no dearth in them of men with a high degree of skill and artistic talent. There will be village poets, village artists, village architects, linguists and research workers. In short, there will be nothing in life worth having which will not be had in the villages. Today, the villages are dung heaps; tomorrow they will be like tiny gardens of Eden, where live highly intelligent folks whom no one can deceive or exploit.

The reconstruction of the villages along these lines should begin now. The reconstruction of the villages should not be organized on a temporary but permanent basis. Craft, art, health and education should all be integrated into one scheme. Nai Talim is a beautiful blend of all the four and covers the whole education of the individual from the time of conception to the moment of death. Therefore, I would not divide village uplift work into water-tight compartments from the very beginning but undertake an activity which will combine different from education I will regard the former as the medium for the latter. Nai Talim, therefore, ought to be integrated into the scheme."[11]

"A village unit as conceived by me is as strong as the strongest. My imaginary village consists of 1,000 souls. Such a unit can give a good account to itself, if it is well organized on a basis of self-sufficiency.

An ideal Indian village will be so constructed as to lend itself to perfect sanitation. It will have cottages with sufficient light and ventilation, built of a material obtainable within a radius of five miles of it. The cottages will have courtyards enabling the householders to plant vegetables for domestic use and to house their cattle. The village lanes and streets will be free of all avoidable dust. It will have wells according to its needs and accessible to all. It will have houses of worship for all, also a common meeting place, a village common for grazing its cattle, a co-operative dairy, primary and secondary schools in which industrial education will be the central factor, and it will have village Panchayats for settling disputes. It will produce its own grains, vegetables and fruits and its own *khadi*."[12]

One can get more information about village *swaraj* and village republic as envisaged by Gandhiji from *Village Swaraj* published by him in a book form by the Navjivan Trust Ahmedabad. The book contains Gandhiji's views on different aspects of rural life including agriculture, village industry, animal husbandry, transport, basic education, health and hygiene. At a time when the Panchayati Raj system put in place in 1993 under 73rd and 74th Amendment to the Constitution of India has failed to deliver the goods it was expected to deliver, Gandhiji's views on village *swaraj* have become relevant again.

The Community Development movement launched in 1950s was to usher in a new era in rural development. But it failed to achieve its objectives. The idea underlying it was imported from the USA; it had no Indian base. The Block Development Officer (BDO) who heads a team of Assistant Development Officers (ADOs) is now as good or bad as any civil servant. In fact, in many States the Block functionaries and equivalent State civil servants are inter-transferable. The system has become so corrupt that whole scheme of Community Development as it was conceived then, has totally collapsed. It is sarcastically said that BDO is an officer who blocks development.

Gandhi's concept of village republics was never put to practice in the country as the leaders like Nehru were so deeply wedded to Marxist and western models of development that considered Gandhian thought on rural development as outmoded. Modern Industrialization was the only solution to India's development problems. Gandhi was wrongly declared as an enemy of machines and mechanization although it is now a well known fact that he was not against mechanization as such; he only objected to 'the craze for machinery'. He welcomed every improvement in small machines which could provide employment to millions of artisans in the villages. In place of mass production by big factories, he advocated production by the masses in their own homes and cottages.

Gandhi wanted that every able-bodied citizen of India should be fully employed; and since a great majority of people of India lived in villages, this objective could be achieved only by organizing village and cottage industries in the countryside. Any economic planning which did not utilize fully the idle manpower in the rural areas could not be termed as sound or rational. "To a people, famishing and idle, the only acceptable form in which God can dare appear is work and promise of food as wages."[13] This ideal of full employment is now recognized by Western economists as basic to planned economic development, particularly of underdeveloped countries with large and growing populations. Prof. Galbraith is of the view that "full employment is more desirable than increased production combined with unemployment".[14]

Mahatma Gandhi strongly pleaded for decentralization of economic and political power through the organization of Village Panchayats. He was of the definite view that Panchayati Raj system in India, if worked on scientific lines, could not only build up the social and economic strength of the countryside but also strengthen the forces of national defence against the risk of foreign invasion. Acharya Vinoba Bhave also stressed on the urgent need for organizing Indian villages on a co-operative community basis through *Gramadana*.

A study of modern economic and political thought in the West would indicate that decentralized institutions are now regarded as crucial to the establishment of democracy on stable foundations. "If man's faith in social action is to be revivified," states Prof. Joad, "the State must be cut up and its functions distributed."[15] In his Fabian Socialism, Prof. Cole maintains that for diffusing widely among ordinary men and women a capacity for collective activity "we must set out to build our society upon little democracies".[16] From this standpoint, the experiment of Panchayati Raj which has been launched in India's countryside with zeal and vigour is a right step towards the goal of "Village *Swaraj*" envisaged by Gandhiji.

Above all, we should be clear in our minds that Gandhiji did not stand for a social and economic order based on material values alone. He always upheld the ideal of simple living and high thinking and worked for a higher standard of life and not merely for a higher standard of living. "Civilization, in the real sense of the term", remarks Gandhiji "consists not in the multiplication but in the deliberate and voluntary restriction of wants."[17]

Unfortunately, this ethical and moral aspect of economic life has often been neglected to the detriment of real human welfare. Modern economists are emphasizing the urgent need for 'investment in man' in addition to 'investment in goods' for achieving broad-based and speedy economic growth. Prof. Schumpeter rightly observes that for the success of economic and political democracy, "individuals with adequate ability and moral character must exist in sufficient numbers".[18] The same idea has been forcefully expressed by Mr. Crosland in the following words: "We do not want to enter the age of abundance only to find that we have lost the values which might teach us how to enjoy it."[19] It is, therefore, this human and moral aspect of our planning which must be constantly borne in mind by all workers, officials as well as non-officials, who are engaged in this great adventure of building up a New India of Gandhiji's dreams.

The time is now ripe to return to Gandhi and his concepts of Gram *Swaraj* and Village Republic. Naturally, there is a long time gap between the first halves of the last century and twenty-first centuries. We should accept Gandhi's thesis that the solution of most of the problems of Indian villages have to be found within the villages. The villages, however, cannot be delinked from cities and towns in the present era of globalization. India needs rural-urban integration with self-reliant villages as the foundation for sustainable development and cities of various sizes as the base for industrial and technological development to meet the export and related needs.

HOW CAN GROWTH FOCI BRIDGE THE GAPS?

India is a land of villages; so says the history. In 2015, India is planning to be a country of smart cities. One hundred cities have already been identified to become smart cities. But the question is: how to develop smart cities without developing smart villages? Streams of people, especially the youths are leaving the villages to find work in cities. Larger and more developed a city, more attractive it is. The smart cities would be filled with rural migrants who would live in slums, road sides and any other vacant place. Within no time, the smart cities would be full of slums and their well-laid roads would be occupied by trollies selling fruits, vegetables and other consumer goods. After 9 PM the road dividers and pedestrian sideways will become *rain baseras* (night shelters). The situation would be much worse than what it is in metropolitan cities of India.

The ruralites leave the villages partly because traditional agriculture can no longer provide employment to a growing population and partly because in the era of mobiles, smart phones and TVs, the youth cannot live in villages whose physical and occupational structure has remained static. Even roads and electricity have not reached many villages. And if they reach, they would alienate the youth more and inspire them to leave the village. The situation has so deteriorated, that the villages which once were pools of labour are not short of labour. One of the new reasons for the backwardness of agriculture is the shortage of labour in villages of India.

India does not need smart cities—the cities with wide enough roads to accommodate growing number of people and vehicles—both two-wheelers and four-wheelers. But the idea of smart cities can fructify only if the smart cities are accompanied and backed by smart villages and towns. In this context, it would be pertinent to recall the author's hierarchic model of human settlements suited to India and which he suggested as early as 1968. The model known as Growth Foci (now renamed as below) would have five levels of human settlements:

I. Global Metropolis (GM)—A first tier city of 5 million or more population,
II. National Metropolis (NM)—A second tier city of 1-5 million population,
III. Regional City (RC)—A third tier city of 2.5 lakh to 5.00 lakhs population,
IV. Rural Service Centres (RSC)—A fourth tier settlement with 10,000 to 25,000 population, and
V. Gram Panchayats (GP)—A village including its satellites covering 5000 to 10,000 population.

The GM is envisaged to be a metropolis, which links the country with other countries of the world economically, technologically and politically and lower level human settlements within the country. It is through these metropolises that the country links itself with other countries of the world and with other cities, towns and villages of the country. Each GM would have 4-6 NMs to serve and in turn, to be served; a NM will have 4-6 RCs to serve and in turn to be served; a RC will have 4-6 RSCs in its service zone; and a RSC will have at least 5 GPs in its service zone. It is through these Development Foci that the top-down and bottom-up processes of development would operate.

The GPs would constitute Gandhi's Village Republics, which would function like Israeli moshavim. They will be cooperative units whose members would be self-employed locally or regionally and thus will constitute the foundation for India's self-reliance in matters its basic needs. Each GP will locally produce much of its basic necessities of life like food, water, transport, and energy. Each GP will be linked by motorable roads to other GPs and its Service Centres. It will have facilities to convert paddy into rice and wheat into wheat flour; it will have tube wells for secured water supply and facilities for harnessing solar energy. Each GP will have a nursery and primary school with teachers from the GP or its nearby areas; it will also have a yoga centre with a teacher preferably belonging to the village. The GP schools will have an attached centre for skill development where students will be trained in selected and locally relevant trades. The employees of the GPs as far as possible would be drawn from within the GP. In case, such qualified people are not available in the GP, arrangements would be made to depute young boys and girls to get appropriate education and training.

The GPs will be managed by a Panchayat of five *Panches* elected for five years. One among the five members of the Panchayat will function as Chairman or Gram Pradhan for a year by turn. The office of the Gram Pradhan will rotate among the five *Panches*. There will be five committees each consisting of five members to manage the affairs of the GP.

1. Committee for Agriculture including Horticulture and Dairying.
2. Committee for Education.
3. Committee for Sanitation and Health.
4. Committee for Handicrafts and Small-Scale Industries.
5. Committee for Cultural and Social Affairs.

Each RSC will function as a service centre for the GPs of its jurisdiction. It will have health clinic with an ambulance. The physician, compounder and other employees of the clinic would preferably belong to the area covered by the RSC. It will have educational facilities upto High School.

CONCLUDING REMARKS

This chapter explains vividly that Gandhi's concept of village republics is not just an idea. It was put into practice in Israel and continues to exist there, various stresses and strains notwithstanding. Had the Panchayat Raj system of India been developed on the lines Gandhi suggested, the shape of rural India today would have been far different and far better.

It is still possible to rehabilitate rural India and take it on the path of socio-economic and human development by integrating Gandhi's concept of village republics and author model of development foci.

What India needs today is two-way process of development: 'development from above' and 'development from below', not just one way process, i.e., 'development from above', as is the case at present. It would be good if the Government of India, Ministry of Rural Development sends a delegation of expert to Israel to study the functioning of Kibubutzim and Moshavim in the era of globalization.

NOTES

1. Bulletproof Innovation: Kibbutz-owned Plasa's Ikea-style, Flat-pack Armour Kits By Nadav Shemer, Fast Company.
2. Shapira, Reuven (2005). "Academic Capital or Scientific Progress? A critique of studies of kibbutz stratification". *Journal of Anthropological Research* from the Navajivan Trust (3): 357-380.
3. *Ibid.* (2001). "Communal decline: The vanishing of high-moral leaders and the decay of democratic, high-trust kibbutz cultures", *Sociological Inquiry* 71 (1): 13-38.
4. *Ibid.-Transforming Kibbutz Research*, Cleveland: New World Publishing, 2008, Chaps. 12.
5. Carmeli Y. and Applbaum K. ed. (2004), *Consumption and Market Society in Israel*, Oxford: Berg Publishers.
6. *Ibid.*
7. http://israelity.com/2010/01/27/kibbutz-changes, 27.1.2010.
8. Segev, Tom. *One Palestine, Complete: Jews and Arabs under the British Mandate*. Metropolitan Books, 2000, p. 255.
9. See James Horrox, *A Living Revolution: Anarchism in the Kibbutz Movement*, Oakland: A.K. Press, 2009. Ch. 3.
10. Gandhi, M.K., *Harijan*, 26-7-1942.
11. *Ibid.*, 10-11-1946.
12. Bose, Nirmal Kumar, (1948).
13. Village Swaraj www.mkgandhi.org, page 3.
14. Galbraith, John Kenneth (1984), *The Affluent Society*, p. 155.
15. Joad, C.E.M. (1964), *Modern Political Theory*, pp. 120-21.
16. Cole, G.D.H. (1943), *Fabian Socialism*, London: George Allen & Unwin.
17. www.mkgandhi.org, page 4.
18. Schumpeter, J.A. (1942), *Capitalism, Socialism and Democracy*, Harper & Brothers.
19. Crosland, Anthony (1956), *Future of Socialism*, Jonathan Cape, p. 529.

REFERENCES

Baratz, Joseph, 1956. *A Village by the Jordan: The Story of Degania*. Tel Aviv: Ichud Habonim, p. 52.

Bettelheim, Bruno (2001), *The Children of the Dream*, Simon & Schuster, p. 15, 243.

Criden, Yosef; Gelb, Saadia (1974). *The Kibbutz Experience*. New York: Schocken. ISBN 0-8052-0511-X.

Gavron, Daniel (2000). *The Kibbutz: Awakening from Utopia*. Lanham: Rowman & Littlefield, pp. 160-168.

Golan, S. (1956). "Upbringing in the Family, in Institutions and the Kibbutz". *Sugiot*. Tel Aviv: Sifriat Poalim, p. 308.

Henry Near (1997), *The Kibbutz Movement: A History*. Vol. II, London: Littman Library, 1997.

Peres, Judy, In 50 years, kibbutz movement has undergone many changes, *Chicago Tribune*, 9 May, 1998.

Rayman, Paula (1981), *The Kibbutz Community and Nation Building*, Princeton University Press, p. 12.

Rosner, Menachem, *et al.* (1990), *The Second Generation Continuity and Change in the Kibbutz*, Westport: Greenwood.

Scharf, M. (2001), A "Natural Experiment' in Childrearing Ecologies and Adolescents" Attachment and Separation Representations, *Child Development*, 72 (1): 236-251.

Segev, Tom (2000), *One Palestine Complete: Jews and Arabs under the British Mandate*. Metropolitan Books, p. 252.

Spiro, Melford E. (1963, 1970), *Kibbutz Venture in Utopia*, New York: Schocken.

The Jewish Advocate, 7 March, 2008.

Index

Acquisitiveness, 147
Advanced Facility Centre, 248
Afro-Asian and Latin American (AALA), 97
Age-old indigenous village techniques, 110
Agrarian challenges, 194, 199
Agricultural country, 152
Agricultural products, 38
Agro-industrial community, 253
Aparigraha, 33–34, 51–52, 147
Artisans, 79, 211, 222, 224, 231, 278
Ashrams, 102, 121, 187, 249
Assistant Development Officers (ADOs), 278
Asteya, 147
Attainment, 59, 82, 101, 118, 151
Aziz, Abdul, 146, 148–49

Basic principles, 10, 20, 49, 87, 111, 133, 136, 175, 240, 268
Basic Tenets of Gandhian Model, 134
Bissell, John, 228
Blasphemous, 14
Block Development Officer (BDO), 278
Bread labour, 33–34, 146–47, 150, 154–56, 163, 171, 187
British colonial rule in India, 193
Business Ethics, 115
Byproducts, 21, 36

Capital expenditure, 202
Capitalism, 1–3, 7, 10, 12, 16, 18–21, 81, 89, 92–94, 127, 132, 138, 142, 147, 151
Capitalist society, 138
Caste system, 80, 241, 251, 257
Categorical conviction of Gandhiji, 214
Centralization, 46, 65, 149
Centralized power, 89
Centralized production, 65
Charkha, 98, 228, 249
Chemical fertilizer, 200, 205–6, 214
Child marriage, 112
Civil magistrate, 5
Civil society, 166, 168
  global, 117
  self-respecting global, 116
Class war, 69, 104, 179
Classless society, 154
Cloth production, 225
Coercive power, 163
Colonial rule, 86, 98, 240, 242, 252
Colonialism, 5, 20–22, 86, 111, 259
Commercial banks, 203
Common Facility Centre, 248
Communal society, 265
Communism, 7, 18, 75, 82, 88–89, 138, 142
Communist country, 127
Community
  development, 278
  disorganization, 252
Confiscation, 152–53

Constitution of India, 89–90, 278
Contemporary Relevance of Gandhian Economics, 85
Cooperative society, 3
Corporate activities, 117–18
Corporate business, 119
Cottage industries, 37, 64–65, 98–99, 135, 149, 172, 278
Crisis
  agrarian, 200, 208, 213
  economic, 127, 173, 268
  environmental, 24, 132–33
Critical Upward Communication (CUC), 122
Crop failures, 201–2
Culmination, 186, 193

Dairying, 167, 239, 282
Dalits, 257
Decentralized mode of production, 22, 149
Deprivation, 3, 110, 127, 212–13
Development foci, 281–82
Development Gap, 162
Dialectical materialism, 7
Discovery of India, 255, 257
Duality, 19

Economics, 1–3, 11–13, 40–41, 51–55, 74, 85–86, 101–3, 139, 141–42, 146–48, 170–71, 173–74, 176, 180–81, 189
  activities, 49–50, 53, 60–61, 64–65, 71, 86, 97, 108, 116, 128, 138, 150, 179–80, 189–90, 264
  capitalist, 2, 136, 142
  decentralization, 149, 171–72, 174
  disorder, 35, 104
  drain, 210, 212
  equality, 77, 154, 156, 159, 172, 253
  functions, 53, 254
  globalization, 169
  growth, 6, 17, 32, 43–44, 54, 76, 91, 94, 108, 181–82, 220, 279
  ideals, 146, 170
  independence, 50, 58–59, 71–72, 135, 179, 211, 222
  institutions, 11, 80, 101, 104
  mainstream, 49–50
  model, 33, 110–11, 133
  national, 71
  organization, 137, 149
  planning, 103, 172, 278
  power, concentration of, 148
  production, 148
  productivity, 104
  progress, 31, 51, 133
  scenario, 31, 183
  security, 35–36, 185
  society, 12, 133, 141
  theory, 8, 10, 43, 47, 101, 133, 147
  transactions, 53–54, 130
Employment generation, 212, 220
Encountering deceleration, 201
Ethical foundations, 17, 60
Ethical principles, 33–34, 97, 99, 170, 179–80
Ethical values, 31, 97, 101, 105, 128, 189

Fiscal autonomy, 210–11
Food
  economy, 194–95
  insecurity, 194
  production, 206
  self sufficiency, 193–94, 207, 213
  sovereignty, 194, 207
Foodgrains, 194, 197–200, 205, 207–8, 238–39
Foreign
  domination, 176, 244
  exchange, 194, 210, 214
  goods, 66, 71, 135, 174–75, 209–12
  investment, 95–96, 129, 134
  supply, 71
Foreign Direct Investment (FDI), 23, 95
Free trade, 207

Freedom struggle, 44, 59, 107, 193, 204, 220

Gandhian concept
of economic development, 145, 151
of global growth, 103
of rural development, 158
of socialism, 92
of *swadeshi*, 173–74, 176, 194
of trusteeship, 51, 70, 83
of village, 87
Gandhian Critique
of socialism, 19
Gandhian economic ideals, 170, 172
Gandhian Economic Model, 133
ingredients of, 49
General Agreement of Trade and Tariffs (GATT), 128–29
Global economy, 178, 188
Global Metropolis (GM), 281
Globalisation, Liberalisation, and Privatisation (GLP), 238
Globalized World Economy, 40
Gram Panchayats (GP), 276, 281–82
Gram Swaraj and Village Republic, 280
Green revolution, 194, 196, 205–6, 208, 213–14, 272
Gross Domestic Product (GDP), 6, 44, 91, 108, 166, 181–82, 196, 205, 221
Gross National Product (GNP), 41, 132, 166
Growth rate of total economy, 197

Handlooms, 72, 146, 223, 225, 228, 249
Harmonious society, 84
Heavy industries, 149, 172, 220, 247–48
Henry Maine's Village Communities, 164
High Yielding Variety (HYV), 200, 205–6
Hind Swaraj (HS), 20, 22, 31, 35, 44, 86, 98, 107, 115–19, 121, 123, 162, 192, 194, 214
Hindu civilization, 257
Hindu village, 257
Hinduism, 21, 80, 168
Home industries, 174–75
Human affairs, 115–16
Human Development Reports (HDRs), 18, 41
Human development, 11, 29, 31, 35, 40, 43, 104, 133, 182, 185–86, 221, 282
Human life, 2, 29–30, 32, 40, 45, 79, 83, 88, 90, 94, 166, 182–83, 185, 187, 189–90
Human settlements, 268, 272, 281
Human spirit, 31
Human survival, 2, 11, 35–36, 54
Humidity, 206
Hunger, 18, 42–43, 46, 159

Immigrants Muslim countries, 273
Imperial country, 160
Impossibility theorem, 79–80
Inclusive Society, 127, 139–40, 143
Independence struggle, 81
India Spinners Association, 220, 249, 275
Indian Agriculture Research Institute (IARI), 206
Indian Institute of Advanced Studies, 165
Indian National Congress, 255, 275
Indigenous industries, 152, 175–76
Industrial country, 3
Industrial education, 209, 277
Industrial revolution, 51, 86, 135, 214, 219, 239
Industrialisation, 54, 117
Industrialism, 17, 20, 22, 107, 138, 172, 194
Institutional structure, 230
Integral society, 139

International economic cooperation, 128
International market, 199, 227–28
International Trade Organization (ITO), 128–29
Israeli society, 266, 268–69

Khadi, 37, 66, 72, 98–99, 109, 135, 146, 148, 152, 159, 166, 218–21, 223, 225, 227–30
Khadi and Village Industries Commission (KVIC), 222–27, 231–32
Khadi production centre, 220
Kibbutz movement, 273

Labour
 abundant country, 79
 exploitation of, 1, 10, 46, 79
 exploiting cheap, 94
 intellectual, 155
 intensive production, 11, 136
 kibubutzim value, 264
 surplus country, 221
 theory of values, 4
Leadership, 121–22, 209, 221, 255
Legitimacy, 21–22, 218

Machineless society, 241
Malnutrition, 43, 148, 240
Management of economic resources, 102–3
Marginal farmers, 195, 202
Marginal variations, 196
Market forces, 91, 164, 184–85
Marxian economics, 2, 7
Materialism, 20–21, 46, 96
Micro, Small and Medium Enterprises (MSME), 224
Mixed Economy, 90–91, 167–68
Modern civilization, 21, 30, 55, 78, 118, 133, 171, 241
Modern economics, 44, 46–47, 53, 133, 162, 189
Monopoly capitalism, 10
Moshavim, 261, 272–75, 283
Muir Central College, 12, 31
Multinational agribusiness, 205
Multinational Corporation (MNCs), 94–95, 130, 225–26, 230, 232, 238–39
Multipurpose centre, 248

Nai Talim, 105, 277
National accounting, 182
National Movements, 3, 111, 265
National Rural Employment Guarantee Scheme, 203, 234
Natural resources, 6, 29, 47, 130, 132, 181
Neo-colonial world, 23
New Economic Policy of India, 176
Non-acquisitive dimensions, 147
Non-agriculture, 196–97, 203
Non-cooperation, 101, 193, 209, 246, 253, 276
Non-economic factors, 166, 207
Non-exploitation, 34, 146, 171
Non-violence, 16, 30, 32–33, 45, 50, 61, 82, 88–89, 104–5, 116, 141–42, 146–48, 153, 170–71, 185–87
Non-violent values, 156
Non-violent world order, 157

Organic fertilizer, 135

Panchayati Raj system in India, 279, 282
Physical labour, 15, 84, 155
Physical Quality of Life (PQL), 238
Plurality, 19
Political power, 41, 148, 150, 173, 239–40, 279
Politico-economic system, 3, 12
Principles of truth, 32, 45, 50, 146
Public accountability, 95
Purdah system, 112

Quit India Movement, 276

Ramrajya, 45
Rapid economic growth, 54
Rational Society, 36
Rational world, 21
Rationalism, 20
Rural development, 61, 109–10, 113, 157–58, 167, 225, 278, 283
Rural economy, 63, 135, 142, 159, 204, 218, 234
Rural industries, 109, 146, 227
Rural masses, 221–22, 225, 229, 232, 255
Rural Service Centres (RSC), 281–82

Sarvodaya, 15, 95, 137, 142, 163, 170–71, 247, 250
Satyagraha, 45, 102, 107, 118–19, 123, 142, 154, 163, 193, 209, 214, 253, 276
Second World War Keynesian, 131
Self melt, 120
Self-government, 62, 244
Self-realization, 15, 105, 107, 151
Self-reliance, 34, 67, 72, 117, 135–36, 156, 176, 194, 207, 209, 218, 221, 232–33, 240, 247
Self-reliant production, 98
Self-reliant villages, 109, 220, 239, 280
Self-sufficiency, 63, 67, 102, 158, 171, 193, 199, 204, 207, 209, 240, 243, 247, 254, 277
Sevagram Ashram, 275
Shining India, 237
Slaves, 36, 64, 89
Smart cities, 237, 280–81
Social control, 79
Social fabric, 54, 178
Social groups, 90, 195, 202
Social organization, 251, 258
Social transformation, 88–89, 242
Socialism, 2, 7, 16, 19, 51, 77, 81–82, 88, 92, 103–4, 127, 154
Socio-economic
  harmony, 101, 104
  principles, 101
Sovereignty, 182, 194, 204, 208–9, 244
Spinning wheel, 50, 98, 155, 158–60, 220, 226, 239–40, 249
Spiritual development, 101–2, 104
Spiritual progress, 15, 38
Stateless society, 154
Subsidies, 207, 225–27, 269
Surplus value, 8–10
Sustainable development, 41, 54–55, 113, 182, 280
Swadeshi, 33–34, 50, 63–64, 66–67, 98–101, 107, 123, 134–36, 152, 158, 171, 173–76, 192–94, 209–14, 242–44
  complete, 67
  dharma, 152
  discourse of, 209
  doctrine, 244
  edifice of, 212
  false, 174
  initiatives, 212
  movement, 107, 209, 212
  observance of, 210
  principle of, 50, 72, 152, 171, 174
  true, 101

Theory of trusteeship, 70, 154
Third World, 156
Touchables, 258
Tourism, 264
Trading companies, 94
Transfer of power, 192–93, 204
True economics, 49, 141, 189
Trusteeship, 15, 23, 34, 50–51, 70–72, 82–83, 86, 89, 102–4, 136–37, 146, 151–54, 156, 165, 179–80

Untouchability, 77, 80, 158, 168, 187, 223, 258, 275–76
Urban centre, 237, 264
Urban handicraft centers, 109

Value education, 105

Village
- cleanliness, 275
- community, 218, 241, 246, 251–54, 256, 258–59, 276
- festivals, 258
- industry products, 109
- level production, 274
- panchayats, 65, 157, 232, 256, 277, 279
- polity, 254
- republics, 237, 251, 256, 259, 275, 278, 280, 282
- *swaraj*, 62, 149, 193, 245, 276, 278–79

Village Industries Commission Act, 224

Violence, 6, 17, 30–31, 34, 46–47, 51–52, 61, 70, 82, 112, 117–18, 132, 147, 153–54, 156

Violent activities, 186–87

Vocational Training, 248

Voluntary organization, 232, 249

Wealth generation, 180, 182, 188–89

Wealth of Nations, 3–4, 74

World Bank, 128–30, 205, 207

World Commission on Environment and Development, 221

World Economic Institution, 128

World economy, 111, 127–32, 135, 178, 185

World Trade Organization (WTO), 128–29, 194, 199, 207–8, 214

Yoga centre, 282

Young India, 78, 145